Anonymous

Questions for a Reformed Parliament

Anonymous

Questions for a Reformed Parliament

ISBN/EAN: 9783337297350

Printed in Europe, USA, Canada, Australia, Japan

Cover: Foto ©Suzi / pixelio.de

More available books at **www.hansebooks.com**

QUESTIONS

FOR A

REFORMED PARLIAMENT.

London:

MACMILLAN AND CO.

1867.

LONDON:
R. CLAY, SON, AND TAYLOR, PRINTERS,
BREAD STREET HILL.

PREFACE.

THE general purpose of this volume of Essays has already been indicated, in the Preface to "Essays on Reform." It is, to show that some of the questions in which the action of Parliament has hitherto been least satisfactory, may be more hopefully approached by a Government representing and carrying with it the whole nation.

Since the publication of the former volume, the question of Parliamentary Reform has made considerable progress ; and there is now a. fair prospect of its being settled within a reasonable time. It may be doubted, however, whether this is not due rather to a sense of political necessity than to a hearty conviction on the part of the present possessors of power that, by a liberal enfranchisement of working men, and a transfer of representation from small boroughs to large and thriving communities, national interests will be promoted.

While the contributors to the present volume are united in this conviction, they desire that each may be held responsible solely for the contents of his own Essay.

The scope of this volume will be reached if it does anything to draw attention to the work which awaits a Reformed Parliament. It is obviously beyond that scope to include the treatment of national questions in detail. The object now is not to present exhaustive or finished schemes for the settlement of the problems of State here discussed ; but to show how they imply in themselves Parliamentary Reform as a condition of their satisfactory settlement. It is no aim of this book to lay down any system for future legislation ; but to consider only what legislation is needed, and to what goal it should tend.

LIST OF SUBJECTS AND AUTHORS.

QUESTIONS

FOR

A REFORMED PARLIAMENT.

I.

IRELAND.

BY FRANK H. HILL.

THE purpose of the following remarks is not to examine the political and economic condition of Ireland
in itself, but only so far as the problems which it involves throw light upon the necessity of a reconstruction of Parliament, in order that they may be fairly
apprehended and impartially decided. I have restricted
myself, therefore, to indicating what these problems are,
and the principles which are applicable to them, without
entering into the details which would be necessary in a
full discussion. The design of the paper will explain
the introduction of some topics, which would be un-
suitable in a disquisition upon the state of Ireland, and
the omission of others, which would naturally find a
place in such an inquiry.

Whatever success may have attended the dealings of the
Reformed Parliament with Imperial and properly English

questions, its government of Ireland cannot be ranked
among its claims to confidence. In 1829, Sir Robert
Peel stated that scarcely a year had passed since the Act
of Union in which Ireland had been ruled by the ordinary
course of law. Lord Derby might say the same thing
now ; nor does there seem any reason to anticipate a
speedy change for the better. At the present moment
the Habeas Corpus Act is suspended in Ireland ; and a
conspiracy which extends wherever Irishmen are found
disturbs the peace not only of Kerry and Dublin, but of
quiet cathedral towns in England, and of border-villages
in Canada. How is this persistent disaffection to be
explained ? To say that the Irish are incapable of constitutional government, is only to say, in other words,
that England has not yet discovered the proper way of
governing them. It is unconsciously to confess a fault
in the language of reproach and insult.

To affirm that the Irish are naturally an intractable
and mutinous race is to beg the question, and to beg it
against the testimony of history and impartial observers.
No people are more easily swayed by justice and affection, as their best rulers, from Sir John Perrot to Lord
Normanby, have found and acknowledged. Their in-
surrections are indirectly of our instigation. Almost
every boon, real or imaginary, ever granted to Ireland,
has been won by the fact or the threat of rebellion. The
independence of their Parliament, Catholic Emancipation,
the Commutation of Tithes, the partial Reform of the
Established Church, the agrarian measures which followed the abortive rising of 1848, the concessions of
various kinds which are promised now, have all been
suggested or hastened by the necessity of disarming or

anticipating violence. It is not strange that a people should be prone to anarchy and lawlessness, when it finds in them the shortest way to mild government and good laws.

The misrule of England in Ireland has not generally been, and is not now, due to evil intentions, but to want of information and sympathy. A wrong once clearly perceived, has not usually waited long for its remedy. But the wrong has scarcely ever been recognised in its own character, and in the earlier stages of its development. When its effects became unmistakeable and unendurable, when the system of which it was a part wholly broke down, then something, but seldom enough, was done in the way of redress. The special abuse was removed, the accumulated growth of evil was cleared away ; but the system of which the abuse was a part, the root out of which the evil sprang, were allowed to remain.

The abuses once more accumulated, and discontent spread with them. The English Parliament, complacently reviewing, from time to time, its concessions and reforms, cannot understand why Ireland is still dissatisfied ; and concludes that it is useless to do anything for a nation which nothing will conciliate. It remains in this mood till the periodic necessity once more presses upon it, beyond all power of evasion or resistance ; and the cycle begins again. The notion has become inveterate in the English mind, that since the redress of just wrongs does not remove the sense of grievance, the grievances are, one and all, imaginary, the creation of bitter memories and visionary hopes. The task of wisely and justly governing Ireland through an English Parliament, which is difficult in itself, will become absolutely

impossible if this persuasion continues to prevail.   There
is imperfect knowledge to begin with.   When to difference of race and of religion, of temperament, of traditions, and of habits, is added the bitter memory of old
wrongs, the barrier of mutual misunderstanding becomes
almost too dense and high to be penetrated or surmounted.

To these intrinsic difficulties, the present constitution
of the House of Commons adds another.   The two great
Irish questions, about which all the rest centre, and to
which they are ultimately reducible, are those of the
Church and the Land.   They are referred to the impartial arbitration of a Parliament returned chiefly by
and consisting mainly of Churchmen and Landlords.   A
nation which is governed by a dominant class in another
country is in danger of suffering the combined evils of
two usually incompatible forms of misgovernment—
oligarchy and foreign misrule.   This is practically the
political condition of Ireland.   Nominally an integrant
part of the United Kingdom, sharing its privilege of self-
government, it is really a dependency on the larger
island, with which its geographical situation and history
have connected it.   Its hundred and five members, even
if they were of one mind, would still form a powerless
minority of the House of Commons.   They might sometimes turn divisions upon critical occasions, and purchase,
by the promise of support, or the threat of secession,
isolated concessions from embarrassed Ministries.   Even
now a fraction of them manages to do this.   But they
could not give shape or effect to a general and connected scheme of policy.   The nature of the influence
which Irish members are almost constrained to wield
degrades Irish politics, and diminishes the moral weight

in the House of Commons of those who are tempted to employ it. Men who trade on the exigencies of Governments, are not likely to be regarded either as very wise statesmen or as very pure patriots. Commercial speculators and party-jobbers anxious to obtain a subsidy for a bankrupt steam-company, or privileges for a sectarian college, form the weights which Irish representation casts, now into this scale, now into that, of the shifting balance of party. Political power in Ireland must always reside with the British, and not with the Irish Members ; with the five hundred and fifty, and not with the hundred and five. The case of Scotland, which is often cited as exhibiting an opposite result in analogous circumstances, is not to the point. The result is opposite ; but the circumstances are not analogous. The retention by the Scotch of their own Church Establishment, their own system of law, and their own methods of local administration, has left their national life free to run in the channels provided for it by their own character and history. The need of technical knowledge for the understanding of most Scotch questions, which is the consequence of the divergence of their institutions and laws from those of England, has created what practically amounts to an independent Scotch Parliament within that of the United Kingdom. In Ireland the forms of law and of institutions are the same as they are here ; and this deceptive outer identity, concealing the most complete difference of substance and spirit, betrays men into the delusion that they know that of which they are most profoundly ignorant. The very light that seems to be in them is darkness. The position of Irish members in the House of Commons is practically akin to that of the delegates from territories in the Congress at Washington : for though, unlike the American delegates, they can vote, their voting-power is, for any good purpose, *nil.* They form a deputation to the governing assembly, authorized to speak the sentiments of their constituents, but unable to give effect to them. The reform which is needed for the better government of Ireland is such a change in the Irish representation as would make it what it is now only very partially,—the reflex of Irish opinion and feeling ; and such a change in the British representation as would dispose the House of Commons to lend a calmer and more earnest attention to the desires and views of the Irish people, and induce it to give effect to what is reasonable and just in them. A more faithful advocacy before a less partial tribunal—this is the essence of the Parliamentary Reform which Ireland requires. The proportion of Irish to Scotch and English members is a matter of secondary importance. At present, and notwithstanding the exodus, Ireland has far less than her share of representation estimated by population, though far more than her share relatively to her territorial revenue and the number of the electors—a state of things which the non-development of the material resources of the country, and the consequently depressed condition of the people, sufficiently explain. That the present constituencies, based on a 12*l.* rating franchise in counties and an 8*l.* rating franchise in boroughs, exercise their franchise with considerable independence, appears from the fact that in the three western and southern provinces, forming that Catholic and Celtic Ireland which is the perplexity of statesmen, the counties, in spite of landlord influence, return 32 Liberal Members against

14 Conservatives, while the boroughs of these provinces
return 23 Liberals and 5 Conservatives. In other words,
the Liberal Members outnumber the Conservatives in
nearly the proportion of three to one. In these provinces Irish grievances are most keenly felt ; and Irish
opinion pronounces by an overwhelming majority in
favour of a remedial policy.

The Conservative strength in the Parliamentary representation of Ireland is derived from Ulster, and from the
Protestant University of Dublin. The province returns
twenty-eight Conservatives, and one Liberal ; the University, two Conservatives. The reason of this geographical distribution of parties lies on the surface. In
Ulster the characteristic grievances of Ireland exist in a
very qualified form. Through the custom of tenant-right
the occupier has a certain degree of security for his capital
invested in the soil. Protestants form a large minority in
the province, and a majority in some parts of it. The
existence in considerable force of various Nonconformist
denominations side by side with the Established Church,
—such as Presbyterians (who outnumber the Anglican
Episcopalians), Wesleyans, Unitarians, and others,—
deprives Protestantism here of the purely political aspect
which it bears elsewhere ; and in so doing removes its
most invidious character in Irish Catholic eyes. Ulster is,
in short, in race, in religion, and in industrial organization, especially in its blending of manufactures with agriculture, rather a displaced fragment of Great Britain than
a portion of Celtic Ireland. Its representatives, therefore,
help to neutralize instead of swelling the protest of the
southern and western provinces against grievances which
it does not share in equal proportion with them.

There is room for a wider enfranchisement—the proportion of the electors to the population in Ireland falling far short of that in England, while education is more generally diffused. There is room, also, for a redistribution of seats—small and dependent boroughs being smaller and more numerous, in proportion to the rest of the constituencies, than in England. Still no pretence exists for saying that, if the Imperial Parliament has neglected the grievances of Ireland, it is because Ireland herself has held her tongue about them. The Ireland which suffers has spoken, and still speaks, but to deaf ears.

Ireland, if we are to believe some politicians, has no special grievances to complain of. She has an Established Church; but so have England and Scotland. The Church may embrace only a minority of the whole population. But this is the position of the ecclesiastical Establishments in the other parts of the United Kingdom also. The Roman Catholics in Ireland are Dissenters—if they could only be got to regard themselves in that light—and are no worse off than Episcopalians and Free Churchmen in Scotland, and Wesleyans in England. The difference between establishing in a Protestant country the most numerous of Protestant sects, though it may not form an absolute majority of the whole population, and establishing a small Protestant minority in a Roman Catholic country, escapes the framers of these parallels. The Churches of England and Scotland are maintained, so far as reason and policy have anything to do with their maintenance, on the ground that they are the best of several imperfect means of bringing the sanctions of religion to bear on the great mass of the people in aid of that morality which is the chief safeguard of law and order, and the basis of national prosperity. As the only religion which can influence a man is that which he believes, the established religion should be that of the people. The Church of England in Ireland rests upon no such basis as this. An Irish clergyman, holding preferment in England, the Rev. Dr. Hume, of Liverpool, published, two or three years ago, a pamphlet, exhibiting the relative social and moral condition of Irish Protestants and Catholics. He shows conclusively that in Ireland " persons of rank and title, those of independent means, and those conventionally known as ladies and gentlemen, or living without labour," —landed proprietors and land-agents, and even farmers, —merchants, and bankers,—surgeons, physicians, medical students, civil engineers, and barristers,—schoolmasters, authors, and governesses,—are in a great majority on the Protestant side. On the other hand, " brothel-keepers and prostitutes exist in unusually large Roman Catholic proportions." So also do " professional beggars, fiddlers, pipers, dog-fanciers, and billiard-markers," and " the inmates of prisons and bridewells." Farm-labourers and servants, and labourers generally engaged in the more menial and unskilled occupations, belong to the ancient Church. Doubtless the zealous compiler of the statistics which are thus generalized sees in the facts which he states conclusive proof of the degrading and demoralizing effects of the Roman Catholic faith. Perhaps a more impartial observer would see in them proof of the degrading and demoralizing effects of confiscation, of social proscription, and of penal laws. In any case, the Church of England is defended as the Church of a rich and educated minority—a minority forming about twelve per cent. of the entire population. To their religious sustenance the whole of the ecclesiastical revenues of the country, amounting to between five and six hundred thousand pounds, is devoted. It is sometimes alleged that the Roman Catholic population has no reason to complain of this arrangement, since nearly four-fifths of this vast sum are raised by a rent-charge on the land of Ireland, and ninety-three per cent. of the land of Ireland is in the hands of Protestants,—who obtained it, however, from Roman Catholics, mainly by force and confiscation. But the burthen does not fall upon Protestant landlords : they acquired their property subject to the charge, or to the heavier burden of tithes. The money belongs to the State as completely as if it were derived from Crown lands, or raised by taxation. The Protestant Church holds it now by authority of the State, which can resume or re-transfer what it once took and gave. The tithes for which the rent-charge is a commutation were of Roman Catholic origin in Ireland.

Regarded, therefore, in the lowest monetary point of view, the retention of its temporalities by the Established Church of Ireland is a grievance not only to Ireland, but to the whole empire. Their equitable distribution among the various communions would in releasing the faithful from some part at least of the voluntary taxation which they impose upon themselves for religious purposes, by so much increase the disposable capital of the country. If it be deemed necessary that the State should use the sanctions of religion for the promotion of social morality and the maintenance of law and order, the only religion which it can bring to bear on the popular

mind is, as has been said, that in which the nation
believes. The condition of the Roman Catholics as
sketched by Dr. Hume shows that they, in an especial
degree, need the benefits which the State Church exists
to confer. The endowment either of the Church of
the majority, or of all Churches in proportion to their
numbers or their poverty, is the only form in which
the continued application to spiritual purposes of the
ecclesiastical revenues of Ireland can be justified on considerations of public advantage. But the fact that the
Roman Catholics, out of the scantiest resources, are able
to provide for the spiritual necessities of a population
more than six times as numerous as that of the Established Church, may to some seem a sufficient proof that
religion in Ireland would not suffer if left to the support of
voluntary zeal. The purposes to which the temporalities
of the Church might be applied need not engage us
here. Capitalized they would represent a sum of nearly
thirteen millions and a half sterling. No Chancellor of
the Exchequer would be embarrassed by having this sum
placed at his disposal. It would materially aid Mr.
Gladstone's schemes, if Parliament should sanction them,
for paying off the National Debt. That part of the ecclesiastical revenues which is drawn from the commuted
tithes would alone far more than defray the whole of the
Parliamentary Grant for Public Education in Ireland.
The reclamation of waste lands, and advances for the
execution of improvements and public works, are among
the possible purposes to which the sequestrated temporalities might be devoted.

It is said that the great body of the Roman Catholics
of Ireland do not feel the establishment of Protestantism

as a grievance. They are on friendly terms with the clergyman, and find him often a useful secular adviser, though they do not attend to his spiritual counsels. They appreciate the advantage of having in nearly every parish an educated gentleman to whom the poor can apply. Every evil has its compensations, and no doubt even the Irish Established Church is not without them. It exists, however, for the purpose of distributing not secular advisers, but religious teachers, over Ireland. If the conversion of the people is the object of the Protestant Church, it is not likely to be forwarded by the exhibition of its ministers in this purely mundane character. The plea admits, however, that the revenues of the Church are practically secularized as far as the great majority of the Irish people are concerned ; and the only question is, whether they could not be secularized in a better way. If they are the indefeasible property of any Church, they belong to the Roman Catholic Church ; and if they are not, they belong to the State, which is bound to em-ploy them for the benefit of the whole people. To divert these revenues from this purpose, for the advantage of a sect, is really to rob the nation of a sum equivalent to the taxation which might be defrayed out of them, or of the wealth which their judicious employment might create.

The Protestant Church Establishment is therefore some-thing more than a sentimental and theoretic grievance; though if it merely offended the reason and conscience, and wounded the feelings, of a sensitive and quick-witted race, the evil might still be not unworthy of redress. The arguments by which its existence is defended are themselves provocatives to disaffection. It is justified as a mainstay of the English connexion, and as an out-work of the Established Church in this country, which would not, it is said, long survive the lopping off of its Irish branch. What is this but to say, that it is main-tained not for Irish but for English purposes? It is de-fended as a Missionary Church, as an instrument for the conversion of the Roman Catholics of Ireland, and as a witness to the doctrines of the Reformation. In all these respects it has been a complete failure. But the objects proposed are not those of modern statesmanship, which does not recognise in the State any organ for the discern-ment of religious truth, nor any mission to propagate it. To employ the property of the Irish nation for the pur-pose of undermining its faith is, not to add to morality the sanctions of religion, but to divorce morality from religion.

Merely to reform what are called the abuses of the Church will not meet the necessities of the case. The Church is itself the great abuse, of which all the rest are logical consequences. The inequitable distribution of property among those who are not entitled to possess any of it is not a matter for the interference of the Legislature. It is no doubt startling to find that while the incumbent of Urlingford, in the Diocese of Ossory, receives 1,200*l.* a year for ministering to thirty persons, the incumbent of Bangor, in the Diocese of Down, receives a gross income of 136*l.* for ministering to a Church population of 1,230 persons. Anomalies such as these—and they are frequent —are legitimate developments of an anomalous institution. If a fractional minority of the Irish people is entitled to all the ecclesiastical revenues of the country, a minority of that minority may as fairly claim the largest share of them. If the Protestant Establishment is a Missionary Church, its chief work is to be done, not where Protestants, but where Roman Catholics are most numerous. If its business is to preserve the faith of its own members by providing them with the ordinances of religion, that provision needs to be made most lavishly where the temptations of habit, companionship, and local sentiment, to apostasy are strongest, and the resources of the faithful slenderest. Rich benefices and small congregations are of the very essence of the Irish Establishment. To object to them is to object to it.

The indirect effects of the Protestant Establishment upon public policy, and especially upon the policy of the Liberal party, are, perhaps, the most serious evils that flow from it. It is the mainstay of Ultramontanism in Ireland. Under its shelter, and in compensation for its injustice, the Roman Catholic *parti prêtre* is obtaining, one by one, almost all the concessions it desires. It is not too much to say that the choice will presently have to be made between its abolition and the abolition of the system of national education, which was, and in spite of injurious modifications, still remains, the greatest boon ever conferred by England upon Ireland. Already great inroads have been made upon that system ; and others are contemplated. The admission of convent and monastery schools under the National Board, the plan for reconstructing the model schools, so as to provide separate education for Catholic and Protestant teachers, the Supplemental Charter forced last session on the Queen's University in the interest of the Catholic University, and the reconstruction of the senate of the former body by the appointment of gentlemen avowedly

hostile to its fundamental principle of united unsectarian
education, are steps towards the establishment of a strictly
denominational system in the schools and colleges of
Ireland. Ireland will not be more easily governed, nor
political and religious feuds become less deadly, when
the young of its various sects are no longer taught together. The Catholic population, educated, from the
primary school to the University, under strict priestly
surveillance, imbued with Ultramontane theories of
society and of government, and restricted to Ultramontane text-books of history and philosophy, will not
enter more readily than they do now into the traditions and the doctrines of English constitutional freedom.
In almost every other Catholic country of Europe, a
liberal and enlightened laity exists, which is prompt to
resist the extravagant pretensions of the priesthood.
But in Ireland, Protestant ascendency, by banding all
sections of Catholics together in opposition to the common enemy, and by inspiring them with a common
resentment of injustice, has prevented the growth and
formation of this politically saving element of society.
The whole Catholic population belongs, if not in heart,
yet for every purpose of action, to the *parti prêtre*.
No one can wonder that sincere Roman Catholics
distrust, and find it hard to believe in, the religious
neutrality of a Government which maintains ecclesiastical ascendancy and subsidizes theological proselytism
in the Established Church. Their suspicion can be
disarmed only in one way—by the establishment of
perfect equality among the Churches of Ireland, whether
that equality take the shape of impartial endowment
or impartial disendowment; and by the abolition of

sectarian privileges in national institutions of education, especially in Trinity College and in the Royal and Endowed Schools. Roman Catholics can graduate, and can obtain non-foundation scholarships, and can even fill one or two of the chairs in the University of Dublin. But they are excluded from its most valuable emoluments and distinctions, and from its governing body. The considerable numbers in which they attend the University make it probable that if these restrictions were removed we should hear very little of the Catholic University except as a plaything of the Bishops, and that lay hostility to the Queen's Colleges would die out. If, on the other hand, the old habit be continued of balancing unjust privileges and inexpedient concessions by privileges as unjust and concessions as inexpedient; if the Royal Bounty to Presbyterians, and the grants to their Professors, be set off against the vote to Maynooth, and both be employed as makeweights to counterpoise the temporalities and academical monopolies of the Established Church, the imbroglio will be inextricable. The good government of Ireland and the harmony of its future relations with England depend upon the promptitude and decision with which a wiser course is taken. That such a course is not to be looked for from the present House of Commons may be inferred from its constitution and from its history. For thirty-five years it has refused any considerable Reform. Tithes were not commuted until they could no longer be collected even at the bayonet's point, and the starving Protestant clergy had to be provided for by a Parliamentary vote. The Church Temporalities Act was passed under the pressure of social convulsion;

and when the doctrine of the Appropriation Clause had
served the purpose of an English party, no one thought
of applying to it for the benefit of the Irish people.
A Parliament of English Churchmen and landlords
cannot be expected to deal vigorously with a branch
of their own Church which is the Church of Irish landlords also.

The chief hope of redress lies in a large and liberal
Parliamentary Reform. The mass of the people have
no motive for desiring that the Church of a rich and
aristocratic minority should absorb the revenues which
might be applied for the general benefit of the nation.
They see no equity in an arrangement which provides that
while the poor support their own religious teachers, the
religious teachers of the rich shall be supported by the
State. Without any ill-will towards the Church of
England, their attachment to it is not so fervent or
undiscriminating as to make them morbidly solicitous
for the preservation of its Irish temporalities. The *élite*
of the working-classes in particular, who must form
the characteristically new element which a considerable
measure of enfranchisement would introduce into the
constituencies, though often sincerely religious, stand
in great measure aside from every ecclesiastical organization. The majority of those among them who
belong to any sect or denomination are Nonconformists.
Rightly or wrongly, they have little faith in the virtue
of Church establishments as instruments of religious
influence and conversion; and are usually devotees of
the voluntary principle. The sympathy of a privileged
few with a privileged few is the mainstay of the present
ecclesiastical arrangements of Ireland. The sympathy of

the many with the many, over-riding the sophistries of vested interests and statecraft, by the homely sense of justice and common good, would facilitate the gradual introduction of a better order of things. The example of English democracy in the United States, in our Australian colonies, and elsewhere, warrants the confident anticipation that the new force which a liberal enfranchisement would introduce into the House of Commons would be directed against the abuse of ecclesiastical ascendency, and to the maintenance of unsectarian education in Ireland.

The adjustment of the land question is yet more imperatively demanded than ecclesiastical reform. Unless a prompt and wise settlement be devised, we shall presently have no Irish people to rule. Since 1851 nearly two millions of people have left Ireland, not intending to return. Within certain limits this movement was necessary and healthy. Its effects were for a time visible in the higher wages and improved modes of living of the labouring poor, who were better clothed, better housed, and better fed than before; in the increase of the deposits in the joint-stock banks and of the investments in Government stock and other securities; and in the multiplication of the signs of business enterprise. The evil days were believed to be over: and a new era was thought to have commenced. These favourable symptoms, however, have during the last dozen years become less and less marked, and now they have nearly disappeared. Irish agricultural prosperity reached its highest point in 1855, fostered by exceptionally favourable seasons, by the new capital and new spirit introduced through the agency of the Encumbered Estates Court, and by the removal of a surplus and half-pauper population, which had increased the consuming mouths without multiplying the productive hands of the country. This progress continued, though at a slackening rate, until 1859. From that time to the present, there has been retrogression rather than advance. The new forces introduced by the social revolution which dates from the famine and by the legislation which followed, appear to have spent their strength. The phenomena which the agricultural economy of Ireland presents are most extraordinary. While vast tracts of available land are unreclaimed, or but half-cultivated, producing nothing, or less than they are capable of yielding, the labour which they seem to invite, and which under a proper system they would reward, is fleeing from the country. Emigration, though it is the salvation of those who escape, has not of late years materially improved the condition of those who remain at home. An opposite impression has been sedulously fostered. It seems to have been derived from a careless confusion of agricultural labour with that employed upon railways and by contractors, and from the assumption that a merely local and temporary improvement, due to the scarcity of farm labour occasioned by such exceptional demand, was permanent and general. From extended personal investigations, Mr. Cliffe Leslie has come to the conclusion that in 1866 the rate of agricultural wages in Ireland did not exceed on the average one shilling a week over the whole working year. This average includes the comparatively prosperous north, as well as the impoverished south and west. Mr. Cliffe Leslie's estimate is confirmed by the following statement, contained in a private letter from an eminent living political economist, himself an Irish landowner, and intimately acquainted with the country: " I have been making particular inquiries (he says) on this subject, and I believe about 6*s.* weekly would express the average rate through the south and west, and from 7*s.* to 8*s.* about Dublin. Taking into account the higher price of provisions, I do not believe that the mass of the Irish labourers are substantially better off now than they were in the period before the famine."

The Poor-law returns confirm this opinion. Notwithstanding the diminished population, they show a large and on the whole steady increase of pauperism during the past ten years. The number of persons receiving Poor-law relief was 44,866 in the first week of January 1858 ; it was 65,057 in the corresponding week of 1866. These phenomena—decreasing population, increasing pauperism, and a declining rate of wages—are no doubt owing in part to a series of bad harvests from 1859 to 1862; but the progress of Ireland had received a check before that date, and it has not been resumed since. The facts admit only of one explanation. Rapidly as labour has decreased, capital has diminished still faster. The same emigration has carried away both ; and the wages-fund has been reduced more quickly than the number of the wage-receivers. The quality of labour has fallen off even more than the quantity. The strong and vigorous go, the old and the infirm remain behind. The consequence is a decline in the birth-rate of Ireland, which in 1865 was only 1 in 39 of the population, or nearly one-third less than the proportion which maintains in England. The consolidation of farms and the conversion of tillage into pasture, which have been in progress in Ireland during the past twenty years, are regarded in England as a necessary and healthy change. They might be so if larger holdings necessarily implied larger capital. But this is not the case. "The increase in the number of the holdings above fifteen acres," says Mr. G. T. Dalton, a very accurate observer and acute reasoner, " has been generally effected in the worst possible way. A ten-acre farmer has been converted into one of twenty acres, on the Procrustean principle of stretching him. With his limited capital he is called upon to do twice as much as he had to do before : and he can't do it. He starves his land, and the consequence is a gradual decrease, since the emigration set in, of the yield per acre of all his crops, root and cereal, without exception." It is remarkable that the productiveness of Irish farming and the prosperity of the agricultural class are greatest where farms are smallest, and the proportion of pasture to tillage is least—namely, in Ulster. In that province the average size of holdings is twenty-five acres, while in Connaught it is thirty-two, in Leinster thirty-seven, and in Munster forty-six acres. In Armagh, one of the most flourishing counties in Ulster, the average size of holdings is only fourteen acres. While the proportion of pasture to tillage over the whole of Ireland is 48 per cent. it is only 39 per cent. in Ulster, and in the counties of Down and Armagh it is respectively 30 and 31 per cent. From Ulster, too, the purely agricultural emigration has been smaller than from any of the other provinces. The theorists who insist that depopulation, the consolidation of farms, and the substitution of pasture for tillage are the causes and signs of Irish prosperity, maintain their thesis in defiance of facts. Where these causes operate least Irish prosperity is greatest; where they are in most active operation the condition of the country is least satisfactory. The facts carry their own interpretation upon their face. Agriculture in Ulster is comparatively flourishing, because in the custom of tenant-right, notwithstanding its vicious and wasteful incidents, the farmers possess a certain degree of security for the investment of their capital. Where this security fails, we see declining production, diminishing population, falling wages, and increasing pauperism. This is the root-evil whence all the rest spring.

To have ascertained it, is to put our fingers upon the remedy, and, I fear, to discover the improbability of its application by an unreformed Parliament.

The security which capital needs, in order to bring it into free and fertilizing contact with the soil, must be either that of ownership, or of tenure under the protection of written agreements or positive law. In Ireland, both these conditions of agricultural prosperity fail. The laws of primogeniture and entail, and the practice of settlements, have the effect of accumulating the land into large estates, owned by a small number of persons, who do not themselves cultivate the soil. They prevent it from freely entering the market; and the artificial scarcity thus produced, of course raises the price of the small portions of land which find their way there. The operation of the Landed Estates Court in Ireland, and of its predecessor, the Encumbered Estates Court, has to some extent, and for a time, neutralized the influence of these regulations. Professor Cairnes mentions that on the sale of the Thomond, Portarlington, and Kingston

estates, a considerable number of the occupying tenants
purchased the fee of their farms. In England, when
a similar opportunity presents itself, it is not less eagerly
seized. Mr. Goldwin Smith has recently asserted that,
in consequence of the entail of the Duke of Buckingham's estates being broken, five hundred freeholders
have been called into existence in Buckinghamshire.
These facts show that the restrictive operation of the
law of entail is real, on both sides of the Irish Sea;
and that a tendency to the formation of a yeomanry
exists, but is combated by artificial legislation. In
Ireland, there are the materials of a class of peasant
proprietors. In a communication to Mr. Mill (published
in the last edition of the "Principles of Political
Economy"), Mr. Cairnes mentions that in cases which
have come to light in the Landed Estates Court, the
price given for the tenant-right—that is, for the mere
goodwill of the farm—has been enormous, being in
some instances equal in value to the whole fee of the
land. Of course, men who will buy a precarious liberty
of occupation, at the ordinary rent, would prefer to
buy the land itself for the same sum. What prevents
them? Mr. Cairnes finds the answer to this question in
the state of the land laws. "The cost of transferring
the land in small portions is, relatively to the purchase-
money, very considerable, even in the Landed Estates
Court; while the goodwill of a farm may be transferred
without any cost at all. . . . But, in truth, the mere cost
of conveyance represents the least part of the obstacles
which exist to obtaining land in small portions. A
far more serious impediment is the complicated state
of the ownership of land, which renders it frequently

impracticable to subdivide a property into such portions as would bring the land within the reach of small bidders. . . . The effect of these circumstances is to place an immense premium upon large dealings in land—indeed, in most cases, practically to exclude all other than large dealings; and while this is the state of the law, the experiment of peasant proprietorship cannot, it is plain, be fairly tried." The round of wrong is complete. The tenant wastes a capital sometimes equal to the value of the fee-simple of the land in becoming a tenant-at-will. He has still to pay rent after paying what, under a different system, would have made him the owner of the farm. He has little or no capital left for its cultivation; and what capital he has, he dares not freely invest, because he has but the imperfect security of the landlord's good faith—a security varying with individual character, temper, and necessities. The seller of the land is a loser also. It is notorious that the same area of land sold in small lots will fetch a larger sum than if sold *en masse.* "The profits of the British Land Company are made out of the difference between the wholesale price which they give for the land and the retail price which they obtain for it; and the profits allow them to pay 15 per cent. dividend, and the shares are selling at 75 per cent. premium." The evil of the land-monopoly affects not only landlord and tenant, but the community at large. The system of peasant-proprietorship which it thwarts, is, as continental experience shows, more favourable to the consummate cultivation of the land than any other. It requires more labour, and yields to it a greater return, not only absolute but proportionate. Mr. Thornton, in his

" Plea for Peasant Proprietors," has shown that while in
Jersey the produce of two and a half acres fed four persons,
and in Guernsey five, in Great Britain it was sufficient
for one person only ; and the number of cultivators was
twice as numerous in Guernsey, and three times as
numerous in Jersey, as it was in Great Britain. But
the present is not the place for the discussion of this
question. The facts stated tend not to the establishment, nor even to the indirect encouragement, by the
Legislature, of peasant-proprietorships, but only to the
thorough carrying out of the recognised economic principles on which the wealth of nations depends. It is
obvious that the advantages derived from free-trade in
the products of the land are imperfect so long as free-
trade in the land itself is refused. It is as if we let the
manufactured article go free, but taxed the raw material
and the instrument of production. To the extent to
which this indirect tax operates, the price of the food of
the people is artificially raised.

The probable effect of a repeal of the laws of primogeniture and entail would be to qualify the present
system of large estates let in large or small holdings
to tenant-farmers by the introduction of a class of
yeomen and peasant proprietors. There is no likeli-
hood that any revolutionary change would follow.
Economic laws, left to their own natural operation,
would bring about arrangements accurately reflecting
the varieties of individual character and social circumstances. It has required exceptional legislation to
produce both the over-minute division of the soil which
characterises the rural economy of France, and the
concentration of landed property in a few hands which

prevails in the United Kingdom. The instincts of trade are wiser than the foresight and safeguards of Government.

The abolition of the laws of primogeniture and entail, and the restriction of the right of settlement, would probably tend to the establishment of more satisfactory relations between landlord and tenant. These relations will not be what they ought to be until they are based on freedom of contract, and determined by written agreements. But it is absurd to talk of freedom of contract with the possessors of a monopoly. Land is now held both in Ireland and in England less as a commercial investment than as an instrument of political and social ascendency; economical considerations occupying only a secondary place in the minds of its owners. Within certain limits, they prefer docile voters to good farmers. So long as this feeling prevails, neither long leases nor the recognition of the tenant's right to the value of his improvements will be conceded by a Parliament in which landlords have a predominant influence. A tenant with a long lease, or tenant with legal security for the enjoyment of the fruits of his own capital and labour, would be politically independent. Therefore leases are out of favour, and tenant right is discountenanced; and capital, wanting security, is withheld from the land, and the means of employing labour fail. Laws for enabling the landlord to improve will not meet the necessity of the case. The extension of the leasing powers of limited owners, who will not use the powers of leasing which they already possess; the application to Ireland of the Scotch Mackenzie Act, enabling the tenant for life to charge his successor for improvements, and advances to the landlords from the public funds,—do not meet the necessities of the case. The real improver must be the tenant. He knows his trade better than any one can teach it him, or he is unfit to exercise it at all. Until he is encouraged, or permitted—for he would need no other encouragement than permission — freely to employ his capital in his own business, in accordance with his judgment of what will pay, there will be no real progress in agriculture. He will not risk money, and time, and labour, without some sort of security for his investment. A long lease would give him all the assurance which he could desire, but this on the present system he cannot expect. The only alternative is to give the tenant in Ireland that which the tenant possesses in many counties in England,—a legal title on ejection to the unexhausted value of the improvements which the usage of the country allows, or the necessities of his business require him to make. The evidence of usage, of expediency, and of value would, in case of dispute, be sifted by a court of justice ; so that wrongful claims would receive no countenance, and a customary law of tenure would gradually grow up suited to the conditions of the country, and corrective of individual misunderstandings. The measures introduced by the late and by the present Government during the last and the present session of Parliament, admit the principle of the right of the tenant to improvements made without the landlord's consent. The charge of communism and subversion of the rights of property is, therefore, no longer advanced against a doctrine which is that alike of Political Economy and of English Law,— namely, that the landowner, as Blackstone phrases it, "has only the usufruct and not the absolute ownership of the soil." It is sufficient, however, without entering upon deeper questions, to urge that if laws framed for a purely political end, such as the maintenance of the power of a particular class in the State, set at nought the received principles of commercial policy, they may justly be met by counter-measures intended to qualify their injurious economical effects. Exceptional legislation in one direction may need to be balanced by exceptional legislation in another ; and privilege to be counterpoised by restriction. A simpler plan is to do away with exceptional legislation altogether.

To neither of these courses can the voluntary assent of a Parliament three-fifths of the members of which belong to the land-owning class be anticipated. The occupation of the land has always been accommodated in Ireland as in England to the increase of the electioneering power of the territorial oligarchy. When the forty-shilling freehold franchise prevailed in Ireland, forty-shilling freeholders were multiplied by the land-owners, who took good care to secure, by private arrangements, the dependence of those whom they nominally enfranchised. The Act of 1829 established various leasehold qualifications, which would have made the tenants politically independent. The landlords practically repealed the law by refusing to grant or renew leases, and in the course of twenty years the county constituencies of Ireland had disappeared almost altogether, being kept alive only by the 10l. freehold franchise. The 12l. rating franchise of 1850 at once raised the number of the county voters from 27,000 to 135,000 ; it now amounts to 172,000. These things tell their own tale. They show that the landlords of

Ireland will not willingly renounce the power of illegally controlling the votes of their tenants. They sacrifice—without perhaps clearly perceiving it—the industrial interests of the country, the comforts of the labourer, the prosperity of the farmer, and their own rent-roll, to the maintenance of a political ascendency which they seldom know how to use wisely. Dr. Johnson justified the law of primogeniture on the ground that "it made only one fool in a family." Unfortunately it gives the "fool" almost absolute control over an important branch of national industry, and predominant power in the government of the country.

The allegations which are commonly made in maintenance of the economical *status quo* in Ireland may be very briefly dismissed. It is customary to assert that the population is in excess of the industrial resources of the country. But, as has been shown, those resources are artificially checked; and to plead this depression as an argument against change is to find in the abuse its own justification. The Irish people have a moral title to require that the social system of Ireland shall be adapted to their needs. As matters stand, their interests and the general well-being are subordinated to the system. The example of the agricultural districts of England is appealed to in proof of the excess of the rural population of Ireland. In proportion to the area of profitable land, the number of persons engaged in the cultivation of the soil in England is, we are repeatedly and confidently told, fewer than in Ireland. The answer is twofold. First, the pretended fact is a fiction. A well-informed correspondent of the *Daily News*, quoting the official figures, says: " The profitable land in Ireland may be taken as

15,832,892 acres. By the Census of 1861, the numbers of the population engaged in agriculture in Ireland are stated to be 988,929, which gives us an average of 31 $\frac{23}{100}$ per 500 acres. In England and Wales there are 32,000,000 acres of profitable land ; and by the Census of 1861 the numbers engaged in agriculture are given as 2,010,454, which shows an average of 31 $\frac{41}{100}$ per 500 acres. In other words, in order to be on a par with England and Wales, Ireland ought to have had 994,728 of her population employed in agriculture in 1861 : that is, she was then 5,799 persons short of her proportion." But during the six years which have elapsed since these statistics were obtained, the emigration has gone on steadily. At present, according to the writer just quoted, the agricultural class cannot number more than 650,000 persons, or about two-thirds of her agricultural population of 1861. "This would give her only twenty cultivators for 500 acres of profitable land, against thirty-one culti- vators on the same area in England and Wales." But if the facts were just the reverse of what they have been shown to be, the parallel would be misleading. A system of small holdings, such as exists in Ireland, demands and will reward the labours of a far larger agricultural popu- lation than can be employed upon an equal area divided into large holdings. To argue from the requirements of *la grande culture* to those of *la petite culture* is absurd. Lastly, the reminder is administered to us that emigra- tion is not a peculiarly Irish phenomenon, but charac- terises in as great, or in a still greater degree, other European nations. While the average of emigration from Ireland, a recent writer has ventured to say, amounted to less than 100,000 a year during ten years, the emigration of Germany alone amounted in a single year to 250,000 persons. The facts are as stated, and they have been very ingeniously selected to convey an entirely false impression. In 1854, the emigration from Germany was about 250,000 ; but it was little more than 162,000 persons in the previous year, and this was the highest point it had up to that time obtained. In the year following, it fell to 81,698 ; and the average of the three next years was between 50,000 and 60,000. M. Jules Duval, in his " Histoire de l'Émigration au xixᵉ Siècle," gives the ordinary annual emigration from Germany as 1 in every 533 of the population, and of Ireland as 1 in every 44 of the population. The Continental States which approach nearest to Ireland are Electoral Hesse and Mecklenburg, from which the emigration was respectively, at the period of comparison selected by M. Duval, 1 in 79 and 1 in 85 of the population. The cause of emigration is to be found in evil social arrangements, and in political mal-administration. In Mecklenburg-Schwerin, the agricultural population are serfs. " The ownership of the soil " (I quote from Mr. Martin's " Statesman's Year-book " for 1867) " is divided between the sovereign, who owns two-tenths of the land ; the titled and untitled nobility, who possess seven-tenths ; and various corporations and monastic institutions for Protestant noble ladies, who possess one-tenth." " In Mecklenburg," says M. Duval, " private property is so rare as to be almost entirely unattainable (*à peu près inaccessibles à tous*)." The misgovernment of Hesse-Cassel is notorious, and M. Duval quotes in regard to it the saying of the Americans, that when a European country is ill-ruled, the

United States are the first to profit by it. The politicians who seek in Germany a parallel to Irish expatriation will find it closer than they supposed. Bad government and a monopoly of the land are the operative causes of the emigration in both.

The classes who rule in the present Parliament cannot be expected to grant the reforms that are needed in the Irish land-laws ; because they perceive that these reforms are in principle just as applicable to England as to Ireland. The only difference is, that what is expedient here is absolutely necessary there. The vicious operation of the land-laws, which on this side of the Channel is disguised by the prosperity resulting from a sound system of commerce and manufactures, is clearly exhibited on the other. There we see the cause operating alone, and are able to dissever its real effects from those which are accidentally associated with it, and to discern its true character. It furnishes a "prerogative instance" for our reasoning. To judge of Ireland in this matter by the English standard, is to try the clearer case by the more obscure. If agriculture employed in Great Britain the same proportion of the population that it employs in Ireland, the outcry for agrarian reform would be loud on both sides of the Channel. The absolute dependence of the tenants on their landlords, and the degradation of the agricultural labourers, prevent the classes most directly concerned in Reform from raising their voices. The influence of the aristocracy and the country gentry in the counties and in the small boroughs gives them the command of the situation. The evil can be remedied only by such a measure of popular enfran-

chisement as will bring the intelligence and right feeling
of the nation to bear upon a question which now rests
with the vested interests and prepossessions of a single
class. No body of men will ever willingly surrender a
monopoly which secures them political power independent
of capacity and deserts.

Ireland has a special claim to redress for her grievances
in Church and State ; since it is in the highest degree
probable that if she had been suffered to retain real
legislative independence for two generations, the evils
under which she now suffers would have been promptly
abated. The much decried Parliament of 1782 gave
constitutional government for the first time to Ireland.
The national movement which abolished at once the legislative supremacy and the military rule of Great Britain,
repealed the restrictions which England had imposed on
Irish trade. The Anglo-Irish colony of landlords and
Churchmen, no longer able to rely on British bayonets,
and brought face to face with the Irish people, were driven
into the path of conciliation. In 1793, the Parliamentary franchise was restored to Roman Catholic freeholders. Had England's necessities continued to furnish
Ireland's opportunity, there can be little doubt that the
admission of Catholics to Parliament would speedily
have followed ; and that the crowning of the, as yet,
unfinished edifice of religious freedom would have been
accomplished by the secularization or equitable distribution of the temporalities of the Established Church. Nor
is it probable that, with a nation of dispossessed peasants
fronting a handful of half-foreign landlords, the laws and
customs affecting the transfer and occupation of the soil

d

would have been suffered to remain on their present basis. The Act of Union, sooner or later, was inevitable, and was ultimately desirable ; but if it could have been deferred for a generation, England might have received Ireland without the dowry of Irish difficulties which still form the embarrassment of statesmen.

After nearly seventy years of connexion, it is surely time that this Union which was at first only political and legal, should become one of heart and mind. To accomplish this result exceptional legislation is not needed. The removal of confessed and notorious abuses, and the consistent and courageous application of recognised principles, are all that is asked. The doctrines of religious equality and of Free Trade, fully carried out, would, in time, redress every Irish grievance, and solve every Irish difficulty. But the British Parliament as it is at present constituted has not the courage of its principles. It is afraid of the social consequences which might follow their unrestricted application. It dreads the diminution of the political power of property. Its fears are gratuitous. If the retention of large estates, no longer tied up by legal restrictions, were associated with the qualities of intelligence and character which first acquired them, the social influence of the land-owning class would be increased by the higher moral consideration which they would command. Their influence would be, what it is not now, legitimate ; and it would be exercised by men, not enervated by protection, but trained, by the necessity of attending to their own affairs, into capacity for the business of the State. The moral gain which would ensue from the substitution of relations of personal independence and mutual respect between different classes, for those of subjection and authority, often degenerating into arrogance on the one side and servility on the other, is beyond measurement. But this is not all. While the Irish, having no hope except in emigration, are but a nomad horde in their own land, the virtues of a settled people cannot reasonably be expected from them. Their exodus is sapping the military strength of the Empire not less than the industrial resources of Ireland. Emigration is a sign of health when it springs from the spirit of enterprise, but not when it is the escape of an entire people from despair. It then indicates a vice in the organization of society, and the need of great social and economical changes. Mr. Gladstone, Mr. Disraeli, Lord Stanley, and Mr. Mill, as well as Mr. Bright and Mr. Maguire, have explicitly recognised in the depopulation of Ireland an evil of the first magnitude. "Against transplantation," says an early writer, whose words with little alteration suit our own time, "the Irish have ('tis strange) as great a resentment as against loss of estate, yea, even death itself. ... Can it be imagined that a whole nation will drive like geese at the wagging of a hat upon a stick?" "The unsettling of a nation," he adds, "is easy work; the settling is not. The opportunity for it will not last always; it is now." The opportunity is now, if statesmen and philosophers who discern the evil and its cure can reckon upon the support of the nation in their enterprise against the vested interests and prejudices of a class. The expedient of patching the existing system has been tried for twenty years, and in 1867 the condition of

Ireland is not sensibly or essentially better than it was in 1847. The only hope lies in an appeal from the Parliament of a predominant order, to the sense and justice of the nation at large. The Reform of the House of Commons is the essential condition of the good government and pacification of Ireland.

II.

WORKMEN AND TRADE UNIONS.

BY GODFREY LUSHINGTON.

ONE feature of the present Reform agitation is the prominent part taken in it by Trade Unions. The movement, it is plain, is not merely political, it is at the same time an industrial one. Industry calls for Reform. Why this is so ; why operatives desire the franchise as operatives even more than as citizens ; what as industrialists they suffer from laws made by others ; what as industrialists they hope to gain from a share in the representation, is the subject of the present paper.

For this purpose I propose to consider in one or two particulars the status and general estimation which the existing *régime* accords to operatives individually, and to operatives associated together in Trade Unions.

To begin with the law of Master and Servant in respect of breaches of Contract. The law of Master and Servant is the law under which the workman works, necessarily therefore it affects every operative every day. It is to him what the Church Discipline Act is to the clergy—what the Merchant Shipping Acts are to sailors. The laws now in force on the subject are not old laws ; they

consist chiefly of statutes passed not fifty years ago.
They were passed for the express purpose of meeting the
situation ; they therefore not unfairly represent what
until very recently were, in the eyes of the governing
classes, just provisions as to the relation of the operative
and employer.

Suppose, then, two men to make a contract in the city
of London in the present month of February 1867, one
an operative, the other a master —the former undertaking
to do work, and the other to pay wages for the work—
how does the law deal with each in case of a breach of
contract ?

If the Master breaks the contract ; if, having had his
work done by an operative, he refuses to pay him wages,
the operative may *summon* either him or his bailiff
before a Justice and recover his wages to the extent of
10*l.* :[1] in default, after twenty-one days, the sum may be
levied by distress ; and in the event of the distress
proving insufficient, the master becomes under a general
statute (called Jervis's Act) liable to imprisonment. But
at any time he has only to pay what is due in order to
procure his release. In all this, of course, the process
is strictly civil.

But if the Operative breaks his contract ;[2] if, having
commenced service, he absent himself, or neglects to
fulfil his contract, or is guilty of any other misconduct
or misdemeanour in the execution thereof, the master
may sue out a *warrant* for his apprehension : under that
warrant the operative may be apprehended in bed, may
be denied information as to the cause of his apprehension
and opportunity to communicate with his friends, may

---

[1] 4 Geo. IV. c. 34, sec. 4.   [2] 4 Geo. IV. c. 34, sec. 3.

be manacled, and so brought before a Justice, who, be it remembered, is necessarily a member of the upper classes, and in a manufacturing district is probably, like the prosecutor, himself an employer. The Justice may sit and hear the case in his own drawing-room, uncontrolled by the presence of any brother-magistrate or of the public : he cannot allow the operative to be a witness in his own defence, and upon conviction may sentence him as a criminal to three months' imprisonment with hard labour at the treadmill or crank, in company, of course, with ordinary felons. Nor is this all : the sentence of the magistrate does not necessarily discharge the operative from his contract, and, if it has not expressly discharged him, the operative when he comes out of prison may be called upon by his master to fulfil his term, and, on refusing, may again be apprehended, tried, sentenced and imprisoned, and so on, *toties quoties.*[1]

I am well aware that I have stated an extreme case, and that the practice is much milder. In England (though not in Scotland) the master almost invariably proceeds by summons, and not by warrant : usually the operative is informed of the offence with which he is charged, and is allowed to confer with his friends. Of course also it frequently happens that the Justice does not sit at home, but sits in open court with his brother magistrates ; and I am far from saying that Justices are always partial, still less that they mean to be so. Also, they have under the Statute an option of inflicting a less severe sentence than imprisonment, viz. abatement of wages, or a simple discharge from the contract. Never-

---

[1] Unwin *v.* Clarke, Law Reports, 1 Q. B. 417 ; notwithstanding, *ex parte* Baker, 2 H. & N. 219 ; Youle *v.* Mappin, 6 H. & N. 753.

theless, the law, as I have stated it, is the law of the land : and a workman subjected to the treatment I have described for breach of civil contract, has no redress.

It is right to mention that these matters have been the subject of a Parliamentary investigation during the last two years, and that the Committee have reported that the present condition of the law of Master and Servant is objectionable, and have recommended the abolition of several of the chief evils which I have pointed out. But how far the proposals of the Committee are from being satisfactory, may be judged from the fact, that they would still leave the operative as a prisoner on his trial, disqualified from giving evidence in his own favour ; that they would still invest the magistrate with the power of inflicting imprisonment for what may seem to him, in his discretion, " aggravated breaches of contract ; " and that they would introduce a new machinery for legal oppression,—namely, a power vested in the magistrate to exact security from the operative for the fulfilment of his contract. It is understood that, founded on the report of this Committee, the Government will in the present session bring forward a measure to amend the law of Master and Servant. Doubtless this measure will be an improvement on the present state of things, but that it will be a satisfactory and permanent settlement can hardly be expected.

I would only add that justice to the operative will be no obstacle to a proper treatment of the peculiar difficulties of the case. Breaches of contract by operatives are injurious to operatives ; and (irrespective of this) when wanton, they are, we may be sure, odious in their sight. Operatives themselves would not wish the cardinal

distinction to be overlooked that, whilst the Master
can almost always pay the damages occasioned by his
breach of contract, an Operative rarely can ; and would
readily affirm the justice of a rule condemning the defaulting operative to imprisonment, provided that he was
imprisoned as a civil debtor only, and damages were
calculated according to a just estimate of the liabilities
incurred under the contract.

Again, Operatives would be the first to admit that some
breaches of contract are crimes, and should be treated as
such. Only let the acts which are to constitute these
crimes be defined beforehand, on some general principles
of criminal law ; let them be defined by the Legislature
after deliberation, in which the interests of both parties
are represented : not abandoned as a matter for the discretion of local magistrates, who are untrained in law,
who with the best intentions can hardly be free from
social bias, and who have to decide on the spur of the
moment, often in the heat of an industrial struggle going
on around them.[1]

The existing law of Master and Servant cannot be said
to be inoperative. The number of prosecutions amounts
to several thousands annually. How many operatives
are convicted and actually sent to prison, I am not
aware ; of these some of course are rogues, and deserve
their sentence ; others again, it is to be feared, have
been guilty of no more than a violent rupture with the

[1] To supersede altogether the jurisdiction of the Justices in this matter
would be very desirable, if possible ; but a summary procedure is doubtless
indispensable to industrial discipline, and a reference to the intermittent
jurisdiction of the County Courts would probably be found inconvenient. But
if the jurisdiction of the Justices must be retained, it should be with the
guarantee suggested by the Committee, that the case should be heard only
before two or more Justices sitting in the public Court-house.

master to whom they have bound themselves, and this
perhaps after provocation; yet they are sent to prison.
Thus does the law deprave its respectable citizens into
criminals! But, of course, the evil of the law is not to
be measured by the number of its victims. Such a law
poisons the daily relation of master and servant throughout the kingdom. It puts into the mouths of masters
brutal threats of imprisonment against any servant with
whom they happen to have a dispute. It dishonours
industry, constituting operatives a degraded class,—but
one remove, as it were, from criminals. Mr. Odger, an
operative witness before the Parliamentary Committee,
truly said, " I think men who are cognisant of this law
say at once, ' There is an inequality in it, and it is
against us :' they say, 'Who made it? Not us ; we had
no hand in making it : it was made by those who employ
us, and by those who govern us; that is evidence of
their justice and right.' " In fact, to appreciate this
inequality, we have only to imagine the case reversed.
Imagine an employer of labour, who has dismissed an
operative before the expiration of the time named in
the contract, placed in the dock before a Proletariat
Magistrate, not allowed to be a witness in his own
defence, and finally sentenced to the House of Correction for three months with hard labour.

I now pass from the status of the operative as an
individual contracting with his employer, to the status
of operatives combining with one another in a Labour
Association. At the outset it is very important to form
a correct conception of the origin and constitution of
Trade Unions, and of the normal operation of a Strike.

Trade Union Associations all spring from one source. Upon the conditions, on which the working man disposes of his labour, depends his working life entirely ; in great measure also his home life, his health, and happiness. But the single operative, without a reserve fund, living from hand to mouth, and more or less bound to the soil, finds that, in dealing with the capitalist employer, he can make but a bad bargain for his labour. He suffers from low wages, or long hours, or unhealthy accommodation, or galling or exacting conditions, and in all he suffers, as he conceives, *unnecessarily.* But he must accept what is offered, or starve. So he accepts. Like poor Esau, he has to sell his birthright for a mess of pottage. Thus it is when he stands alone : but might not he and his comrade labourers co-operate and help each other ? Hence the Trade Union. Operatives in a trade, fewer or more, join together, meet from time to time, and by the light of what education, information, or experience they as operatives, and as operatives in a particular trade, are possessed of, consider what conditions as to wages, hours, and other particulars are essential to their welfare, and practicable for them to obtain from their masters. By dint of divers discussions, and in some trades, of repeated ballotings, some result is arrived at, by the majority at least, which is acquiesced in by the minority, as the rule fixing the conditions upon which every member of the society shall give his labour. The members further agree to make common cause with one another in procuring compliance with these conditions, both from masters and other operatives, and for this purpose to make a common fund by weekly or other subscriptions out of their wages. Accordingly, if in any establishment the conditions are not observed, the usual course is for a remonstrance to be made by the Union, through either its delegates or one of the workmen: and, that failing, for a notice to be sent announcing a strike unless a change be made: at last, if no change is made, the strike does take place. Straightway the Unionists (as well those who are obtaining the trade terms as those who are not) leave the establishment in a body, and are supported by the funds of the Society till the master comes to terms, or they themselves are obliged to yield. The above is an instance of a strike against a single master, but a general strike against all the masters of a trade is in no way different, except in extent.

Several remarks here naturally arise. In the first place, it is obvious that a Union, thus organized, enormously multiplies the force of a single operative, and helps to place him upon an equality with the capitalist employer in respect of the power to ask for reasonable, and to refuse unreasonable terms. It is equally obvious that a Union without power to strike, or a strike without a strike fund, would be nugatory. In the next place, it is apparent that in the result the rules of the Union affect those who were no parties to their being framed, viz. non-Unionist operatives, and employers generally. But—not to speak of the fact that these rules are tacitly made subject to the practical consent of the masters— it is most important to observe that, both in form and substance, they are agreements, binding members only, and the force of them upon others depends exactly upon what proportion of the skill and industry of the trade is comprised in the operatives of the Union. If a small proportion only, the rules are freely disregarded by others : masters find they can carry on their works without Unionists. But if, on the other hand, the Union represents the great majority of the operatives, it may go hard with a non-conforming master to find hands, or with a non-conforming operative to find a master : but then the rules so made are *primâ facie* good for the whole body of operatives. The masters, indeed, have not been directly consulted ; and there are no bounds to the terms which a strong Union may demand from employers : but neither are there any to the terms which employers may seek to impose on operatives : the fact is, that each party is really necessary to the other, and therefore it is the interest of neither to insist upon unreasonable terms, which the other is in a position to refuse. Lastly, the fact of the force of a Union consisting in its numbers fully explains the feeling with which Trade Unionists regard the operative who, with a view to his private advantage, holds aloof,—a feeling much akin to that which defenders of their country have to a citizen who deserts to the invaders for the sake of better pay.

Trade Unions differ very much in detail, but the above, as a general description of their constitution and *modus operandi*, may suffice to indicate why the employer hates them ; why the operative will spend his last sixpence in their defence; also how they are liable to generate abuses —abuses of ignorance, abuses of violence. I will only further point out the obvious need that any law on the subject of Trade Unions should be especially simple, in order to meet the comprehension of those whose conduct it has to govern—the whole operative class ; and that it should be well weighed, considering the magnitude of the interests concerned—the interests, namely, of several hundred associations, comprising several hundred thousand operatives, reaching to almost every trade and town in the kingdom, and possessed of or capable of calling up funds, in the aggregate, of an enormous amount.

And now for the law. If at the present day a person were called upon to give advice to operatives about to enter a Trades Union, as to the legal consequences of their so doing, he might address them to the following effect :—

" You may meet if you like, and agree about wages and hours of labour; and so long as your discussion is confined to those two subjects and your agreement ends in talk, you are safe : but I must warn you that any steps to make such an agreement effectual, are dangerous. If you strike you may possibly, if you threaten to strike you will certainly, be liable to three months' imprisonment with hard labour. Beware then of negotiation : negotiation may too easily be construed into intimidation.[1] I see your rules contain provisions for other matters than wages and hours of labour, and provisions for the organization of strikes. It is doubtful whether these do not render your Union from the first illegal—an indictable conspiracy at Common Law. It will be only prudent, then, to keep all such provisions secret. If the question is raised, the result will probably depend upon who is the Judge before whom it is raised. I am sorry I cannot inform you what is the Common Law of Conspiracy, beyond this, that there are some acts which it is lawful for one man to do, but unlawful for several to combine to do ; but your ignorance of the law will be no excuse.

---

[1] This is clearly shown by the cases of O'Neill v. Kruger, 4 Best & Smith, 389 ; Wood v. Bowron, 2 Law Reports, Com. L. 21 ;—although in each of these the result was that the conviction for intimidation was quashed.

" Further, I see you consider your Trade Union is a means of developing trade : the Judges, however, consider it in restraint of trade ; and, if they have the chance, will certainly designate your Union as contrary to public policy and as illegal in this sense, that your rules are not enforceable in a court of law. Perhaps you think that this makes no matter, that you can do without the law ; but you are mistaken. If your treasurer embezzles your strike funds, the law will decline either to punish him or to protect you. Your Union is illegal, and therefore may be robbed.

" Lastly, I observe that your Trade Union is also a Benefit Society. You naturally think that care for an operative as an individual, and as a member of a family, should go hand in hand with care for him as a member of a class : and, therefore, besides subscriptions for strike funds, you make subscriptions out of your earnings for a fund which is to provide for the evil day when sickness or accident or old age overtakes you. But I am bound to tell you, that if the law loves Benefit Societies much, it hates Trade Unions more. In the eyes of the law the Trade Union element poisons the Benefit Society element, and taints it with illegality, and your treasurer may rob you of your benefit fund, as he may of your trade fund, with impunity.

" In a word : if you are not prosecuted as criminals, congratulate yourselves on your good fortune ; but at least make up your mind to stand without the pale of the law."[1]

[1] Readers, to whom this statement of the law may seem incredible, are referred to the Note at the end of this paper, in which the statutory provisions are set forth and considered, together with, as I believe, all the cases decided upon them by the Superior Courts.

But shameful as the law is which regulates the status of the operative, whether contracting with his master or as combining with his fellows, I am convinced it is not . . the law of which Trade Unionists most complain. It is the general misunderstanding and misrepresentation to which these societies are subject, and the impossibility of setting their case right before the public. The public of themselves know very little of the working man : his very honesty and independence keep him in the back ground, whilst the pauper and the criminal come to the front. Still less do the public know of Trade Unions and their ordinary operations. They become cognisant of them chiefly on special occasions, as when they suffer inconvenience from street demonstrations, or are shocked by news of a trade outrage at Sheffield, or by the spectacle of the evil passions and misery of some general strike, which is set down to the door of Trade Unions, just as English children believe that in every French war France has been the aggressor. Now in general, persons or bodies of persons who find themselves misunderstood are able to obtain redress by having recourse to dis-interested tribunals, such as independent thinkers, the Church, the Law, the Press, and the Legislature. But from these appeals Trade Unions are cut off. Advanced Liberals, as a party, are prejudiced against Trade Union-ism. Many of their distinguished chiefs have been and are capitalist-employers of labour, and, as such, have been vexed by strikes. Their revolutionary doctrine of individualism, which has done such great service in delivering commerce from oppressive laws, leads them to confound voluntary organization of operatives for external legislative interference. Political Economists might have been expected to study Trade Unions, and, whilst freely exposing their errors, to do justice to their legitimate and necessary function; and the best have done so. But the school as a whole have chiefly furnished the advocates of employers' interests and caste-prejudices with sciolistic watchwords. The cause is not far to seek. They have allowed themselves to be hastily scared away by some rules of some Trade Unions, which undoubtedly rest upon the exploded doctrine of Protection. Again, their just pride in their newly acquired science, and the general emancipation which that science has effected from a false system of artificial production and artificial prices, have led to the natural errors of dogmatizing upon a theory without due regard to modifications required by practice, and of confounding a natural tendency of wages to be regulated according to supply and demand, with an absolute and universal law. They would have us believe (despite experience to the contrary) that at any given time and place the market rate of wages must as necessarily obtain as the mercury rises and falls with the change of the atmosphere, and consequently, of course, that all intervention is an unnatural cause of disturbance. This closet theory blinds them to the fact that this natural tendency is always slow, frequently unequal, in operation; that one cause of its inequality may be the disposition of the master, and that a master who is under-paying his men is more likely to awake to a sense of the market rate by a summons from the Union, than by a humble application from a single-handed operative.

The Benevolent world feel that their calling is not with men who are fighting sturdily for themselves, and ask for

nothing but fair play. As for the Clergy, not only is
their ministration impotent to reach the moral difficulties
of the labour market, but their whole habit of mind and
their social position alike place them on the side of
authority; and, whatever sympathy they may have for
the poor, they have, as a class, none for the operative
striving towards intellectual, social, and political emancipation. The Law, as we have seen, is made for employers: nor are the Magistrates, and very Judges on the
bench, more free than other men from the prejudices of
the class to which they belong. The Press of course, at
least such as tends to form public opinion, circulates
amongst, and is therefore written to suit the tastes of
the upper classes—capitalists, employers, tradesmen—in
short, for anybody but the operative. I can scarcely
recall having seen in any journal (the *Beehive* excepted),
with reference to any strike, so much as a hint that the
Masters might possibly be refusing the fair market-rate
of wages. It is always the Union which is in the wrong.
Lastly, as to the Legislature. Of the House of Peers, it is
perhaps unnecessary for me to speak.[1] The House of
Commons may be said to be composed exclusively from
the Master-class, not a few Members being employers of
labour on a large scale: it contains no Member of the
wage-receiving class, scarcely two elected by the suffrages
of that class: and what with its morbid fears of unduly
interfering with the labour market, and its natural apathy
to a topic which neither makes appeal to party nor pro-
poses a charge upon the public purse, is inclined to ignore
the subject of Trade Unions altogether.

[1] It should be mentioned, however, that Lord Lichfield, in a grave industrial conflict, has acted as an impartial mediator; and Lord St. Leonards
has done good service in his repeated advocacy of courts of arbitration.

Such being the case, should we wonder that the public
is in profound ignorance of Trade Societies, their numbers, funds, rules, objects, and doings—or of the causes,
operation, and effect of Strikes? Unfortunately this ignorance does not prevent the public from passing the most
adverse judgments, although a judgment of any value
would obviously require an intimate knowledge of the
origin and operation of Trade rules, the conduct of the
workshop, and the state of the market. Thus strikes are
put down as failures, by persons who have not the least
idea how many of them have succeeded. In any particular strike the operatives are condemned unheard.
They are denounced as demanding wages beyond the
market rate by critics who know nothing of the market
rate, either what it is or how it is ascertained. Some
accuse Unions of wantonly promoting strikes, nor stop
to inquire what provisions Unions have to prevent
strikes, how a strike usually comes to pass, or in what
proportion of cases Unions have tried, with success or
otherwise, to prevent or stop a strike by negotiation or
arbitration. Others vilipend Unionists as dupes of design-
ing leaders, without ever having had cognizance of the
operations of a single society, and forgetting that their
words, if they mean anything, mean that more than
half a million of grown-up men in different trades, in
different towns, and in different circumstances, after a
daily experience for years of the results of the Union, are
habitually duped in matters which intimately concern
their purse and person, their workshop and their home.

Others point to rules prohibiting piecework, and
enforcing a standard wage as betraying the aim of
Unions to reduce all workmen to one low level of

industry and skill. But if such persons were to inquire, they would find that these rules had no such object, but that, whether just or unjust, they, like other rules of Trade Unions, have originated and are maintained as a protection to the operative from some real and unquestionable abuse on the part of his employer.

Others, again, cite the trade outrages at Sheffield as conclusive proof that Trade Unions, as a system, are based on violence and intimidation. It does not occur to these people that they should at least suspend their judgment until they have acquired some notion on one hand of how many trade outrages have been actually committed, and on the other of how many strikes there have been, and how many persons have been engaged in them : and until they have made allowance for the fact that, whilst the strike lasts, men of the operative class, out of work, exasperated, and sometimes starving, are congregated in masses in the streets and daily meet masses of rivals of the same class, whom (whether with justification or otherwise) they must regard as neutralizing their efforts, and trading on their misfortunes.

" Well," but persons may say, " this state of the law, this ignorance concerning Trade Unions are very bad, and, maybe, would never have been, if the working classes had been represented in the House of Commons. But is it not now all going to be set right ? Is not the law of Master and Servant about to be amended ? Has not a Commission been issued, which will give to the public full information of Trade Unions, and will suggest all proper improvements in the law ? Why then a Reform Bill ?" To such I would in the first place

answer, that the possession of the franchise by the working classes is a necessary guarantee that the requisite law
reforms should be made. Without that, it is almost vain
to expect either the establishment of perfect equality,
before the law, between the two parties to the contract of
service, or free licence for combinations amongst operatives, subject only to due precautions to prevent breach
of contract, or breach of the peace ; or full power to
Trade Unions to prosecute their treasurers for embezzling
strike funds. Add to this that, however satisfactory be
the result of the Commission, it would always be expedient for the State that the working classes should have
representatives in the House of Commons, by no means
necessarily either artisans or partisans, who should make
it their special duty to acquaint the public through the
great organ of publicity—Parliament—with the truth of
passing events in the world of industry, and to watch over,
and, if needful, to initiate legislative action in respect of
the relations of capital and labour.

But, in the second place, it is impossible not to see
that this agitation for the franchise arises not solely from
political motives : that, behind the political question lies
a great social one, the status of industry. The fact is,
that the acquisition of the franchise is regarded by the
working classes as the first stage of their formal incorporation into the body politic. That hitherto they have
been socially excluded, and that the time is ripe for
their admission, it needs but a glance at the past and
the present to show. The wilful and almost universal
ignorance concerning Trade Unions is of itself a clear
proof that working men are an unfamiliar, an un-
considered class, whose inner life is hidden from society,

—in short, without the pale. The law of Master and Servant which renders breach of contract by the master a civil matter and a breach by the servant a crime ; the law of Trade Unions, which confines them by tightly-drawn cords, surrounds them with vague terrors, stigmatizes them as contrary to public policy, and denies them protection for their property : the insolence of masters who choose to ignore the officers of the Union as the representatives of its members ; the general prejudice that Unions are gatherings of the disaffected, and strikes open mutinies of the lower order of society : all these spring from the same sentiment, that the working classes are an alien, inferior race, that they have no business to be independent ; that they are born to do as they are bid, that they are not quite free to think for themselves, not quite free to give or withhold their labour.

Again, the very fact that the existing laws respecting them are felt to be too unjust to be carried out, and are on the eve of abolition; the whole march of industry, the working man developing from a slave into a serf, from a serf into a free man, and now asserting his right to political power ; the history of Trade Unions or Labour Associations—their spontaneous origin amongst the people ; their struggles against public opinion, against lock-outs by employers, against statutory prohibitions; the exchange of these prohibitions for the present bare and doubtful toleration, coupled with offensive and harassing disabilities ; the great fact that through all, and despite all, they have increased and multiplied, growing ever stronger and stronger, and now are strongest of all, insisting upon the attention of the public, the ministry, the legislature, becoming national and almost international—all these are signs of the times which he who runs may read. The demand for the franchise is but a knocking by the working classes at the portals of society claiming to be let in. And they will be let in. And one of the earliest results of their being made depositaries of political power will be a change in the public consideration shown to operatives and their associations. Justices of the Peace, even if allowed, will not be so off-hand to commit operatives to prison for breach of civil contract. Judges on the Bench will shrink from declaring Associations of Labour contrary to public policy. Public opinion will desire to be informed before it condemns. It will be felt that to deny to operatives the right to associate together, to agree together as to the terms on which they will work, and to act together to procure those terms in any way not involving breach of contract or breach of the peace, is to deny them the rights of free citizens ; and that the workman is as much entitled to his Trade Unions as merchants to their Chamber of Commerce, barristers to their Inns of Court, brokers to their Stock Exchange, medical practitioners to their College of Physicians. Unions will become recognised social institutions, and be accepted as necessary to put the individual operative upon a level with the capitalist in settling the rate of wages and other conditions of employment. People will then do justice to what is valuable in Trade Unions; to the recognition of the common interest of the class ; to the public deliberations on class interests ; to the making of regulations for the good not of the few, but of the many, for the protection of the weak, not for the enrichment of the strong ; to the sacrifice of individualism ; to the legal submission

of the minority ; to the public morality of holding each
operative responsible for the effect upon others of the
disposal of his labour ; to the heroic struggles for the
permanent good of their order. Society at large, which,
so long as the working classes have been without the
pale, has really desired them to be kept down, will, when
they are once admitted, be as eager that they should
become strong and prosperous ; and will then be thankful
to Trade Unionism, so far as it has procured to operatives better wages and better conditions of labour, and
has made them more intelligent, and more independent
of their masters ; it will then rejoice to see the extension
of the same principle of association to trades where it
is still weak, and amongst agricultural labourers and
domestic servants, to whom as yet it has been unattainable.

On the other hand, when the social incorporation of the
working classes shall be completed, the peculiar abuses
of Trade Unions may be expected to diminish. The
ignorance of workmen of political economy, and even
of the market in which they work, which so frequently
prompts a false policy or leads them to make impracticable demands, will be met by expedients, obvious
enough, but which at present do not recommend themselves to those who are loudest in their denunciations of
the ignorance of Trade Unions—I mean improved education of the operative class, and circulation of statistics
of the labour market. These again, in their turn, would
inevitably lead to increased candour on the part of the
master ; quickened in his sense of duty by a more active
public opinion on industrial questions, and dealing with
more intelligent operatives, he would give information

which he now too often withholds. Unjust or tyrannical rules of the Union will be rarer, because the operative, when his social position is recognised, will be rightly influenced by public opinion. The public will be more impartial and better instructed; it will therefore be more fit to give advice; and the Trade Unions will be more willing to listen to it. Everything savouring of violence will be felt to be repugnant to civilization, to which the working classes will then more consciously and therefore more really belong.

The hostile animus of Trade Unions towards employers, the odiousness of which has alienated many liberal men from their cause, will be much softened. One source of bitterness will be removed. The social sore that sometimes exalts grievance-mongers to the leadership of Trade Unions, that sometimes renders the operative in dealing with his employer quick to declare war and slow to make peace, will be healed. No longer will he see in his master the representative of privilege, he will feel himself secure of equal laws, and of a fair hearing from the legislature and from the public.

Breaches between employers and employed will cease to be felt as feuds between class and class, and will be reduced to simple industrial disputes. As such no doubt they will run high. But even these will be moderated in consequence of the recognition of the working classes by Parliament and by society. Both parties, employers and employed, will become more awake to the partnership which exists, whether recognised or not, and under all hindrances and interruptions must exist between them—the great partnership of Capital and Labour. Each will endeavour to co-operate accordingly. Trade

Unions will be more careful that the terms they demand shall not interfere with the management of the
master.   Masters, in their turn, will feel that the days
of absolutism are over: that absolutism is to be re-
placed by a relation more honourable to employers
as well as to employed : they will cease to be unapproachable, recognising that partnership disputes are not
to be concluded by the authority of the master, but are
matters for settlement between the two parties by means
of negotiation and compromise.   Public opinion will
exercise a more active moral control over these industrial disputants : will demand open dealings between
the parties : will institute courts of arbitration, and put
forth its whole force to compel recourse to them, and
will declare both strikes and lock-outs to be, like wars
between civilized nations, disgraceful to one at least of
the parties concerned, because, as mere trials of force,
they are barbarous expedients for the settlement of questions which in their nature plainly admit of a solution
by peaceful and rational means.

NOTE.[1]

During the first quarter of the present century combinations of
workmen were strictly prohibited, with this result only—that they
became secret and more violent ; darkness, as usual, producing deeds of
darkness. In 1825, a statute was passed exempting operatives from
punishment for engaging in combinations and strikes ; but in the very
next year this statute was repealed, and the statute now in force substituted for it. It is impossible to state the general effect of this
statute without considering its provisions in detail. The principal of
these will be found printed at length below. The statute opens by re-
pealing the statute of 1825, and all the statutes—some thirty-three
in number—which before 1825 were in operation against combinations
of workmen.

[1] I wish to acknowledge my obligations to Mr. F. D. Longe's excellent pamphlet
on the Law of Strikes.

The 3rd section, to which I must presently recur, so far as it affects operatives, holds out the punishment of imprisonment for three months to operatives who shall be guilty towards master or brother operatives of " violence to person or property, threats, intimidation, molestation, or obstruction."

The 4th section exempts from punishment or liability to prosecution or penalty workmen who meet and enter into agreements for the purpose of fixing the wages and hours for which they shall offer their labour. Now it is obvious that besides the rate of wages and hours of labour there are many other matters which concern operatives in their daily work, which, equally with those would, in the ordinary course of things, be subjects for discussion and agreement,—I mean the general conditions of employment. These conditions, of course, vary in different trades, but in every trade there are always some which ought to be or are considered. Such, for example (I purposely take the instances promiscuously), are questions whether the members of the society shall offer their labour to masters who employ non-unionists, or an unlimited number of apprentices, or use machinery, or execute bad work ; whether they shall stipulate for wholesome workshops and other accommodation, for proper measurement or weighing of work done by the piece ; whether they shall resist truck, fines, sub-contracts, employment of women and children, and so forth. · The statute is silent as to whether workmen may meet and agree for any of these purposes.

The statute is also silent as to how such agreements as the 4th section permits workmen to make with impunity,—agreements as to wages and hours of labour,—may be carried out. It does not go on to say that it is, lawful to carry them out in the only effectual manner—viz. by strike.

It is clear, then, that this 4th section does not expressly authorize, even to the extent of exempting from punishment, the great bulk of Trade Unions, which, as a matter of course, have regulations as to other matters than wages and hours of labour, and have general provisions as to strike.

The result of these lacunæ, whether intentional or unintentional, of the statute is tremendous. Learned judges are at issue,[1] whether all combinations, not expressly exempted by the 4th section, are not open to the Common Law against Conspiracy. The opinion of the late Mr. Justice Crompton[2] amounts to this, that an ordinary Trade Union is an indictable conspiracy. Mr. Justice Blackburn[3] (in 1867) will not say that it is lawful, will not say that it is unlawful. Chief Justice Cockburn,[4] Lord Campbell,[5] Lord Cranworth, when Baron Rolfe,[6] and

[1] Wood *v.* Bowron, decided in 1866, per Mellor, J., 2 Law Reports, Common Law, 28.

[2] Walsby *v.* Ancoft, 30 *Law Journal*, M.C. 123. Decided in 1861.

[3] Hornby *v.* Close. *Times*, Jan. 16, 1867.

[4] Wood *v.* Bowron, decided in 1866, 2 Law Rep., Com. Law, 25 ; Hornby *v.* Close, Jan. 16, 1867.

[5] Hilton *v.* Eckersley, 6 Ellis & Blackburn, 63 ; decided in 1855.

[6] Regina *v.* Selsby, tried in 1847, reported in the notes to Reg. *v.* Rowlands, 5 Cox, Crim. Cases, 495.

Chief Justice Erle,[1] seem to have considered that every combination is permitted by the 4th section, which does not promote acts prohibited by the 3rd section of the statute, or otherwise unlawful ; but the value of these opinions is almost nullified by the interpretation which has been put upon the words of the 3rd section, or by what has been deemed to be unlawful.

I have said that it is a question whether the Common Law of Conspiracy applies to Trade Unions ; and here I stop. What constitutes conspiracy at Common Law I despair of explaining to my readers, for the best of reasons, that I do not understand it myself. So far as I can learn[2] it is an undefined crime with an indefinite penalty attached to it. The general principle[3] which underlies it seems to be that acts which would be lawful for one man to do may be unlawful for several men to combine to do, when the act tends to do *harm* (N.B. not *wrong*) to another. But what these acts are is nowhere specified. An eminent authority on criminal law informs me that a conspiracy is best defined as any combination which a judge and jury think deserving to be punished ; and the judge, wielding the full powers of the Common Law unfettered by Statute, may inflict upon the offender any term of imprisonment which he may think reasonable.

To return to the 3d section, which imposes a penalty for " violence to persons and property ; threats, intimidation, molestation, obstruction." The words, " violence to persons and property," call for no observation : they are words that can be understood only in one sense, and as to whether such acts shall be penal, there can be but one opinion. But the words, " threats, intimidation, molestation, obstruction," are of a more ambiguous character, and, of course, the important question for masters, men, and the public, is whether these words are to be interpreted to apply to any of the steps of an ordinary strike.

Lord Cranworth,[4] when Baron Rolfe, seems to have been of opinion that the threats and intimidation mentioned in this 3d section, had reference to the words which immediately preceded : that is, meant

---

[1] Hilton *v*. Eckersley, 6 Ellis & Blackburn, 60 ; decided in 1855.

[2] See Chitty on Criminal Law, iii. p. 1139 :—" Perhaps few things have been left so doubtful in criminal law as the point at which a combination of several persons in a common object becomes illegal. Certain it is, that there are cases in which the act itself would not be cognisable by law, if done by a single individual, which becomes the subject of an indictment when effected by several with a joint design." So Lord Cranworth, when Baron Rolfe, in opening his charge to the Jury in the case of R. *v*. Selsby (5 Cox, 496 *n*), in which workmen were indicted on eighteen counts of conspiracy in the conduct of a strike, said :—"The case is one of extreme difficulty ; and, although the indictment should state the charge in such a way that anybody having heard it read might be able to say conscientiously, ' Guilty ' or ' Not Guilty,' implying of course that he understood what was read to him, it would be quite trifling to pretend that the defendants could have had the smallest notion of the details of the charge against them." Those who wish further to fathom this pitfall of the Common Law, I must refer to Mr. Longe's pamphlet.

[3] Per Crompton, J. in Walsby *v*. Ancoft, decided in 1861, 30 *Law Journal*, M.C. 123 ; approved of by Blackburn J., in O'Neill *v*. Longman, decided in 1863, 4 Best & Smith, 383.

[4] R. *v*. Selsby, decided in 1847 ; 5 Cox, Crim. Cases, 495 *n*.

threats or intimidation of violence to person and property. But this opinion does not prevail.

It has been ruled to be "threatening and intimidating" to a *master* for the officers of the Union to give him notice that his workmen will strike against him.[1] It has been ruled to be "threatening and intimidating" to *operatives*, for a man to tell them that if they dare work they shall be struck against.[2]

Then as to "molestation" or "obstruction." The simple striking against an operative, *i.e.* refusing to continue to work with him, has been punished as illegal—I presume, though it is not expressly so stated, as constituting, under the Act, molestation and obstruction to the operative.[3] It would follow as a logical consequence, that striking against a master, *i.e.* men in a body refusing to work for him at his terms, is also "molestation and obstruction" to that master. And it is very doubtful whether actual striking is in any manner sanctioned by the Amending Statute, 22 Vic. c. 34, which provides that no workman, by occasion merely of entering into an agreement to fix wages, shall be deemed guilty of "molestation" or "obstruction," or be liable to an indictment for conspiracy. As yet, however, I believe no master has ventured to seek a decision on the point.

This is not all. It can hardly be believed, but it is the fact, that in the year 1851 Unionists were found guilty of "molestation and obstruction"[4] for (amongst other things) peaceably persuading their companions to withdraw from the service (without breach of contract) of a master who gave less than the trade wages, and the convictions on this ground were maintained by such excellent judges as Chief Justice Erle[5] and Chief Justice Campbell.[6] This result, however, was too monstrous even for Parliament, as at present constituted, to endure, and such an interpretation was prohibited for the future by an Act made for the express purpose in 1859 (22 Vic. c. 34), but the words still remain the law of the land.

The effect which the Statute has upon combinations amongst masters is not so important, since masters rarely combine ; competition amongst them for the most part producing a policy of isolation. The Statute, however, is silent altogether as to lock-outs by masters, whether singly or in combination. Hence these consequences. A master may dismiss from his works any number of men for no cause except that they are Unionists, whilst the 3rd section might be interpreted by the Judges

---

[1] R. *v.* Bykerdike, decided in 1832, per Patteson J.; 1 Moo & Rob. 179.
    R. *v.* Rowlands,   ,,   1851,   ,,   5 Cox, Crim. Cases, 493, 4.
    Walsby *v.* Anley   ,,   1861,   ,,   30 *Law Jour.* M.C., 121.
    O'Neill *v.* Longman   ,,   1863,   Blackburn, J.; 4 Best & Smith, 386.
    O'Neill *v.* Kruger   ,,   1863,   Cockburn, C.J.; 4 Best & Smith, 395.
    Wood *v.* Bowron   ,,   1866,   ,,   2 Law Rep. Com. Law, 29.

[2] Perham's Case   ,,   1859,   Pollock, C.B.; 29 *Law J.* M.C., 31.
                                                5 H & N, 35.
    O'Neill *v.* Longman   ,,   1863,   Blackburn, J.; 4 Best and Smith, 388.

[3] R. *v.* Hewitt   ,,   1851 ; 5 Cox, Crim. Cases, 162 ; Campbell, C.J.
[4] R. *v.* Duffield   ,,   1851 ; 5   ,,   404.
[5] 5 Cox, Crim. Cases, p 431.   [6] *Ibid.* p. 489.

to prohibit the Unionist from striking against him for employing non-Unionists. As to lock-outs by a combination of masters, whether the Common Law of Conspiracy is let in by the Statute or not, the consequences are equally intolerable. If it is let in, every such combination of masters may be an indictable conspiracy; but then, so is every Trade Union, except such as are exempted by the 4th section of the Statute, *i.e.* except such as simply *talk about* wages and hours. If on the other hand the Common Law of Conspiracy is shut out, then masters may combine to lock-out their workmen, whilst it is possible that men, by reason of the interpretation of the 3rd section of the Statute, may not combine to strike against their masters.

But if it be doubtful that Trade Unions are illegal in the sense of being punishable, it is certain that they are illegal in the sense that the law refuses to support them. The law regards them as contrary to public policy. Not, indeed, that there is any Statute to this effect. But by the Common Law any contract contrary to public policy is to be adjudged void; and the Judges are left[1] to decide for themselves, according to their own notions, what is or what is not public policy. In the exercise of this power the English Judges have pronounced (and indeed it is now settled law) that any agreements, whether between operative and operative, or master and master, not to accept, or not to give employment except upon certain fixed terms—even those agreements which by the 4th section of the Statute persons are permitted to enter into without being liable to punishment—are contrary to public policy as being in restraint of trade.[2] All Trade Unions are thus contrary to public policy: the restraint of trade consisting, it would seem, in this—that operatives by agreeing with their comrades as to the terms upon which they shall work thereby deprive themselves, as individuals, of liberty to work upon any other terms.

Space does not permit me to enter upon the legal arguments against this piece of Judge-made law, or to show the impropriety of Judges being allowed to make rules of Law upon such questions as those of Free Trade and Protection. I care only to call attention to the fact that the Judges as a body (with one distinguished exception[3]), have declared themselves against Trade Unions, that the law brands Trade Unions as contrary to public policy. And to the operative it is of little or no satisfaction that the same disability is imposed upon combinations of Masters. For as combinations of Masters are usually disadvantageous to their individual interests, they are as rare as combinations amongst operatives, being beneficial to operatives, are common: however equal therefore the law may seem, its equality is illusory. The doctrine amounts to a sentence of outlawry against Trade Unions. The agreement as to wages, &c., into which the operatives have entered, is void, and the law declines to do anything which may

---

1 Hilton *v.* Eckersley, decided in 1855, per Campbell, C.J., 6 Ellis and Blackburn, 64.

2 This decision was first made with reference to a Combination of Masters in the case of Hilton *v.* Eckersley (*supra*): it has since been extended to Trade Unions, Hornby *v.* Close. *Times*, Jan. 16, 1867).

3 Chief Justice Erle, in Hilton *v.* Eckersley; 6 Ellis & Blackburn, 64.

indirectly tend to give it effect; it will therefore deny all protection to the corporate property of the society; and if the treasurer make away with the funds, the society is disabled from prosecuting him.

The effect of this is of course to imperil the funds of all the Trades' Unions throughout the kingdom. But the doctrine has lately [1] been carried to a still higher pitch. The Court of Queen's Bench have decided that if a Trade Union is also a benefit Society, the members shall *ipso facto* be deprived of the right of suing a defaulting treasurer, to which as members of a benefit Society they are expressly entitled under the Friendly Societies Act.

The third, fourth, and fifth sections of the principal statute (6 Geo. IV. c. 129, passed in 1825) are as follows :

III. " And be it further enacted that from and after the passing of this act, (1) if any person shall by violence to the person or property, or by threats, or by intimidation, or by molesting, or in any way obstructing another, force or endeavour to force any journeyman, manufacturer, workman, or other person hired or employed in any manufacture, trade, or business, to depart from his hiring, employment, or work, or to return his work before the same shall be finished ; or prevent or endeavour to prevent any journeyman, &c. not being hired or employed, from hiring himself to or from accepting work or employment from any person or persons ; or (2) if any person shall use or employ violence to the person or property of another, or threats or intimidation, or shall molest or in any way obstruct another for the purpose of forcing or inducing such person to belong to any club or association, or to contribute to any common fund, or to pay any fine or penalty, or on account of his not belonging to any particular club or association, or not having contributed, or having refused to contribute to any common fund, or to pay any fine or penalty, or on account of his not having complied, or of his refusing to comply with rules, orders, resolutions, or regulations made to obtain an advance or to reduce the rate of wages, or to lessen or alter the hours of working, or to decrease or alter the quantity of work, or to regulate the mode of carrying on any manufacture, trade, or business, or the management thereof : or (3) *if any person shall by violence to the person or property of another, or by threats or intimidation, or by molesting, or in any way obstructing another, force or endeavour to force any manufacturer or person carrying on any trade or business, to make any alteration in his mode of regulating, managing, conducting, or carrying on such manufacture, trade, or business, or to limit the number of his apprentices or the number or description of his journeymen, workmen, or servants :* every person so offending, or aiding, abetting, or assisting therein, being convicted thereof in manner hereinafter mentioned, shall be imprisoned only, or shall and may be imprisoned, and kept to hard labour, for any time not exceeding three calendar months."

IV. " Provided always, and be it enacted that this Act shall not extend to subject any persons to punishment, who shall meet together

[1] Hornby *v.* Close. *Times,* Jan. 16, 1867.

for the sole purpose of consulting upon and determining the rate of wages or prices, which the persons present at such meeting or any of them shall require or demand for his or their work, or the hours or time for which he or they shall work in any manufacture, trade, or business, or who shall enter into any agreement, verbal or written, amongst themselves for the purpose of fixing the rate of wages or prices which the parties entering into such agreement, or any of them, shall require or demand for his or their work, or the hours of time for which he or they will work in any manufacture, trade, or business ; and that persons so meeting for the purposes aforesaid, or entering into such agreement as aforesaid, shall not be liable to any prosecution or penalty for so doing ; any law or statute to the contrary notwithstanding.

V. " Provided also, and be it further enacted that this act shall not extend to subject any persons to punishment who shall meet together for the sole purpose of consulting upon and determining the rate of wages or prices which the persons present at such meeting or any of them shall pay to his or their journeymen or workmen for their work, or the hours or time of working in any manufacture, trade or business, or who shall enter into any agreement, verbal or written, among themselves for the purpose of fixing the rate of wages or prices which the parties entering into such agreement or any of them shall pay to his or their journeymen, workmen, or servants, for their work or the hours or time of working in any manufacture, trade, or business ; and that persons so meeting for the purposes aforesaid or entering into any such agreement as aforesaid shall not be liable to any prosecution or penalty for so doing, any law or statute to the contrary notwithstanding."

The following is the operative part of the Amending Act (22 Vic. c. 34, passed 1859) :—

"I. No workman or other person, whether actually in employment or not, shall, by reason merely of his entering into an agreement with any workman or workmen, or other person or persons, for the purpose of fixing or endeavouring to fix the rate of wages or remuneration at which they or any of them shall work, or by reason merely of his endeavouring peaceably and in a reasonable manner, and without threat or intimidation, direct or indirect, to persuade others to cease or abstain from work, in order to obtain the rate of wages or altered hours of labour so fixed or agreed upon, or to be agreed upon, shall be deemed or taken to be guilty of ' Molestation,' or ' Obstruction,' within the meaning of the said Act (6 Geo. IV. c. 129), and shall not therefore be subject or liable to any prosecution or indictment for Conspiracy. Provided always that nothing herein contained shall authorize any workmen to break or depart from any contract, or authorize any attempt to induce any workmen to break or depart from any contract."

III.

THE POOR.

BY MEREDITH TOWNSEND.

The House of Commons, which is supposed to represent England perfectly, so perfectly that, as Mr. Roebuck once said, even the foibles of national character are exactly reflected in its proceedings, is made up in the main of four classes of members,—proprietors of large blocks of land (with their sons, nephews, and nominees), successful traders, large employers of labour, and men who have risen nearly, but not quite, to the top of professions. It would be difficult to obtain statistics quite precise, but it is safe to say, that of the 658 members, the odd fifty-eight would cover the men who do not really belong to one or other of these classes. There is but one tenant farmer in the House. There is not one working man. There is not one man elected by English agricultural labourers, or representative in any way of their special interests, but one who can be said to be at once selected and returned by skilled artisans. There are, no doubt, a few men, chiefly from Ireland, who represent tenant feeling as against landlord feeling; one or two who understand

f

from experience what cottage life is; and a few who have learned in their own careers what artisan wishes are; but the overwhelming majority occupy some one of the four positions enumerated. That majority, moreover, is very rich, probably the richest body of men ever collected under a common denomination. It has been calculated that the income of the Commons, distinguishing income from property, is greater than that of the Lords; and, if by income we understand annual receipts which can be spent at discretion, the statement is probably true. At all events, the House is a House of rich men, of men who may feel a commercial crisis, or a fall in rentals, but who know poverty only by observation and report.

Naturally such a House, though open to some non-political inducements, is almost entirely free from pecuniary temptations, much more free for example than Congress, or the French Chamber under Louis Philippe; very bold in dealing with taxes, very unselfish when well led in regulating the incidence of taxation. Gross things have been done occasionally by the majority, as in the matter of compensation for cattle under the Cattle Plague Act; and at least one abuse of taxation remains untouched: but the members taken collectively have endured very equably an income-tax pressing only on themselves and their constituents, have allowed poor-rates in rural districts to fall mainly on the land, and met the only great war for which they have had to provide by large deductions from the incomes of the well-to-do. On the other hand, the Reformed House has shown almost throughout its history an incapacity of comprehending the poor,—that is to say, all classes below the income-tax level,—their needs, wishes, and projects, which has made its action at once weak and unsympathetic. This incapacity displays itself in all kinds of ways, sometimes in positive acts, sometimes in refusals to act, most often in failures to act, and now and then in simple oddities of procedure. Among these last may surely be reckoned the long resistance to the removal of the " taxes on knowledge." I do not believe that the mass of members cared one straw about the financial aspect of that question or series of questions. They knew very well that the treasury would be filled whether journals were stamped or not, or the advertisement duty abolished, or paper makers released from the excise ; but, not understanding the poor, they were harassed by a latent fear that penny papers would be sure to be either " subversive," *i.e.* hostile to property, or irreligious, or indecent, and wanted to make it difficult to establish them. The " poor " were to them an abstraction which they regarded very much as some women regard men, as beings to be humoured no doubt, but also to be guided and controlled and counselled, lest from inherent perversity of nature they should break out into excesses at variance with the fitness of things. We all know how the matter turned out, how suddenly, when the taxes were actually removed, the violent unstamped press disappeared, how conservative and moral, not to say "Philistine," the penny papers became; how, for the first time, the Tories secured a really popular organ. The root of the odd blunder was not bad feeling of any kind, but the total inability of the rich and cultivated to understand what the poor and uncultivated would do with power.

This inability displays itself every day in almost every

f 2

department of legislation, but most visibly in the action of the House with regard to the Poor Law, to the organization of municipal life, and to the regulation of labour. The Poor Law, as it now stands, was framed by the Reformed House, and was on one side an immense improvement upon the ancient system. It saved property from demands which threatened to make it worthless and to destroy the motive for accumulating wealth. But its working was impeded from the first by two mistakes, strikingly characteristic of an assembly too rich to feel where the shoe pinched the poor. The initiative of administering relief was confided exclusively to the ratepayers; and no distinction was drawn between the willing and the unwilling recipient. The consequence of the first mistake was an administration solely conducted in the interest of the payers without influence from the receivers, a defect shown in the towns by a penuriousness often verging on cruelty—as, for example, in the treatment of casuals and of the sick; in the country by a use of the law to keep down wages. When all has been said that can be said, the refusal of the metropolitan Guardians to obey the law about casuals, and the cruel reluctance to make pauper hospitals decently comfortable, resolve themselves into the ratepayer's dislike to spend money for other people's benefit. Such a feeling is neither unnatural nor unreasonable; and it may be admitted that no representation of paupers was possible at the Boards. But it was quite possible to represent the State as impartial arbiter, and a really sympathetic House of Commons would long since have done it, either directly by appointing good chairmen, as executive officers of the Board, or by enabling the ordinary courts of justice, on complaint and evidence, to enforce obedience to the intention of the law. As it is, a parish can get its rates by a very swift legal process ; but the poor of the parish cannot in the same way get due hospital accommodation —pillows, for example, for bedridden old inmates. Parliament has readily consented to establish the jurisdiction most effective for assisting petty traders ; but the pauper is left to the ratepayers, without any trustworthy arbiter between him and them.

Again, to the Members of Parliament, looking down from their height, one poor man seems much the same as another—a tramp like a " labourer," a labourer like an artisan ; and the same system is consequently applied to all—to the decent ploughman who has broken his leg, and the ditcher ruined by drink, to the artisan out of employ, and the rascal who never will work while anybody will feed him. It is true that, the practice of men being often better than their laws, this mistake is in the country remedied by a system of out-door relief, lenient to the very verge of the law, and worked by men who understand individual wants ; but in towns it is not remedied, and every period of distress breaks up thousands of decent households, which might have been saved by judicious discrimination, such as impartial officers would exercise.

There is scarcely a defect in the working of the Poor Law, which is not traceable to one of these two mistakes, which between them have made a vast national system of charity, such as no other nation possesses, an object of loathing to those who receive its benefits. The defects which cannot be so referred, are due to the reluctance of the House of Commons to distribute the Poor Rate like every other direct tax, in proportion to wealth. So strong is this reluctance, that no statesman would dare to propose such a course, or venture to tell the House, that the rate in aid at all events, which is levied whenever rating proves insufficient, ought to be raised like the income-tax. The consequence is, that the rate falls on the small grocer, whose rental is at least half his income, as it falls on the villa-dweller, whose rental is not a tenth of his expenditure, and in time of distress is only collected by summons and distraint. It is not certain that a House of Commons elected by the whole people would be very lenient to pauperism ; but it is certain that it would distribute the burden of rates in a manner much more just and much less oppressive to the poor.[1]

A similar defect runs through the whole of our municipal legislation. With very few exceptions, members of Parliament are too rich to live in towns, too comfortable to realize how far life in Bethnal-green could be alleviated by legislative action. They are inclined to think of dirt, disease, and overcrowding as evils incidental to civilization, with which it is nearly impossible to deal, which, if dealt with at all, must only be dealt with cautiously, so as not even to seem to menace any "rights of property." Parliament readily gives railways power to evict poor people by the thousand, and to take land against the will of its owners, because railways benefit trade ; but Parliament hesitates to give the same authority to improvers, because it is only the poor who would be benefited by the reconstruction of cities. Par-

---

[1] I shall be greatly surprised if a reformed Parliament does not make the purchase of Mr. Gladstone's deferred annuities universal, and in this way make thrift compulsory upon all.

liament readily gives water companies exceptional powers
to recover their debts, because a good supply of water
makes middle-class life more pleasant ; but there is no
enactment securing an adequate supply for the poor,
who are individually powerless ; although, as in the long
run the poor pay their full share of city taxes, they have
a clear right to all city advantages. For Parliament
holds that water, like shoe-leather, is a thing to be
bought, if the buyer has the means ; and forgets that
the monopoly which makes it so dear was made by
Parliament, and that if the poor man contributes under
compulsion more than his share of the cost of grand
improvements—which in London, under the coal-tax, he
certainly does—he is fairly entitled to its aid in obtaining
one of the few necessaries of life. Parliament might
as fairly decree that a non-householder should not be
protected by the police, because he pays no police-rate,
as that a poor householder should have no water to keep
him clean. The one is as necessary to civilization as the
other ; and a House of Commons in which the poor were
sure of an audience, would at once see to such a matter
as this.

The present House of Commons will see that a lodging-
house Act is enforced in the great cities, because over-
crowding begets fever, and fever may reach every
class ; but it will not rigidly apply the principle of that
Act to cottages in the country, because to do so would
be inconvenient to the landowner, and would interfere
with his authority. Parliament has very recently been
persuaded to allow State credit to be employed in securing
better lodging for the masses, but it is lukewarm and
careless in the matter : does not *urge* its employment

—does not force on reconstruction as it forced on the measure for the better prevention of poaching. If a Home Secretary were convicted of always selecting magistrates with a bias against the game laws, he would be dismissed ; but he may allow the health Acts and building Acts to fall into desuetude with perfect impunity. As to going a step farther, and making city life what it might become, a society in which the individual, however poor, should reap the whole advantages of association—the great majority of Members on both sides of the House would proscribe as visionary and " unsafe " any statesman who let it appear that such a conception was in his mind. Parliament does not even consent to leave the municipalities independent, with power that is to do anything not opposed to the laws of the land, fearing lest the majority of poor should burden the minority of rich ; and, while representing only landowners, and the middle-class, the House of Commons has now existed for thirty-five years without creating one village municipality. In New England every township is a corporate entity, able to do for its residents what they deem expedient ; in England the village is an aggregate of houses ruled exclusively by the owners of property, with no power of corporate action for any secular object, however beneficial. No village, for example, could bring water from the stream, and pay for it by a rate. The poor, in fact, get along as they best can, without any sufficient assistance or guidance or recognition from the State, or from Parliament, though Parliament is supposed all the while to be attending, and boasts that it attends, to their interests. A really representative House of Commons would at once address

itself to the improvement of municipal life, to forcing on
the reconstruction of great cities, to securing for every
citizen so much fresh air, good water, and freedom from
miasma, as would give him the control of his only capital
—his strength. If it could not accomplish this end
without putting a burden on property, as it did when it
enfranchised trade, it would impose that burden, and
with even better results. It would, in fact, insist that
the social organization, which is supported by the toil of
the multitude, should benefit the multitude, and not
favour a class; that the political organization for which
the masses contribute half the expense should be at least
as beneficial to them as to their co-partners in the
expenditure.

It is, however, in its relation to labour that the class
character of the House of Commons is most strikingly
manifested. It does not indeed at all dislike agricultural
labourers. Its theory about them is that as long as they
are content with their wages, and respectful to their
superiors, they are to be kindly treated, and even allowed
under the Poor Law (which for them is worked with
comparative lenity) some exceptional privileges. But
the House of Commons maintains a law under which a
man who wanders away from his own village, or group of
villages, in search of better pay is compelled to forfeit his
right to poor relief, that is, to maintenance when he is past
the time of daily toil. It retains on the Statute-book
a law under which a ploughman who refuses to work
can legally be flogged—which indeed is never done—or
legally be imprisoned and made to work with felons
—which is often done; while if his employer suddenly
dismisses him, the ploughman can seek redress only by

a civil action, for which he cannot pay. It jealously maintains a system of local self-government under which the laws are in rural districts administered solely by large employers of labour and by clergymen who mostly share their opinions. It is resolved determinately that rent shall not be an ordinary civil debt to be paid like any other debt, and legislates to give the landlord priority over the baker and butcher and every other tradesman who supplies things as necessary as shelter; and it strenuously resists every suggestion of legislation of the kind most likely to bring it within the power of the industrious and thrifty ploughman to become the proprietor of a piece of land. It refuses absolutely to consider the labourer the best judge of his own interest, though it admits that everybody else is; and its leading members whenever they are compelled to express an opinion on the subject, openly argue that it is better for him to live hardly as a servant, liable to dismissal and imprisonment, than to live equally hardly as his own master, liable to no dismissal at all. They hold distinctly, and sometimes avow openly, that a dull monotony of daily toil on wages so insufficient that they have to be systematically supplemented by national alms, is the inevitable and perpetual destiny of the masses who till the soil; and that any other order of society would be injurious or unnatural. They hold this so unreservedly that when Mr. Simon, an official surgeon, reported that one-fifth of the population of England had not enough to eat, the House showed neither sorrow nor surprise, and never ordered an inquiry into that tremendous statement. Towards other departments of labour the House manifests the same feeling, though in a different way. In trades

not directly dependent upon the land, the workmen
have learned to see that in a thickly-peopled country the
individual labourer is no match for the individual employer. He must therefore either unite with others, or
hunger will ultimately force him to accept any terms
the distributor of wages may choose to offer. The House
of Commons, which recognises every other form of
organization, which has authorized unions of barristers
and of doctors, which has devised special rules of examination to prevent free entry into the Civil Service, and
will permit no person to rise in the fighting services
except in accordance with the regular rules—so unjust
to the able and the industrious—of those services, does
not even recognise unions of labouring men. For years
it prohibited them; and even when, finding that secrecy
led to deeds of violence and terrorism against the
masters, it abolished all legal restrictions, it still refused
to recognise and regulate the Unions, and still left the
law in such a condition that if the officers of a Trade
Union rob its till, the Union cannot obtain the summary
remedy open to any individual or co-partnership. Its
purposes being "in restraint of trade," are illegal. Any
medical practitioner can prosecute and punish a com-
petitor not duly qualified; but a skilled mason trying to
restrain the unskilled mason who undersells him is liable
to imprisonment. It is quite right that violence should
be subject to this or any other punishment which may
be found effectual. No man should be debarred from
selling his labour to the best advantage; but then there
should be equal measure for all. And the state of the
law itself indirectly debars the agricultural labourer from
selling his labour to the best advantage.

The strikes which are so often brought about by Trade Unions may be as mischievous as employers of labour think, but, if so, the House of Commons is bound thoroughly to discuss a matter so serious : and to provide some other form of arbitration between labour and capital. The House of Commons has but just now recognised this duty, and until labour is more fully represented it will not give its whole mind to the subject, pressing as it is. And it cannot be impartial. Its inclination has hitherto been either to avoid the discussion, or failing that, to show that its sympathy is entirely against combinations among the poor ; not so much because combinations raise wages, nor even because they may sometimes embarrass trade, but because they confer a power on workmen which the House, in its ignorance of them, assumes that they will misuse. It may be doubted whether the House as at present constituted would endure county Unions of agricultural labourers ; whether it would not put them down with a strong hand. At present the most powerful interest in the House is in that matter disinterested. It is quite possible that a popular representation might discourage or suppress Unions, but it is certain that it would discuss them first with a keen desire to understand the workman's idea of the matter as fully as the capitalist's. At present the House of Commons simply legislates on the ideas of one side, tempered by individual kindliness of feeling towards the other, and without receiving the other's ideas at all. The notion of the workman, that the State should " organize labour," should compel just compromises between masters and men, should be through its agents or its courts the universal arbiter, seems to the House of Commons to be an impracticable or rather dangerous dream. Very likely it is, but if it were a dream of the constituencies its meaning would at least be thoroughly discussed.

It is the same with education. It would not be true to say that the House of Commons is now indifferent to the education of the people. On the contrary, it sees in education, besides other considerations, a great safeguard for property. But it understands the population below the constituencies so little that it does not comprehend how earnest they are in the matter; how strongly they would support, if it should be necessary, even compulsion; how readily they would for this end sanction expenditure. The House is half afraid of appearing too liberal. It was assumed, for example, all through the debates of 1865, that 600,000*l.* a year was quite a large sum to pay for education, that one halfpenny on the income-tax was an extravagant allowance. The House granted the money, but thought it much; never realized that to the poor education is the question of questions, that three times the sum, or five times the sum, would only increase their contentment with the government, for spending so much to remove the ignorance which, as they know, is the main obstacle in their path. The feelings of the tenant farmers who still dislike an educational system which benefits everybody but them, of dissenting ministers who are afraid for the general interests of Christianity, and of the regular clergy jealous of their right to insist upon Church principles, weigh twice as strongly, ten times as strongly with the House of Commons as those of "the masses." About the Conscience Clause or other comparatively unimportant details, there is debate after debate. But on the poor man's perhaps impracticable ideal, of compulsory and gratuitous education, so organized, that the unscrupulous man may not, by making his children toil, undersell the scrupulous who makes his children learn,—we never hear one word.

It is this incapacity to understand the thoughts, or unwillingness to meet the requirements of the poor—*i.e.* of seven tenths of the population—which seems to me the weakness of the present House of Commons. It may be rash to predict that a more popular House will clear us from the reproach uttered by no demagogue, but by Mr. Disraeli himself, that England contains two nations —the rich and the poor, but experience in some degree warrants such a hope. In 1831, the middle class was bound in fetters legal, financial, and moral—fetters so heavy that to shake them off they were inclined to upset the Constitution. In 1832, they took power. In thirty-five years they have done their work so completely that they have to look round for a grievance, and are inclined to think the cumbrousness of legal proceedings the one most prominent. Why should it be unreasonable to expect that the class at present excluded, if they are admitted to a fair share in the representation, and so gain power, will do as the middle class before them have done, and while respecting the rights and interests of others, will insist upon a more considerate, a more effective, and a less tardy recognition of their own—thus at last making our legislation, which tends even now to be wise, merciful and unselfish, truly national ?

IV.

THE LAND-LAWS.

BY W. L. NEWMAN.

FEW departments of legislation give the legislator a
more fatal sense of omnipotence than the regulation of
the transfer of land. He seems to have reached the
mountain backbone of the State, from which the streams
flow down on either side. The slightest inequality of
surface seems enough to trace their channels—to guide
the distribution of wealth in this or that direction. The
indestructibility of land, its limitation in point of
quantity, the ease with which it is reached by the hand
of the law, mark it out as the bronze of legislation—
ductile, yet durable. Every variation of the conception
of property in land—every limitation, or extension of
proprietary right—develops a new type of human
character. If the proprietor, the lessee, the tenant-at-
will differ in extent of proprietary interest, they differ
also in moral feature. Men's grade and occupation is
a more powerful, because a more unfelt and less obtrusive,
influence in forming their character than education, and
the legislator is hardly less supreme over the one means

of moral development than over the other. It is natural that legislators have generally failed to withstand the temptations of such a position. Especially in the early days of social development, before the great professions have arisen, and when the landowner is the sole figure on the social horizon, the State, in its own name, or in that of religion, descends upon the land, and casts its proprietors in the mould which it prefers. The Hebrew monotheism, the polytheism of Greece, had each a sacred land-law of its own. The Greek city states, small and artificial, mostly long devoid of distinct professions, carried interference with the land far down into advanced periods of their development. The more professional organization of Roman society enabled the State earlier to dispense with a formed and moulded land law; but, as the State relaxed its hold upon the land, it fell more and more into the hands of the class of capitalists which the career of Roman conquest had developed. " Latifundia perdidere Italiam, immo et provincias." As the Empire grew weaker, it returned, in the infirmity of age, to the system of its youth; it connected special pursuits with the tenure of land, till industry died under its fetters, and, with one exception, the great professions wholly disappeared. That exception was the Church. But the Church proved unequal, or indisposed to the secular duties with which it was loaded by Charlemagne; and feudalism, when it reconstructed society, recurred to the traditions of the sinking Roman Empire, throwing them into a Teutonic form, and framed the most elaborate system of State intervention in the transfer of land, which the world has ever seen. The law books, no doubt, exaggerate the completeness and consistency

of feudal law ; they give us rather a Mercator's Pro-
jection of feudalism, than its actual form ; they sink
successive stages of its development, and lose the
historical perspective of its formation ; but still feudalism, and especially English feudalism, presents a
logical neatness and coherence characteristic of the
age of scholasticism. It made merit a condition of
property in land ; it put patriotism into men's title-
deeds, and petrified it into tenure. The land was not
placed in the hands of those who had an industrial
title to its possession—of those who could cultivate it
best—but of those whose counsel in peace or service
in war were of most value. As feudalism accomplished
the object for which it existed ; as progress developed
beneath the comparative order it brought with it, tendencies betrayed themselves in the institution, which
had always existed within it, but which had been more
or less concealed by the powers which had been vested
in the king. It was found to have brought into being
a serried array of great families, consecrated to the
service of the State. Under Henry II. Primogeniture
assumed a stricter and more absolute form, partly in
the interest of the State, partly in that of the family.
Meantime the legal profession had developed, and with
it the power of the Crown. By the end of the thirteenth century, the State felt surer of its footing. Its
control over the transfer of land ceased to be so strict,
because it had ceased to be so all-important as it had
once been.[1] Entail had already arisen from the decay of
feudalism. The Statute *De Donis* proved by degrees

[1] See a tract on the History of the Law of Entail and Settlement, by
Charles Neate, Esq. M.P. 1865. Ridgway.

g

the germ of the system of Entail, by which land was wrested from the control of the State, only to be placed under the still more interested control of the family. It is true that the family rose but slowly to a consciousness of the value of the weapon thus placed in its hands. Mr. Neate has shown good reasons for his belief, that the importance and effect of the Statute *De Donis* have been considerably overstated. In any case, the slight and simple system of entail, which existed at this epoch, was shattered by the device of recoveries and by Henry the Eighth's Statute of Fines. Thus ended the first rude and ineffectual epoch of entails. It was not till the Restoration that the reconstructed edifice assumed its final and most scientific form. Bridgman and Palmer perfected the device by which the father was made tenant for life, and the eldest son tenant-in-tail in remainder. The entail could now be disturbed only by the combined action of two generations of proprietors.

The Family had thus acquired the control over the transfer of land, once exercised by the Sovereign, or his servant, the tenant-in-chief. Yet, if the free passage of land from hand to hand is to be interfered with, it would appear to be better that that interference should proceed from the State than from the Family. The action of the State is founded on better and wider information, on wiser and calmer judgment. It is more open to modification in case of need, and is more patiently submitted to, than that of the proprietor, or pair of proprietors, who make an autocratic disposition in what they have been brought mechanically to believe the interest of the Family. Yet it is not necessary to accept, with the *Code Napoléon*, the too narrow dilemma between control by the Family and control by the State, and, in order to escape from the caprices of family legislation, to subject inheritance to one fixed and iron rule. The State will, on the whole, sufficiently perform its function with regard to the transfer of land, if it rests content with expressing itself on two main points. First, it must regulate Intestate Succession : Secondly, it must secure, that, as far as may be, each generation shall have that full control of its landed wealth, without which full responsibility cannot exist. The State stands between the living and the unborn, and it may reasonably declare within what limits it will permit the existing generation to imperil the general welfare by imposing fetters on itself, or its successors.

How does the law of England stand with respect to these two points ?

1. " If a man possesses an estate-in-fee in England, and dies without having settled his land, and without having made a will devising it, the law of England prescribes, that all the land shall, after the death of such person, except in certain rare exceptional cases, descend in one undivided mass, either to the eldest of his sons, if he has any, or, except in certain cases, if he has no sons living at the time of his death, to the nearest of his relations, according to a table of affinities prescribed by law. "[1]

It is sufficient to say of this law, that it adheres more strictly to Primogeniture than the practice of the Primogenitary class. Few settlements omit to charge por-

---

[1] Social Condition and Education of the People in England and Europe. By Joseph Kay, Esq. M.A., Barrister at Law. Vol. i. p. 42.

tions for the younger children. It is needless to add that its incidence on the great masses of the non-primogenitary middle-class is frequently attended with peculiar hardship. One may well be content to quote on this subject the honest, vernacular indignation of Mr. Lowe : [1]—

"They could avoid making a will for a man, which no good and wise man would make for himself. And yet that was what the law did at the present time. Every right-minded man would feel it to be an insult to be told, that he had made a will which would give all his property to his eldest son, and none to his younger children."

And, though Mr. Lowe would apparently be satisfied if the law charged the land for the benefit of the younger children, yet he went on to state emphatically, that "the simple object of the Bill" (Mr. Locke King's Real Estate Intestacy Bill of 1859) "was to do what every honest and honourable man would do, and for that reason he should give it his support."

2. The rule of the English law in restriction of perpetuities enables the owner of an estate-in-fee-simple "to grant by his settlement, or to leave by his will, different interests in his land to a number of persons, and so to arrange the succession to the ownership of the property by his settlement or will, that no person or persons shall be able to sell any portion of the land, until some person, who was an infant at the time of making the settlement, or at the death of the person having made the will, has grown up, married, and had a son,

---

[1] Second Reading of Mr. Locke King's Real Estate Intestacy Bill, March 2, 1859.

and until that son has attained the age of twenty-one years, and not even then, so as to confer a right to the immediate possession of it, unless all those who have any interest in the land prior to that of the last-mentioned son, are dead, or join in the sale." "It may be stated generally, that these laws enable an owner of land, by his settlement or will, so to affect his estate that it cannot possibly be sold, in many cases for about 50, and in some cases for even 60, 70, or 100 years, after the making of the settlement or will."[1]

Nor is this all. The strict settlement, even in its simplest form, by suggesting re-settlement, tends, as we shall see, to perpetual entail. "If we look," says Lord St. Leonards, "at the frame of a common marriage settlement," we shall find the following arrangements :—"The estate is limited to the husband for life—then the wife, if she survive him, is to have a rent-charge for life, and, subject to that, the estate is to go (1) to the first and other sons successively in tail male—remainder (2) to the first and other sons successively in tail general." We need proceed no further with the remainders, but simply remark that "portions are provided for the younger children." "With his father's concurrence," Lord St. Leonards adds, "the son may," on attaining twenty-one, "bar all the remainders over, and acquire the fee, subject to the father's life estate. If a son marry in his

---

[1] Kay, i. 39. It is true that every well-drawn settlement or will contains a power of sale, and that, where this is not the case, the want is to some extent supplied by the Leases and Sales of Settled Estates Act (19 & 20 Vic. c. 120). This, however, is not of great importance, as the purchase-money is liable to be re-invested in other land to be settled to the same uses, and thus the power is mainly useful in rounding off the estate by the sale of its outlying portions.

father's lifetime, with his approbation, the power to bar the remainders is constantly exercised, and a new settlement is made."

Thus the existing practice of settlement and re-settlement in most cases results in what may readily be put forward as a solemn appeal from one generation to another, whether the settlement shall be renewed. Even if such an appeal took place, the common interest of the nation would be unrepresented in the more than diplomatic privacy of this negotiation between father and son. But, on a closer examination, the supposed solemn appeal to each generation dwindles to a hasty compact dictated by somewhat sordid considerations of momentary interest, to which the law lends the sanction of irrevocability. "Where there are younger children of the first marriage," says Lord St. Leonards, " the father is always anxious to have the estate re-settled on them and their issue, in case of failure of issue of the first son. This he cannot accomplish without the concurrence of the son, and, as the son, upon his establishment in life in his father's lifetime, requires an immediate provision, the father generally secures to him a provision during their joint lives, as a consideration for the re-settlement of the estate in remainder upon the younger sons. Thus are estates quickly resettled." "As," again, "the son can, with his father's concurrence, acquire the fee and make a new settlement, few indeed are the instances in which the mutual interests of the father and the son do not lead to an equitable adjustment of their rights, when the proper time for a new disposition arrives."

In entering on the discussion in which these passages occur, Lord St. Leonards places two statements in somewhat uncomfortable proximity. "Our law," he says, "allows no dispositions which tend to perpetuity;" yet, "the present plan of a strict settlement, within reasonable limit, enables the owner to transmit it to all his posterity, and from its very nature leads to successive settlements, which alone have kept many estates in the same families." We can now judge which of these two rather inconsistent propositions is nearer to the fact.

Mr. Cliffe Leslie [1] places the circumstances of a resettlement in a far truer light, yet one which merely amplifies the picture of Lord St. Leonards. "Take," he says, "the case of an ante-nuptial settlement in which the son joins with the father. It is commonly supposed that the son acts with his eyes open, and with a special eye to the contingencies of the future and of family life. But what are the real facts of the case? Before the future owner of the land has come into possession—before he has any experience of his property, or of what is best to do, or what he can do, in regard of it—before the exigencies of the future, or his own real position are known to him—before the character, number, and wants of his children are learned, or the claims of parental affection and duty can make themselves felt, and while still very much at the mercy of a predecessor desirous of posthumous greatness and power, he enters into an irrevocable disposition, by which he parts with the rights of a proprietor over his future property for ever, and settles its devolution, burdened with charges, upon an unborn heir, who may be the very person least fitted or deserving to take it."

Yet one may venture to feel a sort of kindness even

[1] *Fraser's Magazine*, February 1867.

for the modern strict settlement. It is of course cumbrous to a degree. The most experienced conveyancers stand aghast with a kind of humorous amazement at the work of their own hands. They launch the stupendous creation of an impossible foresight, but they cannot tell how it may act in the future. If the limit of prevision in statesmanship is six months, in conveyancing it is never less than a generation. Yet the very cumbrousness of the instrument indicates a moral progress. As has been said, the practice of the Primogenitary class is far superior to the Intestacy Law of the State, and half the intricacy of settlements is due to a vain effort to make them consistent with the performance of the duties of a father and a proprietor. We trace in the settlement the sense of new exigencies, which cannot really be satisfied, but which it is creditable to recognise. As the rise of legal fictions and of equity foreshadows an approaching change in legislation, so we may see in the elaborate arrangements of the modern settlement the first symptoms of a change, which in the interest of the family, of agriculture, and of society cannot safely be withheld. " The object," says Mr. Cliffe Leslie, " of settlements in tail renewed in each succeeding generation is to accomplish ends " which are inconsistent—" to give each generation a free disposition over land, yet to bind the land from generation to generation in the feudal line of descent—to give all the family property to the heir, yet not to ignore those claims of nature and justice, which feudalism, in its naked and consistent barbarity, boldly set aside. The consequence is, the practical retention of the old evil of perpetual entails, and, along with it, the new evils of heavy incumbrances on land, of

increased incapacity of its owners to improve, of an
unparalleled complexity and uncertainty of title, and of
a division between law and equity carried into intermin-
able fresh ramifications." [1]

We can now appreciate at its just value the twofold
contention of the advocates of the existing laws. They
allege in the same breath that, on the one hand, the law
leaves the individual free to regulate the succession as he
chooses, and that it does not secure a Primogenitary succession, or maintain the possessions of the family : and
yet that, on the other hand, it prevents the alarming
consequences of equal inheritance, "makes only one fool
in a family," and insures the existence of a certain
number of families possessed of stable wealth and culture.
It is obvious that both these lines of argument cannot be
together just. What the law in reality does is this—it
gives the proprietor just that amount of illusory freedom
which will serve to mask but not to countervail the immemorial bias of the State. It is possible to use coercive

---

[1] It is even probable that recent legislation as to entail has stimulated the
father's consciousness of the part he is expected to play. It has created the
title of Protector of the Settlement. " Recent changes," says Mr. Neate, " in
the Law of Entail are apparently only in matters of form, and their object
certainly was only to supply simpler and more rational modes of doing that,
and that only, which could have been done before by an absurd and cumbrous
process. But it seems to me that these changes have in truth imported a
new principle into our law, or, at least, have recognised as a principle that
which before was only a fact. The reason why before the Acts of 3 & 4
Wm. IV. the consent of the tenant for life was requisite to enable the
remainder-man in tail to enlarge his estate into a fee, was purely a technical
one " (it was this, that not being seised for an estate in possession, he could
not be the defendant in a real action, and therefore could not suffer a recovery), " and did not assume in any way the right of the father to control the
acts of the son in dealing with his inheritance ; but the Legislature has now
for the first time recognised that right, and has even seemed to impose the
obligation on the father to enforce it, by conferring on the tenant for life,
who is usually the father, the title of Protector of the Settlement."

legislation in an economical way. If a law has existed
so long, that it has created a class sentiment in harmony
with it, the State is too wise to maintain a useless scaffold-
ing; it blurs the hard and severe outlines of the law
with a safe and skilful recognition of individual freedom ;
it steps gracefully into the background, and the proprietor
plays his part all the more willingly, because he believes
himself uninfluenced. Half the defensive power of
English institutions lies in the fact that they are un-
obtrusive. They have never been " clarified " by violent
and organic change. If there has been revolution, it has
never sought too scientifically to analyse the spirit of the
Constitution, and as it is impossible to subdue forces which
are not clearly identified, movements have rather tended
to modify the holders of power than the profound organic
elements of the State. Thus, in a perfectly simple and
natural way, the very length of time, during which the
tangled and intricate web of the Constitution has been
in process of formation, has preserved its central forces
from attack by disguising them under a variety of accumulations. They have been shrouded in a defensive
Homeric mist. Something has been struck from their
original direct *naïveté*. Two tendencies have been
allowed to run side by side in legislation, the one carefully subordinated to the other—the one fresh with the
strength of success, the other blunted and shattered, but
just allowed a sufficient reality and prominence to deaden
the movement of attack. It is impossible to be suspicious
of so illogical and unambitious a Constitution. Nor have
any but legitimate forces been used to attain this result.
It would not be so complete, or so successful, if it had
not been achieved unconsciously. The great dominant

NEWMAN.]   *THE LAND-LAWS.*   91

interests of England have seldom lost a certain degree of
sobriety. They have never been so blinded to a sense
of their own sectional position—they have never been so
swallowed up in a grotesque and honest fanaticism, as,
like the corresponding classes on the Continent, to raise
their own claims to the rank of a religious creed. When
they have been threatened by movements in the world
outside them, they have usually made the shadow of
concession to the movement which was necessary to
pacify it.

It is easy to underrate the influence of a law which
events have allowed to assume this blurred and ambiguous outline. Cramped and scarred as it may super-
ficially appear to be by the collision of conflicting
influences, it may yet exercise a power in no way
diminished by the fact, that it has lost its primitive
strictness and severity. Its very success in creating a
sentiment, the strength with which political events have
told in its favour, may be the very cause which has
permitted its mitigation. There can be little doubt that
this has been the case with the English law of succession
and entail. Its advocates are conscious that it does its
work. They point quite truly to the obvious fact, that
the adoption of the rule of Primogeniture in intestacy
in no way limits the freedom of devise, but they forget
that the law exerts a moral, no less than a coercive influence, and that it may encourage where it does not
command. They point quite truly to the fact that, in
many cases, the settlor's exercise of the large powers
which the law entrusts to him may be revised every
generation, but they omit to notice the circumstances
which make this revision commonly little better than

illusory. But, while they seek to disguise the effectiveness of the law, they urge in the same breath the
desirability of the consequences to which they will
hardly admit that it leads.

It by no means weakens the case against the law if we
admit that much of its effectiveness is derived from the
dominion which the past has given it over the minds of
a class in England. Even in producing the result which
might most naturally be ascribed to it—the concentration of land in a few hands—it does not operate alone.
The whole history of England has worked in the same
direction. In the sixteenth century the Crown felt
sufficiently sure of a recently created and dependent
nobility to throw it upon the landed wealth of the
Church. In the seventeenth, the middle class, which
had borne the main brunt of the struggle with the
Crown, broken by its own heroism, demoralized by its
momentary success, strayed into the sectarian path of a
noble but mistaken Puritanism, and abdicated its glorious
headship of England to the aristocracy of 1688. In the
eighteenth century, India, prize-money, salaries, contracts,
raised a squirearchy round the aristocracy which had led
the way to victory and fortune, while the common arable
field with its belts of pasture and woodland, which
formed so prominent a feature in the English landscape
of last century, largely disappeared, and its wrecks everywhere went to augment the mass of land already in the
hands of the large proprietors. By the side of these
political causes, which have acted in the past to increase
the accumulation of estates, others exist which continue
to operate in the present. High among these comes the
costliness of conveyancing. The majestic period for

which title must be proved—the elaborate dispositions
which the law permits to one generation of proprietors
at the cost of the freedom of the next—the entire
absence of compulsory registration of title, and, till the
other day, even of permissive registration, make the
transfer of land expensive and hazardous. Then again,
the singular contrivance which is accounted the representative system of the country throws vast legislative
power into the hands of the landed interest. They
exercise an undivided control over one chamber of the
legislature. They dominate the other through the
counties and small boroughs. If we turn from the
central to the local institutions of England, we shall
find land supreme in the administrative and judicial
system of the county. Less factitious attractions of
landed property lie in the semi-feudal colour which still
invests the most ancient type of industry—in the comparative security of its returns—and in the vigorous
rural tastes of Englishmen, stimulated, no doubt, by
elaborate game laws, but yet in the main legitimate and
healthy elements of the social system. Overlaid though
they are with artificial additions, it is easy to see in the
natural attractions of land a sufficient pledge that a
considerable portion will always remain in the hands
of the wealthier class.

The succession laws follow in the wake of these multifarious agencies. What they achieve, the succession laws
crystallize and render permanent. The State intervenes
in the interest of the victorious and omnipotent class, as
it intervenes in favour of the helpless pauper, the factory
child, or the lunatic. "Entrench yourself," it says, "in
the position you have won—the slothful man roasteth

not that he took in hunting—distrust the prudence of
your descendants—construct a cage to fetter their caprice,
not indeed a cage which they absolutely cannot open,
but one which in the long run, and on the average,
will resist and neutralize extravagance and caprice, if,
indeed, your mechanism does not unfortunately double
the danger of prodigality[1]—use the great powers I give
you, and if you ask me how, follow the example the
State sets you in regulating intestate successions."

These considerations enable us to view the existing
distribution of land in its true light. We do not shut
our eyes to the proportion of influence exerted by natural
causes in lending to land more than its agricultural value,
and tending to lift it in places beyond the reach of the
cultivator ; but we find these causes overlaid and intensified by artificial legislation, which checks the free circulation of land even among the rich, and which so blocks
the flow of land to the market, that the diminished
quantity forthcoming falls most commonly to the political
purchaser, to whom the existing anomalies of representation open a path to Parliament through the land ; or
to the aspirant to social greatness, who seeks a place
among the privileged body, to which, by a strange
deviation from ordinary practice, we confide the administration of the county. The tendency of this
legislation to fix land in the hands that hold it goes
far to stereotype historical influences, and to involve us
for ever in the shadow of the past. The reign of George
the Third seems still imaged in the distribution of the
land. We trace in it the footprints of the great war—
of the specially close connexion which the last century

[1] See Mr. Neate on this subject.

created between land and political power—of commons
inclosure carried on at a time when the rich were
exceptionally enriched, and the poor exceptionally impoverished. " The ghost" of the dead Protection still
seems to "sit crowned upon the grave thereof."

The succession law of England, in fact, stands out
from the dead level of English legislation, a monument
of the audacity of ancient politics—an ambitious effort
to guide into certain channels the social and economical
development of the nation. It is strange that this relic
of abandoned political methods—for its sister institutions, sumptuary, usury, labour laws, have gradually
dropped away from its side—should be hailed by a
school of economists, however small, as the last result of
economical wisdom. Happy the institution, we feel,
which forms a valued link in the iron fabric of mediæval
society, and which commends itself to the nineteenth
century as an economical revelation. But, in fact, in
England we are too well used to this kind of argument.
We are rich in ingenious, acute, uncritical Julians, who
rationalize in order to defend. There is a type of English
intellect, stronger in advocacy than in analysis, which
likes to feel its energies limited to a definite circle. Give
it data to defend, and it will clothe them in an elaborate
garb of perverse logic, only not sophistical because not
consciously untrue. It is a serious matter, when this
eccentric spirit plays round subjects so grave as those of
economy and law. The moral force of nations is their
most precious possession, and we cannot afford to have
it shattered and pulverized by a half humorous cynicism,
which would defend compurgation and frank-pledge, if
duller and less ingenious statesmanship had not long ago

given them their *quietus.* But in truth these elaborate
apologies are seldom successful. Somewhere or other,
sooner or later, the essentially archaic and unphilosophi-
cal character of the institution makes itself perceptible,
and the unsound construction topples to the ground.
The effort to find an economical wisdom in our succession law is one of these afterthoughts, and meets with
the usual ill-success. It is claimed that Entail and
Primogeniture encourage industry by investing the proprietor with great powers, and, still more, by establishing in the centre, as it were, of each family a magnifi-
cently fed and coloured drone, the incarnation of wealth
and social dignity, the visible end of human endeavour,
a sort of Great Final Cause immanent in every family.
It may seriously be doubted, however, whether the ingenious contrivance produces its due effect. The object
of adoration lies too often far beyond the reach of his
younger brothers. Nor is his magnificent repose less
suggestive of elegant idleness than work. We may
doubt whether, in the following passage, remarkable for
its *naïveté,* an eminent man has not more correctly
appreciated the consequences of the law, and the exigencies of the younger son's position. "We know,"
says Dr. Chalmers,[1] "that there is a mighty force of
sentiment and natural affection arrayed against the law
of Primogeniture. But here is the way in which we
would appease these feelings, and make compensation
for the violence done to them. We would make no
inroad on the integrity of estates, or for the sake of a
second brother take off to the extent of a thousand
a year from that domain of ten thousand a year which

[1] Quoted in Laing's Notes of a Traveller. First Series. P. 26.

devolved by succession on the eldest son of the family.
We should think it vastly better, if by means of a
liberal provision in all the branches of the public service, a place of a thousand a year lay open to the
younger son, whether in the law, or in the Church, or
in colleges, or in any other well-appointed establishment
kept up for the good and interest of the nation."

As to the powers which our succession law places in
the hands of the proprietor, it is perfectly true that they
are very great. It holds up to every capitalist, whether
his fortune has been acquired in meritorious services to
the State, or by the mere chances of lucky trade, the
magnificent prospect, if he acquires land, of writing his
name, not in the "water" of personalty, but in the "brass"
of real property. Here, it says to the fortunate specu-
lator, is the world of indestructible existences; a word
whispered in this magic realm will practically determine
the future of a string of people, born and unborn : the
most illiterate may rise to the dignity of a social Solon,
and issue ordinances like an autocrat, which, though
nominally liable to repeal, will be practically so borne
out by the family pride cultivated and encouraged by
the State, as to be less disturbed than the works of far
more ostentatious legislators. Settle stock, settle personalty, and the very object settled may melt like snow,
as it is passed from the hands of one generation to those
of another. To settle such property is like writing in
the sand. Settled land is carven brass. It must be
remembered, however, that these vast powers cannot be
given to one generation without being withdrawn from
its successors. It is only the founder of the family who
enjoys this splendid and autocratic privilege. His suc-

h

cessors find themselves lodged in the meshes, and maintained in idleness by the safeguards, of a strict settlement, which practically they do not venture to break
through; and the great powers of the original proprietor
dwindle in succeeding generations to the painful and
accurate observance of an artificial system. If, however, it is doubtful whether the provisions of our law are
effective in stimulating industry, it is not at all doubtful
that such artificial encouragements are no longer needed.
In the early ages of the world, slavery and caste, the
whip or the priest, were perhaps necessary inducements
to labour; but in the days when Belgium beats us out
of the market under a law of Equal Inheritance, and
under the same law the westward expansion of the
United States—the greatest economical achievement of
the century—has been effected, such elaborate contri-
vances for giving industry a needless stimulus are surely
quite uncalled for.

The real effect of these laws on the family relation is
something very different from what these theorists would
have us believe. "I have more than once heard," says
Mr. Neate, "and I believe it to be true," that the relations of father and son "are upon a better footing in the
richer families of foreign nations than they are amongst
us in the same rank of life." "The state of our law is
just that which is best calculated to put enmity between
father and son. The son is in a far higher degree master
and owner of the estate than is the father. Nothing
that the father does by himself can extend his power
beyond the limits of his own life; but the son, if he
survives his father, is absolute owner, and he may even
in his father's life dispose of the estate, subject to that

contingency, which he may provide against by means of
an insurance." This dualism of proprietorship, while, as
we shall see, it cramps cultivation, is very commonly destructive of the peace of families. If the father needs
to raise money, if he contemplates second marriage, he
comes before his son for his approbation. "Their mutual
necessities become a matter of discussion and negotiation" between them, placing them "towards each other
in a most unnatural position. It is a hard thing for a
father to have to confess and excuse his extravagance to
a son," or to diplomatize about his re-marriage. "It is
a worse thing for a son to judge of his father's excuses,
and to decide, virtually as head of the family," whether
they are to be allowed. "The position is morally aggravated (though legally simplified) by the power which the
father has of stopping his son's allowance, and so putting
on him an undue pressure in the bargain. What wonder
is there, we hear so often of the cold and unfrequent
intercourse between the present and the coming holder
of great settled estates. If we looked only to the happiness and morality of families, the old system of Scotch
entail, which denied alike to father and son, either solely
or jointly, all power of alienation, is better."

It is to this singularly constituted class—a stranger
by its own act to entirety of ownership and proprietary
freedom—the slave of its own creation, the title-deed—
fettered by that family legislation which is the most
inexorable kind of legislation—that we commit the vast
issues of the food supply. They are to us what Egypt
was to Rome. Vast and hungry cities, swarming with a
starving population, look to them to be fed. These

h 2

cities have risen side by side with the growth of the large estates. They have opened careers independent of agriculture to the middle and lower classes of England, and have alone made these vast accumulations of land possible. Their rise has softened the consequence to which, among other causes, the law has led, and saved the archaic system, which dates from days when the land had no such pressing and difficult economical function to discharge as it has now. The clamour of these cities for food is marked in the familiar fact of the rising prices of meat. Nothing, it seems, but increased home produce can really fill the gap in the production of animal food. In the infancy of agricultural statistics, surmise and conjecture are already rife as to our recent progress in this department of production; schemes abound for the increase of it in the future. An experienced agricultural inquirer,[1] comparing the returns of the home supply of cattle to the Metropolitan Cattle Market in the years 1853 and 1863, draws but a gloomy picture. "The increase," he says, "in home-fed beasts was trifling in the extreme." There was an absolute "falling-off in the supplies of English sheep." Some districts are noticed as having increased their contribution; others, as having fallen short of their achievements twenty years before. Scotland largely increased her supply within the ten years from 1853 to 1863, and in Scotland nearly the whole of the land is let upon a nineteen years' lease. "Need I say," the writer adds, "that the Scotch grazier has an immense advantage over the English breeder, who is merely a tenant-at-will?" The conclusion is,

---

[1] Mr. Robert Herbert, in a Paper read before the Statistical Society of London in December 1864.

that nothing short of an enormous outlay of capital in the less successful counties for drainage and other purposes, together with a more general system of letting land on moderately long leases, will permanently lower the price of meat.[1] It is by no means necessary for the purpose of this paper to assume the correctness either of this conclusion or of the data on which it is based. Sound or not, these speculations point very decisively to one inference, which is, that there is the most intimate connexion between the food supply of the great cities and the freedom of the land. In whatever degree our agricultural system checks the outlay of capital, or militates against security of tenure, it tends to diminish the productiveness of agriculture, and to raise the price of food in towns. Let us inquire how we stand in relation to these points.

Let us trace, however hastily, the fortunes of the great estate. Let us accept the plea of its advocates—a doubtful recommendation—that the great estate makes great farms. Let us take the *grande culture* at its best, the better to criticize the form of it with which we are familiar. Shake it free from the trammels of Entail and Primogeniture ; rescue it from all artificial augmentations of its attractiveness, which raise its price above the limit of agricultural value ; let it pass freely to the hands most competent to wield it; leave those hands unfettered by limitations of proprietary interest to back the tenant-farmer with the most lavish and most skilful use of capital ; give the farmer a sufficient lease ; educate him

---

[1] " If," observes the same writer (*Agr. Journal*, 1866), the supply of sheep has declined, about which I have no doubt whatever, the present dearness of butchers' meat may be readily accounted for, and its cause is too deep-seated to be affected much by even increased importations of foreign stock."

well.; man the farms with labourers well fed, well paid, well housed : under these conditions the *grande culture* may well rise, not, probably, to the highest limit of productiveness, but to a very considerable efficiency and success. Yet even in its highest form it has its weaker side. First, the owner is not the cultivator. Just that element of human passion and emotion—the proprietary sentiment, or, perhaps, madness—which makes the greatness of the small estate, is lost; the small proprietor is broken into the hierarchical trio of landlord, farmer, and labourer, and the actual cultivators of the soil are not acted upon by the "magic of property." Secondly, the steps of the agricultural hierarchy are apt to be severed by a social and economical interval, which checks the rise of the labourer to the place of the tenant, or that of the tenant to the place of the proprietor. The motives for industry are *pro tanto* diminished. Thirdly, the system is subject to the ordinary weaknesses which beset the severance of labour and capital. Strikes may suspend production, and discourage the capitalist.

If the large estate, even in its highest form, is attended by these drawbacks, we may readily imagine the essential feebleness which marks its fettered and bastard phase in England. The great settled estate, is, as has been shown, in its origin largely factitious—the growth of exceptional conditions of the land-market, during the great war— the product of a law which permits land to be directed in special channels. Even when the owner has himself purchased the land, he has most often been attracted to do so, not by interest in agriculture, or by a sense of agricultural capacity, but by the protection and power which the law lavishes upon the position of the land-owner. Nor is this all. The great estates of England are often so colossal in magnitude, that, even if they were in the most skilful hands, a sufficient supervision would be difficult. Under actual circumstances, the active control over the vast area rests with the agent; and the last opening for the special zeal and interest which might be expected from the proprietor, is closed. The cumbrous mechanism is still further enfeebled by the practice of strict settlement. Parliament struggles in vain with the proprietary dualism of tenant for life and tenant in tail. With an exceptional liberality, it places public money at the command of the tenant for life, for drainage purposes; but even this inducement has failed to secure the proper drainage of the highest-rented county in England.[1] In truth, Primogeniture raises a painful dilemma in the mind of the tenant for life between the improvement of the land, and the interests of his younger children. "The owner," says Mr. Fawcett,[2] "though possessing a large income, must be considered to be a poor man, because, since all his property is settled upon his heir, he is able to make no adequate provision for his other children. A poor landowner has not the requisite capital to carry out improvements on his estate; and, even if he has the capital, he has every inducement not to spend it, because by doing so he enriches his eldest son, who will be wealthy, at the expense of his younger children, who will be comparatively poor." Indeed, the landowner himself,

---

[1] See Mr. W. J. Moscrop's Report on the Farming of Leicestershire. Journal of the Agricultural Society. Second Series. Vol. ii. part ii. No. 4.
[2] Economic Position of the British Labourer, p. 21.

and especially the poorer sort of landowner, is often the first sufferer by the strict settlement. It makes him a tenant for life, and binds him for a time to his land. He must rest content with a third of what might be his income, if he could change the investment of his capital.

Descend from the proprietary class to the tenant farmer; it will still be found that the freedom of agriculture is crossed and cramped by considerations alien to the pursuit. "*La haute politique*" forbids security of tenure. The tenant-farmer of England most commonly holds no lease. Mr. MacCulloch even apprehends the subversion, in the race for political influence, of that "system of giving leases for nineteen or twenty years certain, that has been the main cause of the wonderful improvement of Scotch agriculture." His estimate of the value of the lease fully agrees with that of other experienced judges. "Taking into account," says one of these,[1] "the increased and increasing outlay in the shape of labour, manure, and implements, which land requires to make it remunerative, I consider the question of security of tenure as no longer doubtful; and that farm leases are essential" to the further agricultural development of England. "Farming under the lease system," observes the authority just quoted, "is progressive; and from the large tenant outlay, which the security of a lease induces, it is no unfrequent occurrence for farms during a nineteen-years' lease to be doubled in value, without any outlay on the part of landlords." Thus, the system which is kept practically out of the field in England, is the very system to redeem in some

---

[1] Quoted in the Journal of the Statistical Society, 1866.

degree the agricultural consequences of the strict settlement. As it is, the land remains in the hands of a
tenant for life, who, often enough, neither can nor does
improve; and of a tenant-at-will, who has but small
security in doing so. We are told, indeed, that
" customary allowances" (a form of tenant-right) give
a security for improvements equal to that of a lease.
" Let any farmer," observes the *Economist*,[1] " holding
his farm under such terms, try it. Let him quarrel with
the gamekeeper ; let him interfere with the game bred
on the farm, and fed on his crops for the landlord's profit ;
and he will then test the real value—the no value—of the
tenant-right panacea." A political proprietary like ours,
which, as the *Times* says, purchases for " influence," has
thrown away its money if it grants security of tenure.
The absence of the lease is, in fact, the pivot of the
rural balance of power. Nothing but tenancy-at-will
could hush the murmurs of the game-beset farmer.
Let the leasehold tenants of Scotland raise their
clamours, if they will, through the Parliamentary representatives they are able to return ; let them defend,
if they will, the cause of agricultural production against
the game-laws of the State ; such turbulence would mar
and distort the tranquillity of agricultural relations in
England. The *Times*[2] points out to these misguided
Scotchmen the incompatibility of agricultural considerations with a civilization so high as our own. Parched
with the dust of London, it darts upon the refreshing
topic of the game and the land. It revels in the dewy
atmosphere of the most delicious of monopolies. Just
as " who rules o'er freemen must himself be free," so a

[1] Quoted in the Statistical Journal. [2] March 8, 1867.

grievance with so picturesque a background must surely, it is hinted, be itself merely picturesque. Yet, on the whole, the *Times* is disposed to allow its reality. " There is something," it says, " almost ridiculous in allowing wild and wasteful animals, such as hares and rabbits, to overrun and devastate a district possessing high cultivation, expensively manured, ploughed, harrowed, and harvested with costly machinery, studded with fine farm buildings, and with the steam-engine rendering its multifarious assistance." Even if the farmer receives, as he often does, due compensation, the *Times* allows that the consumer receives no satisfaction for his loss ; and the consumer means England, the whole kingdom, the world. Let the consumer be content. " Take that thine is, and go thy way." The landowner has bought the land, with all its privileges : the State, if he can help it, shall not spoil his bargain. It is hard-hearted to ask him to part with that which he does not fully utilize ; it is wicked to provoke him to fail in his proprietary duties, and to become an absentee.

Such is ever the language of protected classes. They never know where to pause in their demands. It is not sufficient that the State should give them special means for maintaining the land in their own non-agricultural hands ; they must further be bribed to reside on their vast territories by a game-law hostile to the productiveness of agriculture. The outer world must be content to feel a poor satisfaction in living under a system which is at least logically consistent and deductively complete. The Game Laws, we admit, are the natural pendant and corollary of Entail.

Turn lastly to the agricultural labourer. What has

the great estate made of the masses of our rural population ? The base of the column is buried deep in misery
and pauperism.

> " Hic vertex nobis semper sublimis ; at illum
> Sub pedibus Styx atra videt manesque profundi."

Unlike the manufacturing artisan—a new type developed
by great and recent inventions, one which has emerged
upon the world in its most civilized moment—the
agricultural labourer belongs to one of those ancient
and feeble classes, which are entangled in the net-work
of the past, and on which tradition lies with a leaden
weight. He is still—in the South of England at all
events—not far from the spot, where the old Poor-Law
left him. The smoke of the great war still hangs about
the class. In the years between 1760 and 1815—fatal
years, the print of whose footsteps is still deep and fresh
upon the social system of England—the great proprietors, while they detached the common lands from the
unquestionably feeble and ineffectual hands of the community, took the agricultural labourer, for the moment,
under their own high protection, guaranteed him means
of support for a family, however large ; and founded a
pauper warren at home, in the effort to secure stout arms
to crush Napoleon on the Continent. A simple blunder ;
yet blunders are sometimes more ruinous than crimes.
Such a past history, viewed in connexion with the
feebleness of the class, should surely have impressed
upon the State the need of stimulating, with the utmost
carefulness, whatever feeble efforts it might make to
react upon the past, to emancipate itself from its
traditions. One would have thought, for instance,
that the State might at least do its best to fit the

labourer for pushing his chances in the towns; yet we know that education still remains the sport of theological faction.

Nor would the improvement and extension of national education alone suffice. If the pressure of poverty is such that the child is removed from school at eight, nine, or ten years of age, the most efficient educational system must prove a failure. The second decade of life becomes merely a painful retrogression from the low standard reached at ten. Whatever may be done by night-schools, half-time schemes, or the extension to agriculture of the educational provisions of the Factory Acts, we may be quite certain that the effect of every kind of educational machinery would be quintupled, if the hope of social advance could be brought home to the agricultural labourer more generally than it is. At present, "If a hired labourer saves twenty pounds, he has no chance of investing it as capital in some profitable employment; the only purpose to which he can devote it is to place it in the savings-bank, where he obtains something below the current rate of interest."[1] What wonder that "an agricultural labourer can rarely be found who has saved even a few pounds?" The ignorance and the poverty of the class react upon and intensify each other. In large districts of England the labourer is so ignorant, that migration to the towns is reluctantly resorted to, and too often brings small relief; so poor, that his children must begin work early, and perpetuate the tradition of stagnation and hopelessness. It is true that, where mines and manufactures positively penetrate and permeate the agricultural

---

[1] Fawcett's Economic Position of the British Labourer.

districts, a far higher degree of rural well-being is attained. The pauperized proportion of the population—a thirteenth in Wiltshire, a fifteenth or sixteenth in the Eastern and South Midland regions—dwindles to a twenty-eighth in Lancashire, a thirtieth in the East and West Ridings, and a thirty-sixth in Derbyshire. In Durham the labourers, having the choice of easy migration to the mineral districts, are all but absolute masters of the situation. It is not, however, by its results in the Northern counties of England that our agricultural system must be tested. In a region so thickly sown with labour markets, few agricultural systems could fail more or less to succeed. The rural districts of the South and East present, no doubt, infinitely various degrees of well-being and wretchedness ;[1] but, on the whole, throughout them the career of the labourer may still be not unjustly described as a more or less circuitous route to the poor-house. He belongs to one of the few classes in England which, if they desire to advance, must do so by breaking through use and wont, and leaving behind them the ground they know and feel safe upon. He sees every day, in many counties, that as the farms grow larger, a deeper chasm is forming between his class and even the tenancy of land. His horizon narrows every day. He is losing, in the Midlands, even the scanty *pied à terre* which the possession of a garden gives him in some districts. " It fortunately happens," says Dr. Hunter,[2] " that a bit of land allotment or a large

---

[1] Shropshire, Devonshire, Herefordshire, and Somersetshire obtain in many respects from Dr. Hunter a more favourable verdict than other counties. " Inquiry on the State of the Dwellings of Rural Labourers." By Dr. H. J. Hunter, in the Appendix to the Seventh Report of the Medical Officer to the Privy Council, 1864.   [2] P. 134.

garden will secure to its owner comfort by an increase of his means in such a form that no advantage can be taken of his wealth to make a reduction of his wages possible; and for this reason;—there are times when a farmer requires all the labour he can get; at others, he thinks it proper to retain a very few hands only. In order to get regular uninterrupted work, men engage to serve during the busy times at a lower rate than those who are to be turned off as the demand subsides. The garden, or allotment, affords these latter something to work at when the farmer provides nothing, and thus, by entering into a sort of half competition with him, enables the workman to maintain his price when wanted on the farm." "But," observes Dr. Hunter elsewhere,[1] "every attempt made by the farm labourer to render himself as independent of his employer as are the workmen in other trades has been too often met with imputations on his honesty or his industry. The labourer's cows have been within this century nearly extinguished, his pig is frequently condemned, and his garden seems likely to follow the common rights of which he has been in this and the last generation deprived." As hope is withdrawn, the ordinary checks on population are withdrawn too. Special coercive checks take the place of hope—the contraction of cottage accommodation, the proprietor's refusal to build. The labourer is cramped in the close parish or poisoned in the open village. Yet the huddle increases within the cottage. We preach in vain "self-reverence, self-knowledge, self-control." And so the old round begins anew. The hopelessness of social advance, improvident marriage, the

---

[1] P. 179, note.

employment of children, the inefficiency of education, the
dread of movement, hang together in a miserable sequence
of cause and effect. When the immobility of Southern
labour is once shaken, the change will come in the crash
of an exodus. Yet the consolidation of farms and the
emigration of labourers will merely complicate, not solve,
the agricultural problem. The scarcity of rural labour is
a real peril of the future. Already, in parts, agriculture
tends to fall into feebler and feebler hands. "Droves"
of children fill ineffectively the places of grown-up men.
Gangs of migratory Irish, who acquire no settlement,
but issue when summoned from the purlieus of some
more or less distant country town, already in places tend
to supplant the resident labourer, and to lower the type
of agricultural industry. If, again, as seems probable,
many of the articles of consumption most needed by a
dense city population, and least procurable by importation,
are best produced by small farms, the "consolidation"
movement will merely remove the pressure of economical
distress from the country to the towns.

At what points, it may be asked, in this long chain of
cause and effect do the laws which we are discussing
intervene? In what way do they help in producing
these results? They do so by contracting the land-
market, and thus adding to the artificial causes which
help to place the land beyond the reach of the cultivator;
they do so by contributing to keep the land in the
hands of a political proprietary, which discourages the
application of capital to agriculture by withholding the
lease, by preserving destructive game, and by mutilating
its own interest in the land. Let us test the great settled
estate in a sphere in which its proprietor is practically all

but supreme. The housing of the labourer suffered in many districts a marked deterioration between 1851 and 1861. In 821 English parishes, according to the last census, a decrease of houses was accompanied by an increase of population. The demolition of cottages has perhaps ceased with the abolition of parish chargeability, but even if close unions were impossibilities, and thus further mischief were prevented, there is nothing in the Union Chargeability Act to undo the mischief that has been done; and Mr. Childers' Act of last year carefully avoids giving tenants for life power to borrow money for the purpose of building cottages for labourers. Though no one can be more interested than the employer of labour in seeing that that labour is well-housed, and housed upon the spot where it is needed, the Medical Officer of the Privy Council[1] seriously expects that a time will come when the question will have to be considered, "whether all land which requires labour ought not to be held liable to the obligation of containing a certain proportion of suitable labourers' dwellings." Between the latter years of last century and 1851, while the rise in the labourer's wages was but 14 per cent. the rent of a labourer's cottage had risen 100 per cent.[2] Since then, the rural cottage has become more overcrowded, and rents have risen as the accommodation has become worse.

The same law which helps to cripple the large farm system plays, as some of its advocates allow, no inconsiderable part in discouraging the small farm. The two great systems of agriculture seem by this time well

[1] Seventh Report, p. 15.
[2] *Fraser's Magazine*, February 1867, p. 148.

content to close their long rivalry with the admission,
that neither can justly claim an exclusive and universal
empire. Some crops favour cultivation on the large
scale ; others require the minute vigilance of the small
farmer. The *petite culture* has never been so vividly
depicted as in the recent work of M. de Laveleye.[1] We
gaze with astonishment at the system which the prophets
of a faction assure us contains no lesson, no significance
for England. Yet it seems especially suited to be the
agricultural system of a manufacturing country. The
strength of Flemish cultivation lies in the growth
of "*plantes industrielles*" (*e.g.* flax)—in the "*cul-
tures dérobées,*" or second crops, consisting of food
for the host of cattle maintained upon the land—in
the skilful and untiring application of the manure
thus gained—and in the vast produce which results
from the minute attention of the infinitesimal farmer.
"Dans la Flandre orientale," says M. de Laveleye,
"chaque cultivateur, n'ayant pour exercer son industrie
qu'un peu moins d'un hectare [2½ acres], parvient à
nourrir presque autant de personnes que le cultivateur
anglais, qui dispose de trois hectares de terrain productif."[2]
It must not be imagined that this productiveness is the
result of the natural fertility of the soil; for while, as
M. de Laveleye observes, "l'Angleterre a ses beaux
pâturages, qui sans frais nourrissent d'innombrables trou-
peaux," he finds in Flanders no such natural advantages
of soil, but, on the contrary, "une stérilité constitutive
qu'on ne peut vaincre qu'au moyen d'une masse énorme
d'engrais."[3] English authorities fully bear out M. de

[1] Essai sur l'Économie Rurale de la Belgique. Par Émile de Laveleye.
Second Edition. 1863.   [2] P. 56.   [3] P. 229.

i

Laveleye's testimony to the "*petite culture.*"   Already, in 1851, Mr. Caird recognised a great future for the *petite culture* in England. "Our insular position," he observes,[1] "with a limited territory and an increasingly dense manufacturing population, is yearly extending the circle within which the production of fresh food—animal, vegetable, and forage—will be needed for daily supply, which cannot be brought from distant countries. They can be produced in no country so well as in our own. Wool has likewise increased in value as much as any agricultural product, and there is a good prospect of flax becoming an article in extensive demand. The manufacture of sugar from beetroot may yet be found very profitable to the English agriculturist. Now all these products require the employment of considerable labour, very minute care, skill, and attention, and a larger acreable application of capital than is requisite for the production of corn. This will inevitably lead to the gradual diminution of the largest farms, and to the concentration of the capital and attention of the farmer on a smaller space."[2]   As the price of meat rises in our towns, we shall probably turn with increasing interest to the somewhat unsavoury ant-hill described by M. de Laveleye. We are told that this garden cultivation is out of the question in most parts of England. Mr. Cliffe Leslie[3] explains to us why. "The causes of the tendency

---

[1] Quoted by Mr. Cliffe Leslie ; *Fraser*, February 1867.

[2] The high rents paid for allotment ground near towns ; the existence of a class of small cultivators, proprietary and other, in districts where the demand for market produce is specially good ; and, in some degree (for the house is not the sole attraction), the great extension of Land and Building Societies, already indicate what would be the future of the *petite culture* in England, if the land were free.

Fraser, February 1867

which formerly existed, and which still exists in many of
the counties of England, towards the extinction of small
farms, have been the following : first and especially, the
inability and indisposition of encumbered inheritors of
great estates, upon the one hand, and of tenants without
leases on the other, to furnish small farms with the
requisite buildings and fixtures ; secondly, the artificial
pauperism produced by causes already mentioned, and
the anxiety of landlords resulting therefrom, and from
the frame of the Poor-law, to clear their estates of the
peasantry ; thirdly, Protectionist legislation in favour of
corn."

If the small farmer finds no sufficient place in our
agricultural system, we may feel quite certain that the
small proprietor is practically excluded. It is claimed
that the concentration of land in the hands of the rich
is wholly the result of natural causes. Even if it were,
the artificial aid which our legislation renders to nature
would be unfortunate, because it would be gratuitous;
because it would distort, even if it seconded, the economical movement ; and because it would disguise in the
garb of class-legislation the irresistible working of a
natural law. But, in fact, if natural causes have been
at work, there can be no question that they have been
reinforced and consolidated by a number of artificial
ones. It is unnecessary to draw again the oft-drawn
portrait of the class of small proprietors which the
fourteenth and fifteenth centuries gave England, and
which declined apparently with the defeat of Puritanism in the seventeenth century. As a cultivating
class, subsisting on the produce of their own land,
they have practically disappeared, except in the hilly

districts of the north ; for their totally dissimilar successors, the small freeholders of the nineteenth century, are rather owners of house property than of land. On the other hand, the creation of a peasant proprietary throughout the two continents of Europe and America dates to a large extent from the present century, though its germs are immemorial. The conflicts of economists have familiarized us with the hard-working, prudent, and somewhat prosaic personage, who answers on the Continent to the English agricultural labourer. He is not relieved by a hopeless social position from the ennobling cares and anxieties of ordinary life. His intelligence is sufficiently developed to make his life anxious and circumspect. He is the victim of the absorbing and impassioned industry which comes with proprietorship ; but yet that incessant industry is more ennobling than the more leisurely activity of the hired labourer. Even in Flanders, where four-fifths of the land is in the hands of tenant farmers, an equal number of agriculturists feeds a larger non-agricultural population than in Great Britain.[1]

We may reasonably expect that the increased security of tenure which gives a zest to proprietary labour, would, in similar circumstances here, produce a still greater result,—a conclusion which the statistics of the Channel Islands, notwithstanding the cavils of Lord Rosse, seem very clearly to support. It is not pretended that small proprietorship is an agricultural panacea, or even that, like Lord Bacon's method, it "*exæquat ingenia.*" It has not enabled French agriculture thoroughly to throw off the shadow of pre-revolutionary methods of

[1] Laveleye, p. 57, note.

cultivation.[1] But it is a system which, whether it re-appeared in the ordinary peasant-proprietary form, or in the more social and organized form of the co-operative estate, might well be left free to make itself a place in England beside the *grande culture*, if it can do so, for at least two reasons: first, because it is the most vigorous type of that careful and minute cultivation to which the circumstances of England seem to point; secondly, because it is the most powerful instrument for the extension of cultivation.[2]

As to the social consequences of the dominant system, there are few who can feel satisfied or even secure. It must be remembered that even yet we have not felt its full effects. Our law of entail acts with redoubled force at every epoch of advance in national wealth. As each millionaire emerges triumphant from the commercial *mêlée*, and by pure weight of capital forces open the gates of the landed Paradise, one more area is withdrawn from the land market, one more small borough won over, one more voice in Parliament committed to the all-powerful system. English land, we are told, is fated to become "the luxury of the rich"—to be made "pleasure ground." If that dangerous result is indeed decreed by fate, let the land at least circulate freely among the narrow class to which it is confined. But, in fact, the quantity of land which comes into the market is so diminished that it acquires a monopoly value.

---

[1] Still, if we trust Kolb (Handbuch der Vergleichenden Statistik, p. 86), it is in precisely those districts in which the subdivision of land reaches its highest point, such as the Département du Nord and those of the Rhine and Seine, that the best French agriculture is to be found.

[2] See Laveleye, p. 82.

Might not the whole aspect of affairs alter if the land were set free? If one purchaser looked to win from his purchase rent, profit, and wages, and the other rent alone, might not the competition be less unequal than is supposed? Grant that the cultivator is still distanced, are there no corners of England so unattractive to the pleasure-resident, so near to some hungry and smoke-begrimed market for produce, that the balance might alter, and the "magic of property" be infused into cultivation? It is quite certain that so long as the existing fetters are maintained, there has been no fair trial of this issue. In any case, there is no need to disguise under an appearance of class-legislation the operation of a natural law.

We have too long looked to the towns to play the part of safety-valves for rural misery. Their exercise of the right of asylum has cost them dear. The indescribably over-crowded state of some of them is notorious enough. They are, besides, entangled in the meshes of the land difficulty. Immense unapproachable estates, overgrown demesnes, restricted rights of proprietorship, defective titles, and all other causes which keep land out of the market, keep out manufactures and trade from many natural homes for their settlement, and imprison them within bounds where space is at once insufficient and extravagantly dear. One of the most flourishing towns in the United Kingdom owes its extraordinary progress in the present generation chiefly to the fact, that it stands upon ground which the sale of the estates of a ruined noble made the property of its citizens, and thus transferred to the many from the one. "Those who are versed in the

published and unpublished history of towns will readily
call up several similar cases."[1]   Yet our towns are still
the sole or main centres of whatever vigorous life exists
in our social system.   As we look beyond their limits,
we find but few classes economically free.   The Roman
Empire became before it fell a skeleton-work of great
cities, scattered over an effete and morally lifeless surface of *latifundia*.   Are there no signs of a similar concentration of moral activity within the cities in the
England of to-day?   The gulf, it is true, is vast between even the most miserable free population and the
rural slave-gangs of Rome; but, on the other hand, the
Roman Empire had the advantage that it stood alone.
A few philosophic observers might draw perilous com-
parisons between the corrupt society of Rome and the
free village-communities of Germany; but Rome had
no rival among civilized states.   The English agricultural system stands surrounded, not merely by countries,
but by continents, which rest on the principle of the
diffusion of landed property.   England alone severs its
masses from the land.   She replied, at the outset of the
century, by her Enclosure Acts to the French Revolution
and the career of Stein.   Her vast and available coal-
fields, her iron mines, the energy of her people, founded
cities in her midst, and their rise saved the succession
law, by opening other than agricultural paths to fortune.
The very misery of agriculture has intensified the flight
from the country to the towns, and given a wild energy
to manufacturing progress.   A gigantic wages-receiving
class fills the cities, and stands arrayed against an
equally powerful organization of capitalists.   Both capi-

---

[1] Mr. Cliffe Leslie, *Fraser*, p. 153.

talist and artisan are so new in point of origin, that
no tradition of immemorial relationship, no softening
growth of custom and habit removes or mitigates the
crude antithesis of the connexion. It is impossible to
say how soon the schism of labour and capital may not
extend from manufactures to agriculture. We stand in
danger, in one respect, of the fate of the ancient Greek
States, where the antagonism of rich and poor made all
excellence of political constitution fruitless and nugatory; where the social weakness overpowered and neutralized the political advance. The Continent, America,
and Australia proclaim with hardly a dissentient voice,
that, in agriculture at all events, the antithesis of labour
and capital need not exist. England follows a path
which diverges more and more from that of the world.
Not content with allowing the market to sever, if so it
must be, labour from capital, the masses from the land,
it helps by its laws to maintain the aggregation of land
in the hands of a few.

It is the least of the objections to this policy, that it
gratuitously withdraws England from the main stream of
European progress. Yet this is no slight objection. It
was one of the most fortunate features of ancient history
that the main States passed simultaneously, each in its
own way, through similar stages of political and social
development. The same problem, in a thousand different
forms, presented itself to all—emancipation from the
iron fixity of early society, a new and more intellectual
basis of order. So homogeneous was the whole group,
that the solution reached by each was the common
advantage of all. There is danger in an isolated, eccentric growth, if it is not the inevitable result of circum-

stances; and even then it is to be regretted. The sense of national peculiarity, of exemption from the rules of good and ill which prevail in the larger world, may deaden and distort both the party of order and that of progress, till Conservatism assumes an irrational type, and abuses become invincible, because they can only be combated with a fraction of European experience. Let us keep, if we can, in the open and public path—let us cease to pride ourselves on the strange and exceptional growths of our political and social system. Every intricacy of our institutions is a screen behind which craft may secure itself from criticism.

Real as this evil is, it is the least of those which flow from the gratuitous intervention of the State in the land-market. We have seen how the operation of the law cramps the progressive forces of urban and agricultural life. It no less weakens the conservative elements of our social system.

For, first, in whatever degree it tends to exclude the small cultivator from the ownership of the soil, it withdraws from the lower class the most powerful of conservative influences. The proprietor, however small, has the conservative interests of a proprietor. His stake in the good order of the country is not, perhaps, greater— it is probably even safer, and less liable to be affected by civil disturbance, than that of the receiver of wages; but it is more tangible. His interest is stronger because it is less mercenary, and more the result of tradition, instinct, and habit. Instinct and habit are less easily overcome by passion than mere calculation of interest. The prudential check on population, again, is stronger in the case of the proprietor than in that of the receiver of wages. It is hard to recognise the limitations of a vast labour-market—it is easy to descry the limitations of the patrimony. Again, a proprietary lower class has more leisure in youth than a wages-receiving one. Some time commonly elapses before the heir succeeds to the patrimony, and during this interval he may win fresh experience and a wider view of men and things in the ranks of an army or a trade. Moreover, education of a general kind is of more use to the small proprietor than to the more purely professional wages-receiver. He has the responsibility of directing a small capital. His daily life calls for more thought and contrivance than the mere mechanical round of the hired labourer. It is more likely to keep alive the results of school-training.

Secondly, in whatever degree the law checks the free circulation of land among the rich, it substitutes for a vigorous land-owning class, exposed to the common risks of life, one accustomed to be at once fettered and sustained. After withdrawing from the masses some valuable elements of order, it places over them an upper class, which heightens the intellectual indolence of wealth by the practice of entail. "At the present time," says Mr. Fawcett,[1] "428 peers have a right to sit in the House of Lords. And yet, out of that number, perhaps not more than forty or fifty have either the taste, or the inclination, or the capacity, to take the slightest part in its deliberations, even when the gravest political questions are discussed." We need not wonder that a class so protected, so exotic, feels some fear of maintaining its due position at the summit of the political wave. Nor does the action of the law stop here. Not contented with

[1] Economic Position of the British Labourer, p. 13.

weakening by State protection the highest class in the
country, it marks it off from other classes of " those that
have " by special rules for the descent of real property—
the kind of property it most usually holds. Thus, after
creating an antagonism between capital and labour, it
divides the capitalists into a primogenitary and a non-
primogenitary class. It deepens unnecessarily the distinction between classes in England, and probably
encourages even a wider tendency to break into classes
than it directly creates. We shall be told that it makes
up for such flaws by its service in maintaining an aristocracy. In reality, what the law produces is not an
aristocracy, but a plutocracy. Without having achieved
the smallest public service, the capitalist finds himself
in a position to play the part of a Rhadamanthus among
the unborn. Yet, even if its results could be limited to
the creation of an aristocracy, the days are past in which
ten just men could save the State. The vicarious virtue
of a few is no longer the safeguard of nations. Other
principles won the day at Richmond and Sadowa. Nor
is the existing law indispensable to the subsistence of an
aristocracy. Aristocracies exist in continental countries
with a very different inheritance law from our own. We
are told, too, by a palliator of the law [1] that "some of
the largest estates" in England are not entailed.
Feudalism never dreamt of the existing absorption of
the land by a class. "If," says Mr. Neate, "it could
have been foretold to one of those Norman lords that the
time would come when there should be ten, or twenty, or
thirty thousand acres of cultivated land lying together,
of which the direct and absolute ownership should all be

[1] *Economist*, December 22, 1866.

in one man, and within which no rights, even of occupation, should be allowed to exist, but those of a yearly tenancy for the farmer, or a weekly tenancy for the labourer—the feudal tyrant, as we call him, would have turned from the imaginary picture, as representing, on the one hand, an excess of power beyond his desires, and on the other, a degree of abject dependence to which he neither wished nor believed the Saxon could ever be reduced." Aristocracy has existed without the strict settlement—it will exist without it again. They are no friends of aristocracy who plead that it can thrive in no soil but that of a society in fetters. Monarchy and Democracy are subject to no such disability.

The question remains—to whom can we look to give us the openness of the land market, the proprietary freedom which the country requires ? There may be still some who feel the injustice and the evil which is wrought by existing laws, and who hope for its redress from a Parliament in which the land-owning element is supreme. Undoubtedly, no class is more interested in an amelioration of the law. The existing law isolates and paralyses the highest class, checks that agricultural improvement which is a safer and healthier source of value than monopoly, and gathers up, or rather pretends to gather up, the conservative forces of the country into the hands of a dwindling class, daily confronted by a vaster and more intelligent proletariate. We might expect that a class in such a position, though it might not be willing to plunge the scalpel deep into the wound, would be strong in the minor preliminaries of social reform. We might expect, for instance, that holding as it does in its hands the agricultural destinies of the country, it would watch with the keenest interest the agricultural progress which could alone justify the exclusiveness of its position, and would feel that statistics illustrating the progress of agriculture were almost among its essential title-deeds. Or, again, we might imagine that such a class would be eager to supply all subsidiary aids to the free circulation of land, would enforce registration of title, limit the period over which proof of title must go back to at least half the existing term, and bring within bounds the intricacies and obscurities of the law. We might look to them, again, to watch over and mitigate, as far as may be, the migration from the country to the towns, to facilitate the provision of dwellings for the immigrants, to check the fearful over-crowding which is lowering the type of our poorest class. Yet we know that the House of Commons shrinks from the mere threshold of social reform. For five-and-twenty years[1] it hesitated over the collection of agricultural statistics for England, and we may thank the Cattle Plague for the first approximation to such statistics last year. If the House quailed so long before the farmers, we need not ask what its attitude has been to the attorneys. All the ability of Lord Westbury was required to carry a mere permissive Act for the Registration of Title, which has hitherto proved but little better than a nullity. There is the same ghostlike and ineffectual aspect about the Act of last Session for facilitating the improvement of the dwellings of the poor (Labouring Classes Dwellings Act, 1866). "The class of proprietors who most need assist-

[1] See a Paper in the Journal of the Agricultural Society, on "Agricultural Statistics, and the Cattle Census." 1866, No. 4, p. 393.

ance in borrowing money for the improvement of their property, viz. tenants for life and persons with a limited interest, are expressly excluded from the operation of the Act."[1] No powers for the compulsory purchase of land are accorded. We have yet to see whether any more masculine effort to solve this frightful question will result from the deliberations of this Session. And yet these questions are but the mere rudiments of social reform. Profounder difficulties do not elicit even puerile remedies. Mr. Locke King's Real Estate Intestacy Bill appears at long intervals on the horizon of Parliament, and vanishes quicker than it came. Majority after majority affirms, that the State ought to make a will for the intestate, which each individual of the majority would deem it an insult to be accused of making himself.

The feebleness which marks the action of the Legislature on social subjects undoubtedly extends to other departments of legislation. While America has successfully grappled with her gigantic problem, while the Continent has been working out in a masculine spirit the ideas sown in what we thought the fruitless agitations of 1848, the last twenty years of the House of Commons have been in the main an epoch of large debate and little action. We may have too much of these discussions, some of which sound as hollow and empty as dialogues of the dead. That moral force, which the "homœopathic" tradition of twenty years is frittering away, will some day be imperiously called for, and may not be forthcoming.

But, while the spirit of feebleness reigns on almost

<hr/>

[1] See a Paper by Mr. Horace Davey in the Journal of the Social Science Association, December 21, 1866.

all topics, a landowners' Parliament labours perhaps
under a special inaptitude for the subject of social
reform. We need not exaggerate the darker causes for
this. It is true, doubtless, that the wanton demolition
of cottages is no school of social morality, or even of
economical wisdom, for that section of the class, be it
large or small, which has engaged in it. It is commonly
stated, again, and may probably be true, that the contributions of landowners to the cause of national education are far outstripped by those of the clergy. But the
more general and profound causes for this inaptitude are
mainly two. First, it is idle to look to those who make
a practice of mutilating their own proprietary interest
in land to restore to us that fulness and freedom of
ownership which we need. Secondly, the class of large
landowners is exactly the class over which social difficulties pass, not most innocuously, but most impercep- ·
tibly. Mr. Bright has expressed this fact in words, the
truth of which will remain whether this generation heeds
them or not. " It is a long distance from castles, and
mansions, and great houses, and abounding luxuries, to
the condition of the great mass of the people who have
no property, and too many of whom are almost always
on the verge of poverty. We know very well all of us
how much we are influenced by the immediate circumstances by which we are surrounded. The rich find
everything just as they like. The country needs no
Reform. There is no country in the world so pleasant
for rich people as this country. But I deny altogether
that the rich alone are qualified to legislate for the poor,
any more than the poor alone would be qualified to
legislate for the rich."

We must strengthen the political mechanism for the elimination of morbid elements from the social system, or we may be entering on a Louis Quinze period, in which problems accumulate and solutions are withheld. We must no longer exclude from Parliament, any more than we exclude from the Trades' Unions Commission, the voice of the classes to which social difficulties are a reality.

It is possible to discern in broad outline, if not in all the minuteness of detail, what remedies a national Parliament would probably apply to the evils which have here been discussed. Its mere existence would do much to still the upper-class thirst for land. Half the fierceness of this fever is due to the advantages with which the anomalies of Representation surround the landowner's position. We may guess, further, that the rigorous and rotund completeness of the Game Laws would suffer. Could the county administration remain an exception to the rule which connects taxation and representation? We may be pretty certain that Law Reform would become a reality. The prophecies of jurists would be fulfilled in the assimilation of the intestacy law of real property to that which governs the descent of personalty. The land would thus tend to fall more and more into the hands of those who would esteem it for its agricultural value, and it is even possible that, as has happened in other ages and countries, the mischievous power of settlement with which the law arms the proprietor might slumber unvalued and unused. It is more probable that the modification of this power, which is theoretically desirable, would prove to be practically necessary. Would it suffice to prohibit limitations to unborn persons? Or

would this prohibition merely impede and not prevent
the perpetuities under which we suffer ? If this change
were, in the view of the law, as Mr. Cliffe Leslie
seems to think would be the case, in no way to modify
the irrevocability of the settlement ; if its only result
were to substitute irrevocable re-settlement after the birth
of a child for irrevocable re-settlement before marriage,
little or nothing would have been gained.   Other and
more stringent remedies would remain to be resorted to ;
among them that proposed by Mr. Cliffe Leslie.   " There
is one way to remedy the old and new evils together,
and at once to purge our jurisprudence, and to emancipate land from its burdens and trammels ; and that is,
to extinguish the force of settlements as binding and
irrevocable instruments, save so far as a provision for a
wife is concerned ; to put family settlements, save as to
a wife, on the same footing as wills, *ipso facto* void upon
marriage, and revocable by any subsequent conveyance
or will ; to enact that each successive proprietor shall
take the land he succeeds to free from any restriction
on his rights of proprietorship ; and, further, to make
provision that all lands left burdened with any charges
shall be sold immediately on the death of the owner to
pay off the incumbrance."

k

V.

POPULAR EDUCATION.

BY CHARLES STUART PARKER.

THE connexion of Popular Education with Parliamentary Reform is twofold.

On the one hand, education prepares the way for the franchise, which in prudence must be withheld where gross ignorance prevails. For political power without knowledge, when it means anything, means mischief. The marked advance which popular education had made since the Reform Bill of 1832, was one of the strongest arguments in favour of the moderate concession of electoral rights to the working classes proposed in the new Reform Bill of 1866. And further progress of education will lead to further measures of enfranchisement. To creating in this way claims of fitness more substantial, and therefore more effective than abstract rights, as well as to asserting them when created, the friends of a wide suffrage should direct their efforts. But this side of the question belongs to the argument for Reform from the " Progress of the Working Classes," which is the subject of a separate essay.

k 2

On the other hand, there are reasons for thinking that Parliamentary Reform will promote Popular Education. The soundness of this opinion cannot thoroughly be tested till Reform shall have been accomplished. But in the meantime, as the question is one of immediate practical interest, it may be worth while to see what light can be thrown upon the future by such considerations of fact as these :—

I. What are the defects of existing popular education in England ?

II. What are the causes of those defects ?

III. What new forces would a Reform Bill (on the scale of the present Bill, or that of last year) bring to bear on the action of Government in this matter ?

The answers to these questions may indicate, whether a reformed House of Commons will be less or more disposed than the present Parliament to deal with national education boldly, prudently, and without delay.

I. First then, what are the defects of existing popular education in England ?

It is often forgotten that in consequence of there being in England no national system of education such as exists in other civilized countries, there are no general reports of education from year to year, to reveal the extent and nature of our shortcomings. The Reports of the Committee of Council relate only to schools receiving Government aid, and in return admitting Government Inspectors, which are the best indeed, but not the whole, nor even one-half, of the schools frequented by the poorer classes. Nor do the Reports of the several Societies connected with education, great and small, supply the want. They say nothing of the private schools, in which, however, one-third of the children of England receive their education. By far the most authentic and most valuable general statement which exists, is the Report (1861) of the Royal Commissioners appointed "to inquire into the state of popular education in England, and to consider and report what measures, if any, are required for the extension of sound and cheap elementary instruction to all classes of the people." By the aid of Assistant Commissioners, specimen districts, of varied character, including about *one-eighth* of the population of the country, were inspected, and within those limits minute information was obtained respecting every school, public or private. The Royal Commissioners considered that averages and proportions, calculated from an eighth part of the population so selected, might be relied upon with confidence for the rest of the country, when there was no direct information. Respecting the public schools throughout the land, they collected from various sources statistics which they believed to be approximately correct and complete.

But there is a startling contrast, if not absolute contradiction, between the general estimates of the Royal Commissioners and facts which have since been brought to light in particular districts. Take first the "gross amount of popular education."

"The whole population of England and Wales," say the Royal Commissioners,[1] " as estimated by the Registrar-

[1] Report, p. 293.

General in the summer of 1858, amounted to 19,523,103. The number of children whose names ought, at the same date, to have been on the school books, in order that all might receive some education, was 2,655,767. The number we found to be actually on the books was 2,535,462, thus leaving 120,305 *children without any school instruction whatever.* . . . Looking, therefore, at mere numbers as indicating the state of popular education in England and Wales, the proportion of children receiving instruction to the whole population is, in our opinion, nearly as high as can be reasonably expected. In Prussia, where it is compulsory, the proportion is 1 in 6·27 ; in England and Wales it is, as we have seen, 1 in 7·7 ; in Holland it is 1 in 8·11 ; in France it is 1 in 9·0."

Yet in Manchester and Salford, in the year 1865, the Education Aid Society found, by careful inquiry, that out of a total number of 104,000 children the number on the books of all the day-schools of every class was no more than 55,000, leaving *in those two towns alone* 49,000 *as the number not attending school.* Nor does this alarming discovery stand alone. In the diocese of London (which includes a portion only of the metropolis) a committee of the Diocesan Board of Education reports, for the same year, that " *the means of education are wanting for from* 150,000 *to* 200,000 *children.*" If to these be added the 49,000 from Manchester and Salford, the sum already far exceeds, if it does not double, the total number reported by the Royal Commissioners to be without instruction.

An attempt to reconcile this apparent contradiction may help to draw out and define for practical use the true meaning both of the Royal Commissioners' general estimate and of the newly-discovered particular facts.

The Royal Commissioners, it will be found, take for the total of those who *ought* to be at school *one-half only of the children between three and fifteen years of age.* That is to say, they accept for the purposes of this calculation the miserably low standard which they found to exist as a matter of fact, *the average duration of school-life in England being, for the lower classes separately, no more than four years,* and for all classes together only six years. And it has further to be remembered that since many of the children, whose names are on the books at any given time, stay much more than six years at school ; many also (in order to make the average) must stay much less than six years, and so have but little more education than the 120,000, who are "without any school instruction whatever."

In the Manchester and Salford Report, on the contrary, the total number of children includes all from three to twelve years. If six years must be accepted as the normal average duration of school-life for England, two-thirds only of these children, or 69,333, ought to be found at school. Subtracting, then, the 55,000 whose names were on the books, the number left entirely without school education (on the standard of the Royal Commissioners) is reduced to 14,333. But of the remainder many will have had next to no education.[1]

In the diocese of London the inquiry, conducted

---

[1] It seemed worth while to clear up this point, as the Manchester facts have been much quoted. Mr. Bruce appears to be well within the mark when he explains that "probably not a third of the above-mentioned 55,000" [49,000 ?] " children have received or will receive no education at all."—*Address on National Education.* Ridgway. 1866.

through the clergy, gave the total number of names
upon the books of all the public schools as 182,025,
being 8⅓ per cent. of the population. The statistics of
the Royal Commissioners give 8 per cent. as the proportion on the books of public schools in the county of
Middlesex, which is disadvantageously contrasted with
almost all the other counties. So far, therefore, the
two Reports agree. The final discrepancy between them
clearly comes from the Report of the Royal Commissioners taking account of "schools which it could hardly
be expected that the parochial clergy should recognise
. . . every sort and description of private academy and
dame school; while only in a small minority of instances,"
say the Diocesan Board, "do the parochial clergy profess
to give an answer to our inquiry relating to schools of
private enterprise." Of the amount of accommodation
in Nonconformist schools, also, the Committee found it
impossible to speak with confidence. But for every
twenty-six children in public schools in Middlesex, as
a matter of fact, there are nineteen in private schools,
receiving this kind of education, which the clergy do not
recognise. (See Report, &c. 1861 : Statistics, p. 673.)
The statement, then, that "means of education require to
be provided, in the diocese of London, for 150,000 to
200,000 children," must be taken with this qualification.
Education in the private schools, however, is admitted
to be generally very bad. And the Committee of the
Bishop of London's Fund came to the conclusion, by an
independent inquiry, " confessedly somewhat vague," that
" about 160,000 more children ought to be at school in
London."

But if Liverpool (with her Irish immigrants) and

other great towns of the North are as Manchester, if the Midland manufacturing districts should tell the same tale, and if the metropolitan population of the diocese of Winchester is not better cared for than the diocese of London, it is plain that many must be added to the number of " 120,305 children without any school instruction whatever."[1]

And now to what class do these unfortunate children chiefly belong ? The Royal Commissioners reply—

" Against this deficiency we have to set off children permanently incapacitated by bodily or mental infirmities, of whose number we have no certain estimate, and children educated at home, the number of whom must be small, except in the wealthier classes. *Most of the children who, being able to attend, do not belong to any school, appear to be the children of outdoor paupers, or of parents viciously inclined.*"[2]

The children of outdoor paupers had not been overlooked by the Legislature.

[1] In confirmation of the more recent statistics, as against the estimate of the Royal Commissioners, it may further be observed, that in their calculation of the number on the books throughout the country, one large figure is conjectural. The number of scholars at private schools is set down at 860,304, on the assumption that the ratio between public and private scholars is the same for the whole country as for one-eighth of the population. But a similar calculation gave the number of private schools as 34,412, whereas the Census gave 30,524. A corresponding correction of the supposed number of private scholars would raise the estimate of children totally uneducated to 217,381.

It may be doubted, therefore, whether much reliance should be placed on the smaller number. The corresponding number in France, in 1863, in a population of more than thirty-seven millions, or nearly double that of England, was supposed to be under 200,000, entirely without instruction ; while the total number between seven and thirteen years of age, missing from the books of the primary schools, was 884,887. (*Statistique de l'Instruction primaire pour l'Année* 1863.)

[2] Report, p. 84.

" The 18th & 19th Victoria, cap. 34, entitled ' An Act
to provide for the education of children in the receipt of
outdoor relief,' enables the guardians, *if they deem proper,*
to grant relief for the purpose of enabling any poor person lawfully relieved out of the workhouse, to provide
education for any child of such person between the ages
of four and sixteen, in any school, to be approved by
such guardians, for such time and under such conditions
as the said guardians shall see fit." [1]

Under this carefully-worded law, the Royal Commissioners found that out of a total number of 228,424, there
were probably "*at least* 100,000 *outdoor pauper children
totally uneducated.*"

" In the nine counties of Dorset, Durham, Monmouth,
Northampton, Oxford, Gloucester, Rutland, Hampshire,
and Cornwall, containing 38,451 outdoor pauper children, the guardians educate 11 children, at an aggregate
expense of 2*l.* 8*s.* 4*d.* a year." Showing what the guardians
" deem proper."

" The 34,955 children in the workhouses, and the
100,000 who receive no education, or one that trains
them to pauperism, vice, and crime, are *precisely the
children for whom the State is responsible.* Their
fathers are dead, or are unknown, or are in prison, or
have deserted them, or are not able even to feed them,
much less to educate them. *To them the State is
loco parentis.*"

This is theory. In practice, the present system of
education " helps those who help themselves ;" "basing
the assistance given by Government upon voluntary
religious effort." If voluntary religious effort (expendi-

[1] Report, p. 380.

ture, not expostulation) should be made in behalf of these outdoor pauper children, it will be met by corresponding amounts of State aid. In the meantime some remain helpless, and the rest contrive to help themselves not quite as society would wish :—" As a general rule it may be said that these children, as they grow up, are divided between the gaol and the workhouse ; *they form the hereditary pauper and criminal class.* If we could withdraw them from the influences which now corrupt them, we should cut off the principal roots of pauperism and crime." [1]

Parliament has not thought fit to adopt such radical measures.

But if this outdoor supply of paupers were cut off, as it might be, by educating one generation, there would still remain the indoor paupers, to illustrate the working of State parentage, in theory, with a voluntary system of education in practice. Mr. Cumin thus describes their life :—

" I know nothing more pathetic than a workhouse school. No human creatures ought to excite a more lively sympathy. Without home, without parents, often without a single friend, they are alone in the world from the moment of their birth. Whilst one of the pauper nurses at Bedminster was sorting the infants in order to distinguish the orphans and the deserted from the rest, I asked the name of one that was rolling about the floor. ' Fanny Step,' was the reply. ' Why Fanny Step,' I rejoined. ' Because, Sir, she was found on a door-step.' Such is the history of many a workhouse girl. Doomed, by necessity, never to know the meaning of that familiar

[1] Report, p. 382.

word, home—cut off from the exercise of the ordinary
affections—many of them diseased in body, and feeble in
mind—these poor children exhibit little of the vigour
and joyousness of youth.   Listless and subservient in
manner, they seem to be broken down by misfortune
before they have entered upon life. . . . One of the most
fatal effects produced by the pauper children being
brought up in close contact with adult paupers is this,—
that the child loses all desire to earn its own living, and
is content to spend its days in a workhouse."[1]

Properly to educate these poor children *in the workhouse*, has been found almost hopeless, and some
of the results of attempting it have been incredibly
shocking.[2]   When they have been transferred to " district
schools," or " separate schools," on the contrary, the
results have been most encouraging.   Mr. Tufnell says
of the former, " The number of failures in these schools
are not on the average more than two or three per cent.,
and I believe that if you test the number of failures in
the highest class schools, even those frequented by the
peerage, you will find a greater proportion of failures in
life than from the children of the district schools."

Very few district schools, however, have been established, owing to causes which seem to resolve themselves
into the petty jealousies and short-sighted economies of
guardians, the viciousness of parents, and " the absence
of any department expressly and imperatively charged
with the duty of endeavouring to effect the objects of
the Acts."

---

[1] Report, p. 356.
[2] See Report, p. 370.   It is better to abstain from quoting the worst case,
as an attempt was being made to remedy the evil.

In the Stepney separate school, a fair sample of
others, out of 229 boys sent out to service, three had
fallen back on the workhouse, and only two had committed crimes, the fall in each case being due to parental
influence.

But both in district schools and separate schools, in
1859, there were only 7,063 out of 44,618 workhouse
children : and there has been no marked increase since.
So little practical regard have the guardians, and the
State, even to the pecuniary saving which might be
effected by keeping them off the rates, and out of gaols.[1]

[1] The statements of the Royal Commissioners on this branch of the subject
have been challenged, and public interest was so far excited, that a Select
Committee of the House of Commons on Poor Relief (which reported in
May, 1864) made inquiries into the state of Pauper Education. Since
1847 workhouse schools had been under the inspection of the Committee of
Council, and Parliament had annually placed at the disposal of the Poor Law
Board a grant of 30,000*l.* for salaries of workhouse teachers. As to the effect
of these measures in improving workhouse education, after sixteen years of
experience, " a great deal of conflicting evidence was submitted." It was
shown, on the part of the Poor Law Board, that the Report of the Royal
Commission under this head was founded chiefly on the official Reports of the
responsible Inspectors ; that the Royal Commissioners thought that was the
best evidence they could have ; and that they did not examine the Poor Law
authorities. Also, that substantially this part of the Report was prepared
by Mr. Senior, and that in his own mind the recommendations which it
contained were the practical application of the following principles, which,
however, his colleagues did not expressly adopt :—

" It is as much the duty of the community to see that the child is educated
as to see that it is fed. Unless the community can and will compel the
parent to feed the child, or to educate the child, the community must do so.
The elementary education of a child costs not less than thirty shillings a year.
There is no reason to believe that that sum is obtainable from the parents.
It is the duty of the State to aid private benevolence in supplying the sum
that is not obtainable from the parents. We ought to recommend a system of
State assistance for that purpose."

Whether the detection of such principles ought to discredit the recommendations, is matter of opinion.

It was further shown, that in the Reports of the Inspectors may be
found passages containing evidence (in the opinion of the Select Committee
" abundant evidence ") of progressive improvement. Mr. Tufnell, for instance,
says :—   [" There

"Till Parliament can give health, strength, providence, and self-control, how can it deal with the evil of
pauperism ? "

The question is Mr. Lowe's (Preface to Speeches, &c.
1867). Of course there is a limit to what may be effected

" There has been a very great improvement of late years, owing to the
improved condition of the teachers that have been appointed since the Parliamentary grant has been allowed. . . In most workhouses the *intellectual*
education is extremely good."

This opinion was confirmed by all the other witnesses. Mr. Lambert was
decidedly of opinion that the *intellectual* education of children in workhouses
is better than that of the same class out of the workhouse.

Industrial training also appears to have been largely adopted, with the best
results. Girls are taught sewing and laundry-work ; and boys (though not so
generally) trades and field-labour.

Even in the Reports presented to the Royal Commissioners by their own
Assistant Commissioners, passages were pointed out which are inconsistent
with a sweeping condemnation of pauper education throughout the country.
The workhouse schools at Dorchester, Cerne, Yeovil, Hereford, and Ledbury
in particular, had received high praise from Mr. Fraser. (See Reports of
Assistant Commissioners, vol. ii. pp. 89, 151, 152.)

If such workhouse schools as these are described to be were more common,
there would be little cause to complain of the provision for indoor pauper children. But the worse case dwelt upon by the Royal Commissioners is that of
the children of outdoor paupers, to which it is replied that somehow they
contrive to pay or to be excused the school fees. And with regard to indoor
paupers, some of the strongest evidence before the Select Committee confirms
the Royal Commissioners' Report. Mr. Tufnell, for instance, formerly an
Assistant Poor Law Commissioner, and for fifteen years Inspector of Metropolitan Poor Law Schools, adhered to his opinion given before the Royal
Commissioners as to the *moral* disadvantages of workhouse education, and
the saving to be effected by establishing district schools, so that the children
might not become paupers, and recommended giving the Poor Law Board
compulsory power to establish district schools in town districts ; which, for
the metropolis, Parliament has since done. And Mr. Farnall, after a long
service as Poor Law Inspector in four widely distant and different districts,
stated that " the whole of the education which is carried on in the workhouses is very inferior to that which is carried on in schools out of the
workhouses, and that consequently the children return more frequently to
the workhouse as their home."

On the whole, therefore, it would seem that the conclusions of the Royal
Commissioners, though expressed in language somewhat sweeping and un-
measured, point to grave and wide-spread defects in the system of indoor, and
still more of outdoor, pauper education.

either by sanitary or by educational measures. But Mr.
Tufnell's evidence may supply a partial answer.

"3154. You think that giving them a good and careful education
tends indirectly very largely to diminish pauperism?—Yes ; and it is
very economical to the country in that way.

"3155. (*Mr. Senior.*) Therefore a district school, whatever it may
cost, is a saving of expense ?—A very great saving of expense,
I believe. I believe that *the pauperism of London in the last few
years has been very much diminished by the effect of these district
schools.* It is perfectly well established, that pauperism has a tendency
to run in families, adult paupers rearing pauper children, and thus the
vice of dependence on the rates becomes hereditary. The good education given in these district schools absolutely stops this hereditary
pauperism, and I have no doubt also diminishes crime, by educating
children out of their vicious propensities. It is well known the larger
proportion of criminals have been orphans early in life, and yet the
orphan class is precisely that which turns out best in district schools.
Thus, *if you do not educate them, they become thieves and paupers ; if
you do, they become well-conducted productive workpeople.*" [1]

Such is the choice presented to the State in its relations with orphans and others to whom it stands as
parent. Among these the Royal Commissioners distinctly
reckon vagrant children taken out of the custody of their
natural protectors, not as convicted of any crime, but to
save them from the consequences of neglect.[2] If workhouse schools were what they ought to be, these children
might be sent there ; the expense, when possible, being
laid on the parent. For children actually convicted of
crime, the provision made by means of reformatories was
considered to be satisfactory.

[1] Report, p. 376.
[2] The Industrial Schools Act of last Session was an attempt to deal with
this case. Whether it will effect more than former Acts it is too soon
yet to judge. But daily advertisements appear on behalf of the homeless
boys of London, who will be left on the streets, it is urged, if private persons
do not contribute for their industrial education.

But having thus traced to State parentage, and to the confidence which Parliament reposes in "guardians," five-sixths at least of the supposed number of totally uneducated children, it may be well before proceeding further to enlarge the field by taking into view those also who receive an insufficient education.

It appears then, that in the year 1858, more than one-fourth of the children of the poorer classes "were attending private schools, which, as our evidence uniformly shows, are for the most part inferior as schools for the poor, and ill-calculated to give to the children an education which shall be serviceable to them in after life." Of those in public schools more than one-half "attend for less than 100 days in the year, and can therefore hardly receive a serviceable amount of education, while our evidence goes to prove that a large proportion even of those whose attendance is more regular, fail in obtaining it on account of inefficient teaching. . . . *We know that the uninspected schools are in this respect far below the inspected; but even with regard to the inspected, we* have seen overwhelming evidence from her Majesty's inspectors that *not more than one-fourth of the children receive a good education.*" [1]   (Report, p. 294.) These figures [2] leave ample room for astounding discoveries of ignorance in particular districts of the country.

And ample room was required. The Manchester and Salford Education Aid Society, for instance, was formed

---

[1] Forty per cent. of the children who pass through the French primary schools remain unable to read, write, and cypher. Mr. Bruce "fears that at least fifty per cent. of our population are practically uneducated."

[2] Mr. Lowe calculated that "of the children that are in the schools which the grants of the Privy Council are intended to assist, *only one-ninth get the benefit of a really good education.*"—Speech of Feb. 13, 1862, p. 14.

in 1864 for the practical purpose of assisting poor parents to educate their children. In doing this systematically, by visitation from house to house, and inquiring at all the schools, they discovered in the first year the lamentable facts which have already been placed in contrast with the Report of the Royal Commission. They have since stated, in a paper contributed to the Social Science Association, that, *judging by the experience of Manchester and Salford, education among the lower sections of the people throughout the kingdom is not on the increase.* In 1834 there was one day scholar for every 10·33 of population ; in 1861 there was only one for every 11·00.[1] Their third Report (1867), states that "good is being done, as the numbers in actual attendance at school are greater by 2,290" (six per cent. apparently) "than in the previous year." Nearly the whole of the poorer and more neglected districts had been canvassed, and again *a majority of the children of school age were found to be neither at school nor at work.* Of 3,940 children sent to school by the Committee, only 446 could read at all, and only 54 could read well. Perhaps the most instructive statistics are those which relate to the parents and young persons from 12 to 20 years of age, belonging to nearly two thousand families, whom

---

[1] The progress of education in Manchester and Salford seems to have been irregular ; in 1834 a little in advance of the average, in 1861 greatly in arrear. But the Committee are probably wrong in generalizing from their local experience. The Royal Commissioners give statistics showing the steady general progress which has been made in education. In 1833 the number of day scholars was one in 11¼, in 1851 one in 8·36, and in 1858 one in 7·7. (p. 294.) The progress, however, has been least among the lowest sections of the people, such as the Education Aid Society visits and Government neglects. France, since 1832, has doubled the proportion of children at school to the population.

l

the Committee have helped to pay school fees for their children. *Nearly one-third of the fathers, almost one-half of the mothers, and about the same proportion of the young men and women could not read.*[1] Ignorance, it seems, is hereditary, as well as pauperism and crime.

The Report of the London Diocesan Board is not based upon a similar canvass or visitation of neglected districts ; but some of the answers from the clergy give precise and telling facts.   In Islington district, for instance, Mr. Davies reports, "Fifty boys dismissed," for want of room ; Mr. Lees, "The want of large rooms obliges us to reject fifteen or twenty applications for admission every week ;" Mr. Stanham, "We could fill a school three times as large as our present one."   In other districts, Mr. Davidson, of St. Paul's, Buckingham Gate, reports "Many hundred children around go to no school whatever ;" Mr. Walsham, Holy Trinity, Paddington, "is obliged to refuse many children of the poor ;" Mr. Chambers states "that the number of children actually in school is far greater than the space justifies."   Mr. Harness's schools are "too full ;" and several churches have "no schools."   Altogether there are 91 parishes in which the clergy state that new schools are at once required.   Facts such as these reduce to its practical meaning the Royal Commissioners' statement that "there is no large district entirely destitute of schools, and requiring to be supplied with them on a large scale."   Very different is the estimate of the Diocesan Board, that "some 250 large schools, for 500 children, require to be built at once to place the diocese

---

[1] These facts appear to rest on the statement of a single visitor, but are vouched for by the whole Committee.

of London in its proper condition in the matter of education."

To take another instance, it is stated that in the Eastern Counties, where agricultural gang-work most prevails, there is a very great deficiency of school accommodation ; and in the diocese of Norfolk there are no less than 120 parishes in which at present no day-school exists.[1]

The results of these deficiencies may be seen in the statistics of ignorance, pauperism, and crime. It has already been stated that in the neglected parts of Manchester, about one-third of the fathers, half the mothers, and half the young people cannot read and write ; and that in the country generally, a large proportion of the children of paupers in the end fall back upon the workhouse, or frequent the gaol. In the prisons, in 1864, out of 126,038 inmates (excluding debtors and military offenders), more than ninety-five per cent. were unable to read and write decently, and more than thirty-five per cent. could neither read nor write. In the Reformatories, about one-half the inmates could neither read nor write, and about nine-tenths imperfectly, if at all. In the Feltham Industrial School, three-fourths could neither read nor write, and four only out of 216 could write and read well.

If any one would take the pains to compare the cost to society of gaol, workhouse, and police arrangements for adults, with the cost of education for children, adding on one side of the account the money given to idle beggars, and the value of goods stolen, and subtracting on the other side a round sum to represent what the

[1] See Mr. Dent's speech on the Sixth Report of the Children's Employment Commission, 2d April, 1867.

revenue and the public interest generally would gain by an increase of thriving productive labourers, he might probably show that the present system is a gross economical blunder. It might then be hoped that some day a courageous and far-sighted Chancellor of the Exchequer, casting about for ways and means to increase revenue and diminish expenditure, and looking beyond the next few years, would take a comprehensive view of the Estimates of the two services, and deal with crime and pauperism by substituting, on a larger scale, intellectual and moral, for physical, prevention. " We shall save in prisons," said a French Minister of Instruction, "what we spend in schools."

In Switzerland a reformed system of education has almost emptied the gaols. In July, 1863, there was not a soul in the prison of the Canton de Vaud ; it was much the same at Zurich ; at Neufchâtel there were two prisoners. In the Grand Duchy of Baden, where great efforts were made in 1834 for the improvement of education, the number of prisoners fell in eight years (1854 to 1861) from 1,426 to 691 ; the number of thefts from 1,009 became 460 ; pauperism decreased by one-fourth ; and gaols had to be closed. In Bavaria improved education was followed by a remarkable decrease of illegitimate births. In Germany generally the number of criminal convictions was diminished between 1827 and 1862 by 30 per cent.[1] In France, and in England, improvement of the same kind can be traced, standing in good proportion to the labour which has been expended on education. But in France there are still 81 per cent. of criminals who read and write imper-

[1] Statistique de l'Instruction primaire pour l'Année 1863.

fectly, and 38 per cent. who cannot read or write at all. The corresponding numbers for England have been given.

In the British army, out of 10,000 soldiers examined in 1856, more than one-fourth could not write, and more than one-fifth could not read; while, in the British Foreign Legion, raised in 1855, four-fifths of the Italians, and 97 per cent. of the Germans, could both read and write. In France a third of the recruits cannot read (Statistique, &c. 1863), but "it is rare for a soldier in the French army to complete his term of service without having learned to read and write; indeed, the instruction provided in the *écoles du premier degré* of the army, is not a little relied on as the means of diffusing primary education through the rural districts of France.[1] Whereas, of some 16,000 who left the British army in the years 1856-1857, about 32 per cent., at the end of their military career, were unable to write their own names.[2]

In Prussia 3 per cent. only of the recruits are uneducated. The French Report of 1863 gives a curious illustration of Prussian vigilance. An officer, whose duty it was to give military instruction to the Landwehr at Potsdam, discovered, in the course of twelve years, three recruits who could neither read nor write. Their case was thought so extraordinary that an investigation was ordered; when it appeared that they were three sons of boatmen, who had been born on the river, and had passed

---

[1] Report by Colonel Lefroy, R.A., quoted by the Royal Commissioners, p. 423. Italians at the present moment insist on a similar reason for not reducing their large and expensive army, regarding it as an instrument both of general and of political education.

[2] Since 1861, all school fees for soldiers have been abolished.

their early lives in voyaging up and down stream, never stopping in any one place.[1]

It is a mistake to suppose that the Prussian system of education is irksome to the people, or enforced at all against their will. It rests upon a much more ancient and broader foundation than police inspections and penalties :—

" Compulsory school attendance dates from the earliest period of the Reformation, and was a recognised religious duty long before it became a law of the State. The schooling is compulsory only in name ; the school has taken so deep a root in the social habit of the German people, that were the law repealed to-morrow, no one doubts that the schools would continue as full as they now are. In the free city of Frankfort there is no compulsory law, and I was assured by persons most likely to be informed that all the children of school age are as regularly sent to school there as in any other town of Germany. In Würtemberg a law was last year enacted, abridging the time of schooling, for the sake of easing the pressure on the existing school accommodation ; but it has not yet (May, 1859) appeared that the people are disposed to avail themselves of the remission of time. . . . The children learn to read, write, and cypher as a matter of course, just as they learn to talk or to dress as neatly as they can afford." [2]

Such a state of feeling and custom as regards education is by no means confined to Prussia, but may be found existing in other countries.

In Baden, for instance, attendance at school is compulsory, but fines are rare. A French sportsman, bent upon amusement, in vain offered a florin a-piece for boys to attend him as beaters. The parents replied that they had to go to school. " In this matter," says a high authority, " we have reached the point at which no more remains to be done."

---

[1] Statistique, &c., p. 9.
[2] Report of the Rev. Mark Pattison, Assistant Commissioner, quoted in the General Report, p. 192.

In Würtemberg the universal diffusion and high standard of primary education is, of all facts, the most notice-
able and striking to a foreigner. There is not a peasant,
not a kitchen-maid, or a bar-maid, who cannot read,
write, and cypher well. Education is compulsory to the
age of fourteen. The first and second time that a boy
plays truant he is punished himself; the third time, his
parents answer for it. Recruits are put through an
examination, and the parents are responsible if their
son cannot write.

In Saxony, it is said, there is not one child to be
found which has had no schooling. The penalty for
non-attendance is fine or imprisonment. At first the
authorities had to fight against the negligence of parents.
But soon the advantages and salutary results of a general
and enforced attendance at school convinced even the
recalcitrant. The present generation of parents, educated under the new law (of 1835) never dream of withdrawing their children from its beneficent control. Thus
the actual enforcement of penalties may be said to be at
an end. Two generations of school-children (school-life
in Saxony lasting eight years, from the age of six to
fourteen) have sufficed to bring about this revolution.
For it was in 1848, a year elsewhere of many promises
and but scanty performance, that the greatest efforts
were made. Nassau, where education has been both
compulsory and gratuitous since 1817, boasts that it has
not one illiterate person in the Duchy. In short, generally wherever the population is German, it will be found
that education is compulsory, and the necessity of inflicting penalties rare.

In Sweden, Norway, and Denmark, parents are fined if

they leave their children uninstructed. Switzerland, except Geneva, Schwyz, Uri, and Unterwalden, is under a compulsory system. In Holland, all relief to pauper families is withdrawn if they fail to send their children to school. In Italy, by a law of 1859, education is gratuitous and compulsory. In Spain, compulsory education dates from 1857, and in Portugal from 1844, though the law is not generally enforced for want of a sufficient number of schools. The principle has been proclaimed even in the Danubian Principalities and in Turkey.[1]

In the United States of America, as is well known, great efforts are made to promote the education of the people. The Royal Commissioners observe that truancy, nevertheless, prevailed in Boston. By a law since enacted (1862), a fine of twenty dollars is imposed throughout Massachusetts for neglect of the school regulations, which apply to all children between seven and sixteen years of age. In Connecticut, by a law of 1858, any person who cannot read is disfranchised. Great exertions will be required, and are being made, to educate the black population[2] of the South : for their white masters, to their indelible disgrace, had passed laws forbidding the education of slaves.

The experience of great part of Scotland and of some happy parishes, perhaps, in England, tends to prove that without compulsory enactments education may come to be regarded as a necessity of life. The best results follow wherever the work has once been taken in hand

---

[1] Statistique de l'Instruction primaire pour l'Année 1863, pp. 9—13.
[2] In Jamaica compulsory education for the negro population has been strongly recommended.

in good earnest, and not allowed to fall into arrear. The great difficulty is to make up arrears. If one generation only could be completely educated, the next would be sent to school as a matter of course, and the blessing would descend to their children's children. But in England this has yet to be achieved.

II. From the defects which have now been pointed out in our existing system of our education, it is easy to pass to their causes. These might be divided under three heads, as they affect Accommodation, Teaching, or Attendance. But it will be more convenient to treat of the two first together, and it will also be found that good schools and good teaching are among the most effective means of producing good attendance.

Now the creation of good school accommodation, and the improvement of teaching, are precisely the two works in which the administration of the Parliamentary grant has been most active and most successful. In round numbers, the total sum expended by the Committee of Council for Education, since its constitution in 1839, now approaches ten millions, of which more than a million and a half have been spent on grants towards building, and more than five millions on training teachers.

The buildings are good, and the teachers are good. If it were to the purpose, it would be easy to say much in praise of the progress which has been achieved, and of the high standard which has been established in both these respects. And although there is room for improvement, it will be convenient here to assume that the schools and teachers approved by Her Majesty's inspectors, are nearly what is to be desired. But the present question is, why they are not more in number, and more equally distributed through the land. And the answer is obvious and simple. It is a fundamental principle of the present system of education in this country, that all is to depend upon voluntary local effort; and in some places those who have the will to promote education have not the means, and those who have the means, have not the will.

These are called "*the neglected districts;*" a name doubly applicable, for they are neglected by the dispensers (though not by the collectors) of the public revenue, in most cases for no other reason than because they are neglected by their own landowners, employers of labour, ministers of religion, or others, who are or ought to be, managers of the schools. In a district which is not neglected, the cost of education for each child may be roughly divided into three equal parts; of which one is paid by the parent, one by local subscriptions, and one by the State. In a neglected district, State aid is withheld, usually because local subscriptions are inadequate or ill applied; and the parents, generally poor, are thrown for the most part on their own resources, with such results as have been described.

The neglected districts included, in 1863, about one-twelfth of the larger parishes, half the parishes with between 500 and 5,000 inhabitants, and nine-tenths of the still smaller parishes. In all, out of 14,895 parishes, more than 11,000, with a population of six millions, derived no direct assistance from the State.[1]

The Royal Commissioners found that for less than a million scholars assisted, there were nearly a million and a quarter whose names were on school-books, unassisted,

---

[1] Report of the Select Committee on Education, 1866. In France, out of 37,510 *communes*, 818, with 262,499 inhabitants, had no schools in 1863. (Statistique, p. 283.)

of the class for whom the grants are intended ; a fact
which in their opinion showed that "the system had not
effected, and was not adapted to effect, a general diffusion of sound elementary education among all clases of
the poor.[1]

The existence of neglected districts at all to this extent
is an acknowledged defect and scandal ; but what makes
the matter worse is, that they are the poorest and least
enlightened districts, and therefore most in need of some
stimulus from without. " It is no discredit," said Mr.
Lowe, in 1862, " to a tentative and preliminary system,
but it would be a discredit to that system which we wish
to render permanent in the country, if we could not meet
this great and pressing want. These districts contribute
to the revenue equally with others, and it is exceedingly
desirable, both on the ground of justice and of policy,
that they should receive back some share of the money."[2]

But the remedy which Mr. Lowe proposed in introducing the Revised Code is likely to be of slow
operation. As is well known, the general principle of
the Revised Code is payment by results of education,
ascertained by individual examination of the children.
The special provision made, as Mr. Lowe explained to
Parliament, " in order to extend the benefits of the
system to country schools "[3] was the addition of an
inferior or fourth-class certificated master, and the permission (in small rural schools only) to employ a pupil-
teacher properly recommended and approved. As the
amount of assistance would depend on the number of
children who satisfy the Inspector, " it will be possible,"

---

[1] Report, p. 295.
[2] Speech on the Revised Code, Feb. 13, 1862, p. 15.   [3] Ibid. p. 45.

Mr. Lowe adds, "for benevolent men and women possessing leisure, but in narrow circumstances, by assisting the teacher to confer great pecuniary benefits on schools, by preparing children to pass the examination."

At what rate are these anticipations being realised? The year 1865 may be regarded as almost the first which has been wholly subject to the influence of the Revised Code. Its working appears to be good, and the outcry against it, which at first was general, and such as required a minister of good courage to encounter, now concentrates itself upon certain points which are most open to attack, and perhaps also to judicious alteration. The increase of certificated teachers was 1073 (more than ten per cent.), almost every one of whom "represents a school brought, not only into receipt of annual grants towards its maintenance, but under the influence of annual inspection, and under those other conditions of efficiency, on which an annual grant, or the amount of it, depends."[1]

But it is not stated how many of these are fourth-class certificated teachers, or represent the most neglected districts. And as to pupil-teachers, "the introduction of the Revised Code has been followed by a great diminution in their number," a diminution since 1862 of more than 28 per cent. The Committee of Council admit that this diminution is "greater than is desirable." But, at all events, it probably leaves few to accept engagements in the small rural schools. "The past year shows a less rapid decline," but still a decline of 9 per cent. in the number of male pupil-teachers; which is serious on all accounts, considering how much they

[1] Report, 1865-66, p. viii.

contributed to the efficiency of education under the Old Code.

And does this gradual process keep pace with public opinion ? " Ces lenteurs," said the French Minister of Education, speaking of a like question in France, in 1865, " ne sont plus de notre temps, et ne doivent être ni de notre pays, ni du Gouvernement de l'Empereur." Is marching in the rear of European educational progress more permissible for England, or less unworthy of the Government of the Queen ?

For the children in these districts to wait for a decent education till wealth comes to the toiling poor, or zeal to the lazy rich, is like the steed waiting for the grass to grow. The opinion of Mr. Lingen, than whom no man is better qualified to give an opinion on this subject, is that " if everything goes on as it is now going on, *in fifty years hence* the want will be overtaken by the action of society alone ; but if adequate provision, even within the life of the present adult generation, is to be made, it must be made by the State." " And if it be made by the State," he was further asked, " do you think that it must be by some system of local rating ? " " I think so, if it is to be done on sound principles," was his answer. (Select Committee on Education, 1865, p. 31.)

The principle of permissive local rating may be regarded as a compromise between pedantic maintenance and rash abandonment of the present voluntary system. It is in human nature, that what men will not do separately for a common interest, lest some who have not paid their share should profit, they will do jointly, when the burden can be fairly laid on all. In order to see how far the facts suggest some such measure, it is necessary to look more closely into the nature of local apathy. Any district may, or may not, have wealthy, benevolent, or stirring residents, but every district with a considerable population has the employer of labour, the landowner, and the minister of religion. The interest which these three classes respectively take in promoting education may be measured roughly by their subscriptions to the school funds. In manufacturing and mining districts, employers of labour for the most part contribute on a very liberal scale, partly from a sense of responsibility for their dependents, partly from an enlightened view of their own interest in the matter, partly also, perhaps, because under the Factory Acts, if schools were not otherwise established, they would be forced to provide them for their own people. It is in agricultural districts that the greatest difficulty is felt. The school expenses there are heavy in proportion to the population. The small employers of labour as a class are by habit and almost of necessity penurious. It has been calculated that on an average not more than five per cent. of persons liable to income-tax are subscribers to schools. The burden therefore comes to be divided, often in most unfair proportion, between the landowner and the clergyman of the parish, who may be ill able to support the larger share.

In a Western agricultural district Mr. Fraser reported on the subscription-lists of 168 schools. It appeared that 169 clergymen had contributed on an average ten guineas each, and 399 landowners about five guineas each, making up between them seventeen-twentieths of the whole subscriptions. The rental of the landowners is estimated at £650,000 a year. The stipends of the clergy are not stated, but if they were a tithe of the rental it will be found that as compared with the land-owners, the clergy had contributed at least eight times their fair share ; besides giving probably their zealous personal service.

Mr. Hedley gives a corresponding return for eighteen schools in an Eastern agricultural district, in which the clergy had contributed much more than half, the land-owners less than one-third, and other persons little more than one twentieth part, of the total subscriptions.

This aspect of the case so well deserves consideration, that it is worth while to quote at length the remarks of the Royal Commissioners.

" The heaviness of the burden borne by the clergy is imperfectly indicated even by such figures as these. It frequently happens that the clergyman considers himself responsible for whatever is necessary to make the accounts of the school balance, and thus he places himself towards the school in the position of a banker who allows a customer habitually to overdraw his account. He is the man who most feels the mischief arising from want of education. Between him and the ignorant part of his adult parishioners there is a chasm. They will not come near him, and do not understand him if he forces himself upon them. He feels that the only means of improvement is the education of the young ; and he knows that only a small part of the necessary expense can be extracted from the parents. *He begs* from his neighbours, *he begs from the landowners ;* if he fails to persuade them to take their fair share of the burden, he begs from his friends, and even from strangers ; and at last submits most meritoriously, and most gene-rously, to bear not only his own proportion of the expense, but also that which ought to be borne by others. It has been repeatedly noticed by the school inspectors, and *it is our duty to state that as a class the landowners, especially those who are non-resident (though there are many honourable exceptions), do not do their duty in the support of popular education, and that they allow others, who are far less able to afford it, to bear the burden of their neglect."*—*Report,* p. 78.

The voluntary system is, in fact, to a great extent,

a system of over-driving the willing horse. And it is impossible to contemplate, with unmixed satisfaction, the sums of money raised throughout the country by voluntary effort, when it is remembered that much of this vaunted benevolence is in truth extorted from the clergy, the friends of the clergy, and others who most feel the sin and scandal of not helping the helpless, often with resentment against those whose duty it was to have done it, and who will profit without so much as knowing that they profit by having it done for them.

Take an instance which cannot be invidious, because the defaulter is the nation. The example which the State (in loco parentis) sets to parents, may be matched by the example which it sets to landowners and employers of labour.

Who (that does not prudently keep his name off every public subscription list) has not been canvassed in behalf of schools for the parish of St. Stephen's, Devonport, or other dockyard parishes, where it is urged that "Government, to the exclusion of others, is the great employer of labour, and the scholars who frequent the schools are the children of its workmen?" Who does not recognise, in substance at least, the familiar statement quoted in the Report of the Royal Commissioners?

" The employer of labour here is the nation, through the Admiralty and Horse Guards, and is therefore *non-resident*.

" The Admiralty and the Horse Guards and Board of Ordnance occupying all the water-side premises of this town, and all the land that would be available for private enterprise in manufacture or commerce, make this town one of the poorest in the kingdom ; the persons who derive profits in trade as merchants or wholesale dealers, in consequence of the articles consumed by the dockyard men and seamen and soldiers and their families, have their private residences and their houses of business in five cases out of six in the adjoining town of Plymouth. I am left in such a parish as St. Stephen's, Devonport, without any residents to whom I can look for aid in the form of subscriptions, and there are not half-a-dozen residents or a dozen proprietors, lessees of my parish, to whom I *could* apply, or to whom in any case a school committee *would* apply. The Admiralty is the great employer and the occupier of the water-side premises, and so the hinderer of commerce and manufactures, and, therefore, conjointly with the lord of the manor, ought to contribute sufficient for the erection of a sufficient number of public schools for the poor of this locality, and sufficient grants to keep all the schools as living institutions in a normal state of efficiency. *Private employers to the same extent, failing, as the Admiralty have hitherto done in this duty, would meet with unanimous condemnation."* —*Report,* p. 445.

So, again, the chaplain of the dockyard at Portsmouth writes :—

" I omitted to mention to you the general view of the educational question in these towns which I entertain. It is, that Government, as bringing so many persons here, should do more for the parochial schools."

But Government seems to view the matter in the same light as that in which most of the London clubs view applications in behalf of the schools of St. James's parish—namely, that individuals may subscribe as much, or as little, as they like, but the body corporate " can only regret that they have no funds applicable to the purpose."

Accordingly the individual has to ask himself whether he can rely on the case made out by parochial clergy personally unknown to him, and either withholds his subscription altogether, or gives, out of compassion for the poor children, with a feeling that the department of Government, through which the national responsibility to provide for these schools is incurred, plainly neglects its duty in not taking the measure of the public obligation, and meeting it by a liberal contribution from the public purse.

Similar feelings cannot but exist also towards other landowners and employers of labour who shirk their public duty; and as such conduct is caused in most cases by negligence, or by want of enlightenment, it would be a good thing for themselves, as well as a relief to others, if the duty could be better defined, and assessment substituted for expostulation and reproach.

One of the chief causes of indifference is non-residence, on which Mr. Fraser has thus reported :—

" 'I hardly know,' he says, 'what is meant by a rich parish or a poor parish, as in every parish (as one sees from the overseers' book) there is a certain amount of annual income going into somebody's pocket, which on all principles of responsibility stands bound, as with a first charge, by certain duties to the place from which it is derived. *The* fact that makes all the difference in the educational, and almost in every other, condition of a parish, is the residence of the owners of the land ; or, at least, this combined with the energy and zeal of the parochial clergyman. Where the proprietor does not live, there, to a very great extent, he does not spend ; and many an owner of property, who is quoted as a benefactor to his kind in the neighbourhood in which he resides, is shabby and niggardly to an extent that is inconceivable towards a parish whose only claim upon him is that he carries off its great tithes or owns half or all its land. The "poor parish," in far the majority of cases, is that which is out of sight, and therefore out of mind. The school is a picturesque feature on the outskirts of the park ; it is an expected feature—one which visitors will like to see, and will be sure to ask after—in the village adjacent to the hall ; and there of course it stands, is tolerably cared for, and duly admired. But rare indeed are the instances of landowners who, wherever they have property, seem to feel it a first duty to do something for the social and moral elevation of the people.' "—*Report*, p. 317.

The natural remedy for this is a rate. And as the relief from burdens such as poor-rates and police-rates, and the increased value of property where there is a

thriving population, which might be expected to result
from an education rate, would accrue to owners of rateable property, they would in course of time be indem-
nified. Nor is it easy to see how any other than the
ordinary mode of levying a rate could be invented, so as
to distribute the local burden among all on whom the
school has a moral claim. Suppose, for instance, it were
thought right that an education-rate should fall on all
persons in the neighbourhood paying income-tax, of whom
at present 95 per cent. subscribe nothing to schools. Would
it be possible to instruct the present collectors of income-
tax to assess an extra farthing or halfpenny in the pound,
and to hand over the proceeds to a local Education
Board ; and would the result to landowners differ enough
from that of an ordinary rate to make it worth while to
attempt such an arrangement ? Or suppose it were desirable to distribute the burden still more widely, say
among all who possessed the electoral franchise, would
it be possible to enact that an annual local payment for
this purpose should be a condition of keeping the name
on the register ? Probably not. These suggestions are
improvised only to illustrate the point, that a local
assessment for the purposes of education must almost of
necessity fall on the same rateable property, to the owners
of which the pecuniary benefits would in time accrue.
The arguments which have been used against this arrangement tend rather to show that some other kinds of property should be made rateable for all purposes, than that
there should be no education-rate. But if it can be shown
that the burden ought in fairness to be more generally
distributed, perhaps the way in which this could best
be done is by increasing the proportion derived from the

national revenue, which at present is about one-third of the total expense ; taking care, however, not so far to reduce the local burden so much as to encourage waste. An increased national contribution would offer a greater inducement to local managers to pay up liberally their diminished share and to lay aside all crotchets and scruples which may have hitherto prevented them from accepting Government aid.

For it is not apathy alone which affects the relations of a district with the Government, and thereby its whole educational fortunes. Besides the apathetic or indifferent squire, or clergyman, an equally well-known character at the Privy Council Office is the controlling squire, who will have things all his own way. Such a man locks up the school, and sends the key to the vicarage with a message that he does not mean to shut up the school, but only wishes to show that he can do so if he likes. Presently afterwards, without consulting the vicar, he dismisses the certificated master, on the ground that he acts in opposition to his wishes. And so the school parts company with the Government system and all its advantages, and returns to the rank of a dame's school. The corresponding rector is perfectly satisfied with having less than 4 per cent. of his population in his parish schools, and refuses to admit even the Bishop's inspector.[1] Or, to take a milder case, he is perplexed by unscrupulous and noisy misrepresentations of " the Conscience clause ; " and while he candidly admits that in practice he would not force the Church catechism upon a child whose parents did not like it, he scruples to enter into a compact to that effect, such as the Govern-

---

[1] Report of the Committee of Council, 1865-6, p. 188.

ment is in justice bound to require, before it spends
public money on a school, which in a small district is
wanted to provide education for the children of Dissenters
as well as of Churchmen.

It is a heavy price to pay for the boasted freedom of a
voluntary system, that the conscientious scruples, stupid
whims, or selfish indifference of one man of unenlightened mind, may cut off a whole parish from all
share in the public grants, with their attendant advantages, and retard, as long as it pleases Providence to
spare him, the salutary progress of education among his
poorer neighbours.

The conscientious scruples, as might be expected, are
felt almost entirely by managers, and not at all by
parents. The evidence on this point collected by the
Assistant Commissioners is conclusive. "The mass of
the poor have no notion as to any distinction beyond
that between Roman Catholics and Protestants." "The
question of religious belief rarely enters into their heads
in choosing or refusing a school." "The truth is that
the religious difficulty, as it is called, does not exist."
That is, it exists only in the minds of the managers; who,
however, under the present system, are the patrons, not
the servants, of the people, and often make use of that
position to enforce their own terms as far as the patience
of Government will allow, and further.

Thus the apathy and whims of landowners and the
conscientious scruples of certain among the clergy, are
the chief immediate causes of bad schools and bad
teaching; and the voluntary principle, which suspends
all the benefits of State assistance upon precarious local
conditions, is the deeper cause that gives such fatal

importance to the personal failings of the rector or the squire.

But bad schools and bad teaching, especially the latter, are in their turn principal causes of bad attendance at school.

The causes determining the limits of attendance, in fact, naturally fall under two heads,—the inducements to go to school, and the inducements to stop away. " The question," say the Royal Commissioners,[1] " as to the feelings with which parents of the poorer classes, who are neither in a state of abject poverty, nor of reckless and intemperate habits, regard elementary education, is one of the most important in the whole range of our inquiry." And it will be of still greater importance when those parents come to possess the franchise.

Especial attention, therefore, may perhaps be requested for the two propositions which the inquiries of the Royal Commissioners tend to establish, as it will be necessary again to confront their general statements with the results of later and more particular investigations.

" The first is, that *almost all the parents appreciate the importance of elementary education,* and that the respectable parents are anxious to obtain it for their children. The second is, that *they are not prepared to sacrifice the earnings of their children for this purpose,* and that they accordingly remove them from school as soon as they have an opportunity of earning wages of an amount which adds in any considerable degree to the family income."[2]

The evidence in support of the first proposition is very striking :—

[1] Report, p. 174.   [2] Ibid. p. 175.

" Wherever a school is established which supplies the sort of education for which the poor are anxious, it is filled with pupils. All the Assistant Commissioners testify to this. Mr. Coode's district is remarkable for the bad state of its education, yet he says, ' It is a subject of wonder how people so destitute of education as labouring parents commonly are, can be such just judges as they also commonly are of the effective qualifications of a teacher. Good school buildings and the apparatus of education are found for years to be practically useless and deserted, when, if a master chance to be appointed who understands his work, a few weeks suffice to make the fact known, and his school is soon filled, and perhaps found inadequate to the demand of the neighbourhood, and a separate girls' school or infants' school is soon found to be necessary.' "

Mr. Foster reports that—

" On account of the inefficiency of the schools, there is considerable indifference on the part of the parents to their teaching . . . but among by far the greater proportion in the district there is a strong desire to have their children educated ; and if this has not issued in sending them to school, it has been chiefly due to the inefficiency and repulsive character of the schools within reach."

Mr. Fraser concludes thus :—

" That all the difficulties which surround the attendance of children do not prevent the efficient schools from being full ; that these, therefore, may fairly be considered to have solved and overcome them, and that the great object, consequently, to aim at, is to place all schools in a state of efficiency."

And Mr. Mitchell says :—

" When I look at the actual instruction too frequently offered in the schools for the working classes, I can only rejoice that parents are so sensible as not to send their children there, for more complete waste of time than one too frequently grieves over in these schools it is hardly possible to imagine."

The experience of the Manchester and Salford Education Aid Society is very different from that of the Royal Commissioners. They say :—

" The thought is depressing that among the poorer sections of the manual-labour classes, so little value is set on education, that even when offered free of cost it is in so many instances impossible to persuade parents to accept the gift. The Committee candidly admit, that when they commenced operations, they were wholly unprepared for such a result."

In five day-schools, where particular inquiries were made into the causes of non-attendance, it was found that of 529 children for whom the Committee were willing to pay the fees, and who had no other reason for not being at school, 304 were absent through neglect of parents. Thus, they say, " the unconcern of the parent constitutes the one grand obstacle to the success of voluntary effort." [1]

Here, again, perhaps the contradiction to the Royal Commissioners is more apparent than real, and the reconciliation of the two sets of facts is instructive. For on the one hand the Royal Commissioners admit the apathy and recklessness of the most degraded part of the population. On the other hand, it is not improbable that in the neglected districts of Manchester in which the Committee's operations are chiefly carried on, the teaching may be inefficient; in which case according to Mr. Fraser's doctrine, quoted above, the efforts of the Committee might advantageously be directed to making the schools efficient, rather than to bringing the children there by other means. So far as they could show that the schools are already efficient, they would strengthen their argument in favour of compulsion.

The Report of the London Diocesan Board, although it states in general terms that " a growing feeling is manifested in favour of some legal compulsion being exercised," affords no detailed information as to the

---

[1] Third Report, &c. 1867. Of 8,427 children absent from school, 4,336 were of parents able to pay the fees.

causes of non-attendance. But their statistics show
that out of 1,085 church schools in the diocese 490
are not under inspection, which strongly suggests that the
instruction in them may not be good enough to reward
attendance. A bad preacher empties his church, and
a bad teacher his school. On the other hand, good
teaching may account for the run upon other schools
in this diocese which has made their accommodation
inadequate. It might be worth while in further inquiries
to note whether this is so.

And now as to the second proposition of the Royal
Commissioners, that parents are not prepared to sacrifice
the earnings of their children. Beyond all doubt, the
greatest inducement to keep a child away from school is
the competition of the labour-market with the school.
It is in this form that the poverty of the parent practically tells upon the question. The poorest parent seldom
finds school-fees an insuperable difficulty. In case of need,
they are often remitted or paid for him by charitable persons, and in any case the amount is comparatively small.
" I can never forget," said Mr. Göschen, in his speech on
education, at Halifax, " that twopence is the price of a
pint of beer." But for a poor man to forego the value of
his children's labour, feeding them without help from
their earnings, is a much more serious matter. " This,"
said the late Prince Consort, " is a delicate question, and
will require the nicest care in handling, for here you cut
into the quick of the working man's condition. His
children are not only his offspring, to be reared for a
future independent position, but they constitute part of
his productive power, and work with him for the staff of
life. The daughters especially are the handmaids of the

house, the assistants of the mother, the nurses of the younger children, the aged, and the sick. To deprive the labouring family of their help would be almost to paralyse its domestic existence." [1]

There can be little doubt that the right mode of dealing with this question turns very much on details. The conditions of skilled labour and unskilled labour, of high wages and low wages, of town life and country life, of healthy and unhealthy, social and solitary employment, are widely different, and demand different practical treatment. But in this matter, happily, considerable progress has been made, and experience gained.

Another essay in this volume describes the first introduction of the Factory Acts, and traces the subsequent extension of protective legislation. And although the successive Reports of the Children's Employment Commission have revealed habitual and long established barbarities to tender children, which are a disgrace to the name of England, and enough to make a man forswear for ever the principle of letting things alone, yet of late years it cannot be said that Parliament has been slow to deal with each case when sufficient information had been obtained. In the present Session, the Home Secretary has introduced two Bills, the operation of which would be to shorten the hours of labour, and otherwise to protect the interests, of no fewer than 1,400,000 young persons, women, and children. And the abominations of agricultural gangs have no sooner been brought to light, than public opinion insists upon an immediate remedy being applied; though delay was proposed, for the purpose of obtaining infor-

---

[1] Address to the Educational Congress, 1857, quoted in the Royal Commissioners' Report, p. 188.

mation enough to bring private with public agricultural gangs under the same protective provisions.

Thus, though public opinion is evidently tending in the direction of compulsory education, its introduction will probably be gradual; and may, perhaps, take the form, suggested by the principle of the Revised Code, of testing by results, and forbidding children below a certain age to be engaged in any such regular employment for wages as can be legally defined, without a certificate that they are able, at least, to read and to write. For a long time compulsory education in factories was a failure, and in some places it still is so; because Parliament, having secured the attendance of the children, took no pains to secure that the teaching should be good. It is fair to say that the House of Commons passed the Factory Bill (of 1833) with clauses not only authorizing, but requiring the Inspector to establish factory schools to be supported out of the poor-rate, wherever he thought them desirable, and empowering him to dismiss a master without appeal. The Bill was altered by the House of Lords. And from that time till the last year of his service (1859), one of the most active inspectors, Mr. Horner, was in vain calling attention to the fact that the education of the children was, "in numerous cases, an utter mockery," enough to have discredited the whole system, if the soundness of its principle had not been shown in other highly satisfactory results.

The principal conclusions of the Royal Commissioners on the difficult question of compulsion were to the following effect :—

"That coupling the present conditions of attendance with the increasing interest felt in popular education, and the prospect of better and more attractive teachers and schools, the state of things in this respect is not on the whole discouraging.

" That the difficulties and evils of any general measure of compulsion would outweigh any good results which could be expected from it under the present state of things.

" That neither the Government nor private persons can effectually resist, or would be morally justified in resisting, the natural demands of labour when the child has arrived, physically speaking, at the proper age for labour, and when its wages are such as to form a strong motive to its parents for withdrawing it from school.

" That this being the case, public efforts should be directed principally to increasing the regularity of the attendance, rather than to prolonging its duration ; and that so far as the prolongation of attendance is aimed at, the division of the children's time between school and labour will be found more feasible than their retention for the whole of their time in school."

The last suggestion would seem to be practicable in many kinds of employment, and the arrangement very desirable. The Royal Commissioners say :—

" We call attention to the point as one which may be of the highest importance not only in cases where the nature of the employment admits of the regular half-time system, but also in certain cases where the child's services are required during the greater part of every day, it being in evidence that if two fresh hours in the morning can by any means be spared for the school, a considerable amount of education may be secured."—*Report*, p. 191.

Another obvious, but most important recommendation suggested by the consideration of this whole question of attendance is, that special effort should be made by means of evening schools, to keep up the education once received. The Royal Commissioners recommend—

" That, inasmuch as evening schools appear to be a most effective and popular means of education, the attention of the Committee of Council be directed to the importance of organizing them more perfectly, and extending them more widely, than at present.

" That for this purpose a special grant be made in schools where an organizing master is employed."—*Report*, p. 547.

It is to be hoped that this important and popular part of our educational system will be developed as rapidly as possible by liberal aid from the State. When Mr. Lowe introduced the Revised Code in February, 1862, he stated that there were only 317 evening schools to nearly 7,000 day schools under the Committee of Education. The last Report (1865) records the inspection of 1,215 night schools. Mr. Barry says, "Night-schools are yet in their infancy. The regulations of the old code were adverse to their establishment; but the new code and the special provisions for the examination of these schools at night and at the end of the winter half-year are likely to lead to their increase and improvement."[1] Mr. Bonner says of the same arrangement, that it "makes the establishment of night schools so easy, that I cannot but look forward to a considerable increase in their number."[2] Mr. Fraser reports that the new minute is acceptable, and convenient. Mr. Robinson states that evening schools are on the increase, and Mr. Sewell, that the number is rapidly increasing : "The new minutes are popular, and are likely to be generally adopted." It is satisfactory to find in the London Diocesan Report (p. 10) that "nearly 10,000 scholars are returned as in attendance in the night schools of the Church of England in London ; a fact particularly gratifying to the Diocesan Board, which has now for several winters done its utmost in support of these useful schools."

But to say more of the advantages of short-time study generally, or of evening schools in particular, would be to discuss the possible remedies, tried or untried, rather than the causes of defective education.

[1] Report, 1865, p. 45.   [2] *Ibid.* p. 81.

It has been shown that the chief proximate cause is the existence of "neglected districts," receiving no State aid or superintendence exactly where it is most wanted; and the consequent absence of such stimulus to attendance as is given by good schools and good teaching. Other proximate causes are the competition of the labour market; the inability of some very poor parents, especially of outdoor paupers, to pay school-fees, or to clothe the children decently enough for school; and the indifference to education of the most worthless parents, and of the State where it stands *in loco parentis;* together with the fact, that compulsory education has hitherto been imposed only on a few pauper and vagrant children, and on those employed in a limited number of trades. And the causes of the existence of neglected districts are, partly the want of flexibility in a highly centralized administration of the Parliamentary grants; but chiefly the apathy, whims, prejudices, and conscientious scruples of local managers, especially of the landowners and clergy, together with the perseverance of Parliament in maintaining a provisional system, which allows State aid to depend on these local contingencies, and the consistent discouragement by Parliament of every proposal to substitute a local rate, and managers elected by the ratepayers.

It appears then that the action of Parliament, though keeping pace, as well perhaps as legislation can be expected to keep pace, with the movement of the public mind, has hitherto been inadequate to the need. But " the public mind " has hitherto meant the thoughts and wishes that prevail in constituencies mainly composed of those classes who do not depend on a national system for the education of their children. And foremost among these have been the clergy, and others under clerical influence, who feared that in a rapid progress, more directly controlled by the State, they might lose the hold which they now have on the education of the people. As an illustration of what is meant it may be not unfair to quote the language of Canon Trevor, in a paper read before the Social Science Association at York (1864). With much truth, but some professional narrowness of view, he represents the present system as being in its very essence a definite compact between the State and ministers of religion. "The mainspring of the whole is *the local subscription, representing the religious element,* and due to the exertions, often to the personal contributions of the minister."[1] It cannot be expected that the clergy should think otherwise of a system which allows the burden to fall so heavily on themselves. But let there be no mistake as to what is meant by the religious element. "*The preservation of their distinctive tenets,* in the importance attaching to them in their own eyes, not in the eyes of others, was the condition deliberately agreed upon with the religious organizations. The State has no right to expect the stipulated co-operation without paying the stipulated price. *Dogmas which a Committee of Privy Council may be quite unable to appreciate or even to understand* may yet appear to good Christians of greater importance than reading, writing, and arithmetic. These will not consent to work for the secondary object, if they are hindered in that which to them is primary and engrossing." It is lest co-operation given on these terms should be lost,

[1] Transactions, 1864, &c. p. 415.

that the progress of public opinion and the procedure of Parliament as at present constituted, have been cautious and slow. Under this state of things, another generation of working men has grown up since the first Reform Bill, in great part without education ; while years have been spent in fruitless and inadequate discussion, or allowed to pass in silent acquiescence, with little perception of the sin and danger of delay.

III. It remains to consider what new forces a Reform Bill would bring to bear upon the action of the Government, and of society generally in this matter.

These would be of two kinds, the direct voting-power of the new electors, and their indirect influence through changes worked in the opinions and feelings of those who already possess the franchise.

One portion of the new electors would differ but little from the present voters in habit of mind or social position. Of these no more need be said than that their accession to the constituencies would probably have a general invigorating and refreshing effect upon Parliament, and through Parliament upon the executive government.

But a moderate, and still more a large reduction of the franchise, would admit to the polling-booths a considerable number of working men, who in several ways would exercise a special influence in this question of education.

In the first place, *they are, and they know that they are, the persons most directly interested,* being drawn from the class which does depend for education on the provision made for them by Parliament.

The grandfathers among them, for the most part, have had little or none ; the fathers more or less, according to

the accident of their birthplace ; with the rising generation, education in reading and writing has been the rule,
rather than the exception. But the children of all these,
and their neighbours' children, are those whose future is
most deeply staked upon the promptness of the Legislature in dealing with this question. " Fifty years hence,"
when the operation of the Revised Code (according to
Mr. Lingen's estimate) may have diffused education
through the whole country, the present generation of
parents will be in their graves, and their grandchildren
will be past the school age. They cannot afford to
wait. For us this has been an interesting but also an
embarrassing question, and one of which only by degrees
we have come to feel the paramount and pressing importance. For them it is a vital question, directly and
manifestly concerning, as but few questions do concern,
their individual fortunes and the fortunes of their class.
Is it likely, then, that so far as it might rest with them
they would permit the enactment of a more comprehensive system of popular education to be any longer
postponed ?

    It may be objected that the working classes do not
know what is for their own interests, and that, in the
case of a great and sudden reduction of the franchise,
there would be added to the electoral roll a large proportion of persons themselves uneducated, of whom it
may be presumed that they would be indifferent to the
question of education. It cannot be denied that these
people have little notion of what education is. They
often neglect to enforce their children's attendance at
the schools which have been provided, or deliberately
choose rather to snatch a small immediate addition to

the family earnings by condemning their offspring, as they perhaps were by their parents condemned, to premature and hopeless toil. Yet that the great majority of poor parents are anxious to obtain elementary education for their children, is in evidence, and more proof might be added. Mr. Cumin, for instance, one of the Assistant Commissioners, gives his experience as follows :—

" I took various opportunities of ascertaining from working men themselves, their opinion as to the value of education. When I asked them whether education was of any use to their children, they seemed to doubt whether I was serious ; or if they supposed that I was, they seemed to consider the question rather insulting.

"An Irishman whom I met driving a cart summed up the case in favour of education, thus : ' Do you think reading and writing is of any use to people like yourself?' I asked.   ' To be sure I do, Sir,' the man answered with a strong brogue ; ' and do you think that if I could read and write I would be shoved into every dirty job as I am now ?   No, Sir ! instead of driving this horse I'd be riding him.' "

On asking another man a similar question about girls, Mr. Cumin was met by the remark, " I don't know, Sir, whether you'd like to have your love-letters read or written by strangers." He mentions a case of an auctioneer's porter, earning 13s. a week, who had five children, all of whom, except a baby in arms, were at school at an expense of 5d. a week ;[1] and of the widow of a cabman, " with five young children, working day and night as a sempstress, to keep body and soul together without aid from the parish, but yet sparing several pence a week in order to send her children to the best National school in the neighbourhood." After describing the evils which result from neglecting children,

[1] Report, p. 95.

he says, " *The working man or woman understands the thing thoroughly ; I have questioned numbers of them on the subject, and I believe it to be an axiom with them that a child left in the streets is ruined.*"

Thus even among the poorest, many will be found in whose minds the desire for education is strong and uppermost; though they can form no more practical conception of it than as an instrument which would lift them out of the dirt and misery in which they live —a road to better and more lucrative employment— a light upon their narrow horizon—next to daily bread, and as a means of securing daily bread, the one thing needful for their children, if no longer possible for themselves.

Notwithstanding their own ignorance, those who thus conceive of education would have their humble but salutary influence in the choice of such representatives as would think it their first duty to insist, in Parliament, that this great want of the nation should at last be supplied. Others, again, who as yet have not even the desire for education, would still be persuaded to join in a movement which their leaders and associates would truly tell them is required for the advancement of their class.

These considerations afford encouragement and ground for hope, even if the party who lately resisted Reform, but now with astonishment find their leader outbidding veteran Reformers, should abdicate their natural function of slow and watchful concession to popular demands ; and with the zeal and clumsiness of converts, entangled perhaps by secret and over-subtle calculations of party advantage, should in effect hurry on a more sweeping measure of Reform than that which would have been loyally accepted in the year 1866, and give the franchise where education has not gone before. But, looking to the more probable contingency of a new Reform Bill on the scale of the moderate proposals then made and rejected, or rather evaded, there is less room for doubt as to what would be its effect on the prospects of popular education. The enfranchisement of some 200,000 of the most respectable working men would bring to bear on the mind of Parliament the convictions of those who have themselves received an elementary education during the period which has elapsed since the Reform Bill of 1832. And it is found by experience that none are so keenly sensible of the degrading effects of ignorance as those who have but lately escaped from it, whose daily life, among their fellow-workmen and neighbours, brings them in contact with it, and whose homes are surrounded by the vice and misery which it has caused. It can hardly be doubted, then, that on the part of these voters there would be an increasing, and if in some degree a latent, yet practically an effective, demand for larger measures of State education. For—

Secondly, *the working classes, more than any other class, are disposed and trained to vigorous united action.*

"It is an observation," says Mr. Lowe,[1] "true of human nature as of other things, that aggregation and crystallization are strong just in proportion as the mole-cules are minute. It is the consciousness of individual weakness that makes persons aggregate together, and nowhere is that impulse so strong as in the lowest classes

---

[1] Speeches on Reform, by the Rt. Hon. R. Lowe, p. 54.

of society. Nothing is so remarkable among the working classes of England as their intense tendency to associate and organize themselves."

In other questions which vitally concern their class, as, for instance, the wages question, and the question of intemperance, it is well known by experience how much they have been inclined to act in bodies, to obey their leaders with the strictest discipline, and to enforce upon each other the sacrifice of individual interests for the attainment of a common good. That a belief in Popular Education as a common good is dominant, if not universally diffused among them, sufficient evidence has been adduced; but as regards their disposition to act together in the matter, further reference may be made to an essay in this volume on the "Progress of the Working Classes," and especially to such instances as that of the Rochdale Co-operative Society, which sets apart more than £500 a year for educational purposes. The conclusion from these premises is evident. "Once give the men votes, and they will probably launch those votes in one compact mass" upon such institutions[1] as our hundred thousand uneducated outdoor paupers, and our ten thousand "neglected districts," with six millions of population, shut out from State assistance by no fault of their own.

Thirdly, *the working classes are notoriously in favour of protective legislation, and shortening the hours of labour,* both of which tend to promote education. They

---

[1] "It is impossible to believe that the same machinery which is at present brought into play in connexion with strikes would not be applied by the working-classes to political purposes. Once give the men votes, and the machinery is ready to launch those votes in one compact mass upon the institutions and property of the country."—*Speeches on Reform,* p. 54.

were active in supporting the Factory Bills, the Colliery Bills, the Bakehouse Bill, and the like, and there can be no doubt that they would expect their representatives to support Mr. Walpole's new "Factory Acts Extension Bill" and "Workshop Regulation Bill, 1867," or other such measures, which might tend to restrain the competition of the labour-market with the interests of education. Indeed, further, and

Fourthly, *the working classes are probably not averse to compulsory education.*

The notion of working men by their votes compelling Parliament to compel them to educate their children [1] is perhaps not so ludicrous as it may seem. It is not unlike petitioning Parliament (as in fact they did) to prevent them from sending their children under eight years of age, or for long hours, to factory labour. Indeed, the compulsory education of children is one great point of the Factory Acts, which were not carried without the help of numerously-signed petitions from the parents. And so successful have these Acts been, that by common consent they are being rapidly extended to include all employments for children of this class which can conveniently be brought under legal definition and official inspection. And not only is this so as a matter of fact, but a deep principle underlies such legislation, a principle which until very lately [2] had not been recognised,

---

[1] " It were ludicrous, if it were not so sad, to hear speeches which urge working men to seek for the franchise, that they may compel Parliament to compel them to educate their children," &c.—*Speeches on Reform*, p. 8.

[2] See a remarkable chapter on " Law in Politics," by the Duke of Argyll. "During the present century two great discoveries have been made in the Science of Government : the one is the immense advantage of abolishing restrictions upon Trade ; the other is the absolute necessity of imposing restrictions upon Labour."—*Reign of Law*, p. 367. Third Edition.

except by practical acquiescence in measures which were supposed to be anomalies indefensible in theory. Experience proves, that in unrestricted competition of labour the natural working of separate individual interests often tends to results which are injurious to all, but which can be avoided either by voluntary compact, or by positive interference of a higher authority, to protect the common interest. Of these· two, voluntary compact is perhaps in some respects the higher form of restraint on individual action ; and it is conceivable that working men might themselves agree to restrict the hours of labour for children, with a view to their education. But it does not lie in the mouth of those who have a bad opinion of trades unions, to say that the working classes ought to choose this way of protecting their children from unrestricted competition, rather than call upon Parliament to do so by compulsion.

In fact, although the name of compulsory education is unpopular in this country, there is already a good deal of the thing ; and there will be more of it if Mr. Walpole's two Bills pass into law. With actual compulsory education of indoor paupers, (to whom might easily be added outdoor paupers), vagrants, and youthful offenders, and short-time labour for children employed in factories of every kind, collieries, mines, bleaching and dyeing works, lace works, the six manufactures of the Act of 1864, and the long list proposed in the Acts of 1867, it would not be a formidable step in advance to make—as Mr. Bruce proposed at Manchester—" one general law that no child under twelve or thirteen years of age shall be allowed to work without producing a certificate that he is able to read and write." And a bill for that purpose, if the country were consulted, would probably be largely supported by the votes of working men.

Fifthly, *opposition would not come from working men to liberal expenditure on education from the public revenue, for the benefit of their own class.* This needs no proof, and

Sixthly, *they would have no such disinclination as the present constituencies to a local rate for education.*

Seventhly, *they would prefer a national to a voluntary system of education.* For working men, from an honourable feeling of independence, dislike to be laid under too much obligation, and although no class is more sincerely grateful for assistance generously rendered, they are disposed to resent injudicious patronage, or excessive clerical interference. It is perhaps for reasons of this kind that so many of their children (one-fourth of the whole number) are sent to places of education where neither squire nor parson has any footing, and where the parent pays the whole expense.[1]

Even the Royal Commissioners have not abstained from representing local subscriptions and also the State aid as " of the nature of a charitable donation ;" though why the latter should be so regarded, more than the whole endowments of the Universities for the upper classes, or of Grammar Schools for the middle-classes, it is difficult to see. But an education-rate fairly laid would not appear to working men in that light; and many of them would send their children with more satisfaction to a school so maintained, than to the present schools ; just as they keep their money with more satis-

---

[1] " Private schools, containing by estimation 573,436 children, are entirely supported by the payments of parents of the class in question."—*Report*, p. 177.

faction in Post-Office Savings Banks, though at a lower rate of interest, than in those which are set on foot by private schemes of benevolence.

Lastly, *the working classes take a broad view of the question of religious education.* Of this fact sufficient evidence has been adduced.[1] It is not that the best of them, or the bulk of them, are at all irreligious, or unwilling to accept the guidance of those who are better instructed in religion than themselves. They are very ready to be taught, and to let their children be taught, whatever they can understand, and not a little that they do not understand. But it seems they are not in the habit of attaching importance to distinctions between one and another Protestant creed. And they do not like that reading, writing, and arithmetic should be badly taught, for some incomprehensible reason connected with " *dogmas which a Committee of Privy Council may be quite unable to appreciate, or even to understand.*" They think that the maintenance of such dogmas might well be left to men of learning and of leisure, and that it ought to be conducted so as not to create difficulties in the education of simple children, who are trying to snatch a little school-learning before turning to their work for life. So far as they must be instructed in disputed doctrines, let it be in the Sunday-schools of each denomination, or from the pulpit, where their spiritual pastor can set before them such food as to himself seems good. But let the week-day school, where the parent pays his children's fees, and foregoes their labour, in the hope of giving them certain humble accomplishments, be made efficient for that purpose by

[1] More may be found in the Report of the Royal Commissioners, pp. 34—39.

obtaining the advantages of Government aid and inspection ; and, let education be rescued from entire dependence on such managers as think it a duty to make the preservation of distinctive tenets their "primary and engrossing" object.

That such are the feelings of parents is simple matter of fact, and need cause no surprise; because, as the Royal Commissioners observe :—

" It was to be expected that the distinctive tenets and separate interests of any religious community would be maintained by its teachers and guides, rather than by their followers, however attached to their leaders and guides the followers might be. Nor need the comparatively passive attitude of the body of the people materially diminish the practical difficulty of introducing a comprehensive system, since it is not with the body of the people, but with the founders and supporters of schools, that those who might attempt to introduce it, under the present or any probable circumstances, would have to deal." [1]

This last remark was true at the time when it was made.[2] But under the circumstances of a wide popular franchise, which are more probable circumstances in 1867 than they were in 1861, it would be with the body of the people, and not only with the founders and supporters of schools, that educational reformers would have to deal. If a strong and wide-spread feeling in

[1] Report, p. 38.

[2] Lord Lytton (then Sir Bulwer Lytton) argued against the Reform Bill of 1866, that there are in England "such strong differences of religious sect, that we should find it impossible to precede democracy by that universal and general system of education, without which it would be madness to make the working class the sovereign constituency of a Legislative Assembly."—*Times,.* April 14th, 1866.

favour of national education can be aroused—and indi-
cations are not wanting to prove that it can—not
throughout the country generally, but in the great
towns, such as Manchester, Rochdale, or Bradford, which
are in the van of working-class progress ; if the great
body of instructed working men should take part in the
movement ; and if veteran educational reformers, or ex-
ministers of education, together with the most enlightened of the clergy and of the landowners, should place
themselves at its head, to encourage and direct its course ;
a state of things might ensue, in which the present
founders and supporters of schools would find their
circumstances considerably changed. With liberal expenditure from the central revenue, local educational
rates, elected school-managers, the popular element
greatly strengthened in Parliament, and around them
the beginnings of corresponding social change, they
would review their position. And finding themselves no
longer sole pioneers or patrons of the movement which
they have been accustomed to lead, but surrounded by
the flowing tide of popular feeling in behalf of education,
secular and religious, for which they have long looked
and waited in vain, what course is it to be supposed
they would pursue ? Is it conceivable that more than a
small discontented minority—by no means the ablest or
the best—of the excellent and public-spirited men, who
have fought the uphill battle, would desert in the hour of
victory because their troops were getting beyond control,
or, because their co-operation were no longer indispensable, would choose altogether to withhold it ? Surely
they would rather accept the new order of things ; present themselves for election to offices which once they

held by prescription ; and in the matter of religion, without any violation of conscience, but rather perhaps with
new enlightenment, learn to enforce less dictatorially
their own distinctive tenets, and not to exercise themselves out of season upon those high things, which are
above the comprehension of the poor and simple.

Enough has been said to indicate what would
be the direct influence of enfranchised working men
upon the question of national education in Parliament,
and their probable relations with the present chief
promoters of education throughout the country. But
their enfranchisement would also have an indirect influence on the question through the minds of other
electors, the more thoughtful of whom, so soon as they
shall see the working classes in possession of political
power, will probably begin to ask themselves, with
various motives, " What has been done, or what is being
done, for the education of these people, on whose virtue
and good sense our interests as well as theirs have come
to depend ? " Some perhaps will ask this question in
alarm, shrinking back from the enfranchised working man as from a monster of their own creation, who
insists upon their giving him a soul ; others, it may
be, with self-reproach for opportunities neglected in
the past ; the larger number (it may be presumed)
with confidence in their fellow-countrymen, and with
good hope for the future. But whether the motive be
low or high, whether they are actuated by fear, or by
prudence, or by sense of fitness, or by generous sympathy
with the cause, all alike will feel that Reform has given
new importance to the question of national education,
and that its practical solution can no longer be deferred.

It may be that to some minds this part of the case is proved, and that what they doubt is not whether the action of a reformed Parliament in the matter of education will be prompt, but whether it will be prudent. It is, of course, impossible to foresee what measure of collective wisdom any future Parliament will display on any particular question ; and anticipations on general grounds will vary with the trust or distrust which different minds feel towards the great body of the nation. But there are several particular facts which seem to make it improbable that the question of Popular Education is one on which there will be rash or mistaken legislative action.   It has been now for a long time before the public mind, and has gathered round it a great mass of valuable experience, ascertained facts, definite theories, and serious, though for the most part abortive, attempts at legislation.   It has a literature, a press, and a public opinion of its own ; and, perhaps more than any other political question, obtains the attention and enlists the services of the ablest and most enlightened men in the country, who would soon unite in opposition if things appeared to be going the wrong way.   The vested interests also which have grown up under the present system, and which showed their formidable strength in the late agitation against the economies and rigours of the Revised Code, might indeed encourage profuse expenditure, but would certainly resist abrupt and ill-advised departure from the accustomed course in which so much good progress has been made.   But even if public expenditure on education became excessive, and its course less steady, the mischief done would be as nothing compared with the continuance of neglected districts, which, without doubt, must last for many years to come if a change is not made in the present system. On this point men of judgment and experience of all parties are agreed, even those who differ from each other strongly on the practical question whether the change should be attempted in the present state of public opinion.

" It is only just," says Mr. Bruce, " to eminent statesmen, to recall the fact that they have acquiesced from necessity in the compromise on which our present system is founded. The names of Earl Russell and Earl Granville, Lord Lytton, Sir John Pakington, Mr. Adderley, and Mr. Milner Gibson " (to which should now be added Mr. Bruce's own name), "may be found appended to measures not identical, differing indeed in important particulars, but far more comprehensive and stringent than Parliament or the country were prepared to adopt. The demand of the advocates of a national system is that the Legislature should provide machinery by which schools should be built and maintained wherever they are wanted. To this demand Parliament has declined to accede. However urgent the need, however absolute the destitution, Parliament refuses to supply, or to enforce the supply, of a single school." [1]

The change of government last year prevented the Select Committee on Education from presenting a report on the merits of the question; as it was undesirable to disturb and unsettle the minds of persons engaged in working the existing system, until it should be known what action a responsible Government would be disposed to take. But the draft-report of the chairman recommended that the Committee of Council on Education

[1] Address on National Education, p. 16. Ridgway, 1866.

should cease to exist ; that in its place there should be a Minister of Public Instruction, with a seat in the Cabinet; that local organization, in connexion with the department, should be established, after the analogy of boards of guardians in connexion with the Poor Law Board ; and that power should be given to levy a rate for the promotion of education, in certain cases to be defined. Important evidence is quoted in favour of this last measure. Among others, " Lord Granville and Lord Russell both contemplate rating as part of an extended system ;" Mr. Lingen " thinks there should be power, though he does not think it would be necessary in every case, to levy a rate ;" and Mr. Lowe " approves of rates, though he doubts whether we can now adopt them." In his evidence Mr. Lowe went so far as to say that under the present system he had never considered the extension of the education of the country as the duty of the Education Office ; and of the Royal Commissioners' plan of a county educational rate levied by a county Board, he says, " We thought it would be impossible to persuade the House of Commons to agree to it."

Yet in his eulogies of the present House of Commons, and in his instances of their being unfairly censured for " things over which they have no control, or which they have done very wisely to let alone," Mr. Lowe is silent on the subject of education. Is this a case in which " such faults as the House of Commons has, will be aggravated rather than abated by *any change in a democratic direction ;*" or rather, to avoid invidious names, by a liberal admission of working men to electoral rights ? Or is it an exceptional case ? At all events it is not one which can be met by the abstract argument, that " what

is wanted is not more power to urge on change, but more
intelligence to decide what that change ought to be."
What the change ought to be in the present system
of education is very well understood both inside the
House of Commons and outside the House of Commons.
The question is whether those who desire the change
can command a majority or not in the present House.
Mr. Lowe appears to be of opinion that they cannot.
But if so, then the question of popular education
stands in precisely the same relation to the Reform Bill
now pending, as that in which many other important
questions stood to the Reform Bill of 1832.   It waits for
" more power to urge on change ; " and that power, there
is much reason to think, will be found, if needed, in the
votes about to be given to the persons most directly
concerned.

In his able speech on the Revised Code, which is not
without touches of irony, Mr. Lowe probably adapted
himself well to his audience when he thus addressed the
present House of Commons :—

" I cannot promise the House that this system will be
an economical one, and I cannot promise that it will be
an efficient one ; but I can promise that it shall be either
one or the other.   If it is not cheap it shall be efficient ;
if it is not efficient it shall be cheap.   The present is
neither the one nor the other. . . .   It is not in my
power to say how far *the people* will avail themselves of
the system.   If it were a Government system I could
force it on them, but as it is a voluntary system I cannot,
and whether they will accept it or not rests in their own
breasts ; but the Government has placed itself in a
proper position when it is able to say, 'We deal with

schools on this principle ; if they are effective in their teaching, they shall receive public aid to the amount which the Commissioners have declared to be sufficient, but if they are not effective they shall not receive it.'"

A Minister of Education who should have to address on the same subject a Reformed House of Commons, may be expected to hold different language :—

"I cannot promise," he might say, "that this system will cost no more than the old system. The House well knows that the estimates for promoting the education of three and a half millions of children throughout the country, must exceed the estimates for assisting one million and a quarter in those favoured districts where there is most voluntary expenditure. But I can promise that it shall be neither inefficient nor partial. The old system was either the one or the other. This shall not be inefficient, because efficient teachers make an efficient school ; and by training, inspection, examination, and liberal salaries, it is in our power to provide efficient teachers. Moreover, means will hereafter be taken, if efficient teaching, together with the present amount of compulsion, should fail to secure regular attendance of the children. It shall not be partial; because, wherever there are families of working men, there it will be the duty of Government to see that schools are provided suitable to their requirements. If it were, in the old sense of the words, a ' voluntary ' system, I could not promise these things, because whether they should exist or not would rest in the breasts of squires, farmers, and the parochial clergy; and with all due respect for these gentlemen, I can neither regard them as ' the people,' nor expect that in every parish throughout the land they would be true spokesmen of the will, or fit judges of the educational wants, of the people. But the Government will not have placed itself in a proper position till it is able to say, 'We deal with schools on this principle : if they are efficient in their teaching, we give, together with their share of public aid, as much freedom as we can to local managers ; but if they are not efficient, they shall be made efficient, whether the great men of the parish say yes, or whether the great men say no.'"

"Experience has proved" (to borrow again the language of a late Vice-President of the Educational Committee, speaking, however, without official responsibility, and to a popular audience) "that the voluntary spirit, in its full power and development, is the growth of certain favourable soils, and that there are wide ungenial regions in which it can find no sufficient nutriment. In districts like the principality of Wales, where the population is not collected in overpowering masses, and the voluntary system is thoroughly organized ; in many of our rural parishes, where the squire and clergymen work heartily together ; in those portions of the country where the rich, poor, and middle classes co-exist in fair proportions, our present system has very nearly supplied the means of education, and may be trusted to make up the deficiency within reasonable time. But in the poorer districts of our larger cities, in parishes where the clergyman struggles in vain against the niggardliness of the landowner and the apathy or hostility of the farmer ; in those places, in fine, which the voluntary system, after thirty years' trial, has failed to reach, some other means, more stringent and peremptory, and independent of individual caprice and illiberality, must be found. The

alternative is the growth of a vast population in ignorance and vice, with ever-increasing danger to the State,
and to the reproach and scandal of a civilized and Christian people." [1]

In presence of such danger to the State, and still more
of such reproach and scandal in our Church—if religious
factions will allow us still to speak of ourselves as a
Church—it has seemed best throughout this paper to
say nothing of the higher interests of popular education,
in order to enforce more strongly the policy and plain
public duty of putting an end to gross neglect of the
lower. If Government would but for one generation
take care of the first elements of knowledge and a sound
understanding throughout the land, the higher studies
would in the next generation take care of themselves.
" Teach the people to read," says the French Minister of
Public Instruction, "and you have only to place the
right sort of books in their hands, to work wonders :
teach them to count, and they will count the cost of a
revolution." In England the point of view is somewhat
different. " Teach the working man to read," we have
hitherto said, "and let him choose his own books : teach
him to count, and he may count the cost of a strike."

But the time has come, when it is important that he
should receive the elements of a political education,
however humble. Those who elect the legislators of a
country, should know something of the nature of its
laws—enough, at least, to understand what is said to them
by the candidates for their votes. Those whose wise or
foolish conduct may affect its future history, should be
instructed in its history of the past. If, as years pass on,

[1] Address on National Education ~ ~ ᵃᵃ

government throughout the great empire of England is to rest more and more upon the consent of the governed, we owe it as a duty to all mankind to see that there be no unsoundness in the base. Even in art, in literature, and in science, our attainments will be higher and more secure in proportion as they are built upon a broader foundation. And in religion, what better safeguard could we have against unworthy superstition on the one hand, and chilling doubt or over-zealous and unpractical dogmatism on the other, than the broad common-sense and common Christianity of a free and well-instructed people? But the promise made through a Hebrew prophet of old, stands as yet unfulfilled in this, perhaps in any Christian land: " The days come, that they shall teach no more every man his neighbour, saying, Know the Lord; for they shall all know Me, from the least of them unto the greatest of them, saith the Lord." Perhaps the history of Christendom could furnish no more painful comment on this text than the revelations of gross heathenism in the great towns of England, in the nineteenth century of the Christian era, which for some years past have been published in the face of Europe, and officially brought to the knowledge of Parliament and of the country.

With experience of other nations and our own, and advice of leading statesmen of all parties to guide us, it has been easy to indicate in what direction the remedy for these evils lies. Reasons have been given for believing that a Reformed Parliament will deal with the matter vigorously and promptly. Whether this would have been done a few years later, or may even yet be done, by an unreformed Parliament, which has been moving slowly in the right direction, and has never been more disposed to bestir itself for good than now in view of approaching dissolution,[1] it is of less practical importance to know, and Parliament itself can best answer. If only a beginning can be made of a truly national system of education,—that is to say, of one which shall at least attempt to train up every child in the land as becomes a future constituent of the English nation, and a member of the Christian Church,—it may be left as an interesting historical question for the accomplished schoolboy of a later age, whether, in the days of Queen Victoria, Popular Education did more for Parliamentary Reform, or Parliamentary Reform for Popular Education.

[1] Within the last few days Mr. Bruce, himself, and Mr. W. E. Foster have introduced a Bill for this purpose, which is understood to embody the views of the most active promoters of education in Manchester. The Act is permissive, and may be adopted in any Borough or Union by a majority of the Borough electors or ratepayers who vote. For each district there is to be an elected School Committee, constituted as a body corporate with the necessary powers, and employing paid inspectors. Schools may be received into union either as " Free Schools " or " Aided Schools." At the former the scholars are to pay nothing ; at the latter not less than what the Committee pays. United Schools must be open to inspection, and free from enforcement of "any religious doctrine, catechism, or formulary " on a child whose parent shall have sent in a written objection. The Committee are not to interfere with a school except to carry out regulations (approved by the Queen in Council) and to inspect : and the managers may withdraw a school from union on three months' notice. The Committee are to inquire into the amount of school accommodation in the district, to publish a report setting forth what additional schools are needed, and to take no further steps for providing them, until private persons shall have failed to do so ; in which case they may provide premises, and either retain the direct control, or transfer it to managers. The payments to managers are to be chiefly on attendance, but partly on examination, and are not to exceed the present customary rates for a free school, or half those rates for an aided school. The Committee may also make building grants. In this case, or where they build a school, the expense is to be charged to the parish in which it is situated. The general expenses are to be charged to the Borough rate or the common fund of the Union. The Bill stands for a second reading after Easter.

p

VI.

LAW REFORM.

BY JOHN BOYD KINNEAR.

OTHER writers have, in this volume, pointed out the shortcomings of Government and Parliament in regard to several of our institutions which are established by positive legislation. I propose in this essay to draw attention to like failings in regard to the structure of the law itself, and the means provided for the administration of justice. It is indeed difficult to deal with this subject popularly, for it necessarily involves a mass of technicality in its details, such as none but the trained lawyer can fully understand. Nevertheless, that the public should have some general idea of its character is very necessary, since, as will be seen hereafter, it is the public which must sanction and enforce reforms even in Law. Nor can we satisfy our responsibility in this matter with the reflection that law is only a luxury for the rich, and that any man who chooses can decline to resort to it. He can do so only at the heavier cost of oppression. In all disputes he must confess himself, beforehand, to be in the wrong. He must resolve to submit

p 2

to gross injustice, he must acquiesce in the forms of law being perverted to his ruin, he must be prepared to leave his fame at the mercy of the libeller, his property a prey to the perjurer, and even to offer his liberty a sacrifice to his determination to resent neither violence nor falsehood. For no man can tell, when or in what way that which he prizes most may be attacked by open or secret enemies, nor in what form it may be needful to appeal for protection to that sole method of vindication which modern civilization allows—an appeal to the tribunals of the country to examine and declare the truth.

If it be answered that, at least, such exigencies are rare, the answer is insufficient as an excuse to those who perpetuate a system that makes deliverance from them difficult, costly, or imperfect. Moreover, in the daily concerns of life there are constantly arising occasions in which small roguery gains an advantage through defects of law, and even honesty on both sides is able to obtain only an uncertain and expensive guidance. No matter how clear a right, every friendly lawyer will at present advise his client rather to abandon than to maintain it, if it is but of small value, and the adversary is litigious. And with perfect good faith on all sides there are perpetually occurring questions in which the exact meaning of an agreement, the interpretation of a will, the ascertainment of a line of descent, involve disputes which only courts of justice can resolve, and in which the interposition of rules that make their action uncertain, tedious, or expensive, amounts to a denial of justice.

If, again, it be suggested that many of the cases last indicated may be met by mutual agreement, by taking the opinion of counsel, or by reference to arbitration, there is a distinct answer to each proposal. Agreement is, of course, always desirable when it is come to without compulsion ; but when it is enforced by knowledge that failure to agree will be punished with the heavy fine of judicial proceedings, it loses at once its Christian virtue and its practical equity. Next, to require men, under the like compulsion, to settle disputes by assent to the opinion of counsel, is to require them to be content with a second-rate judgment when they are entitled to ask for the highest. And lastly, the idea of arbitration, while equally subject to this objection, is attended with its own peculiar disadvantages. The arbiter, like the judge, must ascertain facts before a fair decision can be given. But as he has neither the same authority, nor is subject to the same control of public opinion as the judge, it is found in practice that such decisions are far more tardy, and even less satisfactory than those of a duly constituted Court.

The obstacles to justice, which are thus oppressive and frequent, arise from two causes. The one is that the whole body of the law is obscure ; the other is that the means provided for ascertaining it are faulty. On the first head common experience is sufficient evidence. Every man is by the Constitution assumed to know the laws by which his conduct must be governed, yet notoriously no man does or can know them. They are sealed up in thirty volumes of Statutes and in thirteen hundred volumes of Reports. There is no work to which a plain man can resort for an authoritative exposition of even the principles which must guide his conduct at every turn. As to the details in which a principle becomes wrapped up in the course of the transactions of life, he finds himself utterly lost in the subtlety of distinctions which have been gradually accumulated by the legal ingenuity of ages. If he has recourse, as he must have, to lawyers, he finds that even they cannot always guide him. Lord Langdale has said, " The statutes are often framed in such a manner as almost to defy interpretation, daily provoking observations in the Courts of Justice upon the carelessness and want of skill of the Legislature." Lord Westbury has called the statute-book " a mass of enactments and of statutes, which are in a great degree discordant and irreconcilable." Sir Samuel Romilly, speaking of the unwritten law which is propounded by the Courts, declared that " the law being unknown till it was promulgated by some decision, it was not possible that men could have conformed to it as the rule of their conduct, and it can hardly be said to have been previously known even to the judges themselves." Mr. Austin declares of the whole that "the law is known imperfectly to the mass of lawyers, and even to the most experienced of the legal profession."

The first great evil, then, of our legal system, and it is surely one of which the magnitude cannot be exaggerated, is the want of a plain and authoritative statement of what the law is. Such a statement would form a Code ; and to this word the prejudices of many lawyers are vehemently opposed. They say it is impossible to construct a Code ; impossible to foresee all the cases of its application, and injurious to lay down fixed rules, which cannot be modified in the necessities of life. The plea of impossibility is, however, disposed of by the fact that it has been done. The Romans had

a Code ; the French have a Code, embodying and super-
seding a most complicated variety of local law, and
which, after experience of its advantages, some other
Continental States have adopted. We ourselves have
made a Code for India ; and a Code of English law has
been prepared for the State of New York, and already
brought into operation. Indeed, to say that it is impossible to make a Code, is not only to ignore experience,
but to condemn civilized law altogether. A Code is
nothing more than a systematic statement of the law, of
which the Courts and Parliament are every day making
partial statements. If the separate principles of law were
incapable of being plainly and lucidly stated, human
society would be impossible, and we should be reduced
to a state of arbitrary despotism. And such is no less
the legitimate deduction from the assertion that a Code
would either be 'imperfect or too rigid. It is, of course,
out of the question to foresee every social modification,
which may need new rules to regulate it. But from
time to time it would be the business of the legislature
to supply such rules, and of the Courts to apply general
principles to the details of life. And, in point of fact,
the Courts do confess themselves bound down rigidly
to the maintenance of certain principles established,
rightly or wrongly (and too often lamentably wrongly),
by the dictum of a great judge, or the " current of
decisions." The difference between such a system and
that of a Code, does not lie in the superior flexibility
of a rule so established ; which would, in fact, mean
its greater confusion and uncertainty. It rather lies in
the fact that no man can tell beforehand at what period
a judge-made rule shall be considered to have become

204 QUESTIONS FOR A REFORMED PARLIAMENT. [ESSAY VI.

irrevocably binding, and that he can very seldom find
it stated with simplicity and precision; while in a Code
every enactment would be always authoritative, and
would, we may expect, be stated with accuracy and
brevity.

But though the want of a clear statement of the
law is the primary, it is not the only want. Fundamental amendment is required, no less than per-
spicuous enunciation. It may, indeed, be said that
the two are in great measure interlaced, for the law
is, in many respects, so absurd, that it could not be
enunciated plainly; and the attempt to do so would
reveal its character in such a light as to make simplifi-
cation a matter which, for very shame, lawyers could
no longer resist.

Take, for instance, the whole subject of the laws of
real property; a subject affecting every holder of land,
from the cottager to the duke. The mere endeavour to
state, in the series of consecutive propositions which
form a Code, the various doctrines of estates legal,
and estates equitable; of remainders in fee, or in tail;
vested or contingent; of seisins and uses; of trusts
executed, and trusts executory; of powers at common
law, and in equity; of mortgages; of terms of years;
and of the infinite variety of complex, conflicting,
fictitious, even contradictory interests, which form the
Real Property Law of this country,—would force lawyers
themselves to see the absurdity of the system. And
when the fact was realized that the whole of this mass
of confusion was applicable to the ownership of every
patch of potatoe ground, and was, indeed, to be found
or traced in nearly every title to small or large estates,

the public would undoubtedly step in and compel
lawyers to reform the system ; to replace, by plain and
simple rules, the pedantic and preposterous structure
of fiction, which the ingenuity, timidity, and bigotry
of successive generations of their craft, have built up
as an obstacle to the free possession and transfer, in the
present age, of property in land.

It would be beyond the scope of a brief and popular
exposition of this subject to enter into the details of
amendment, or into the more recondite entanglements
of our existing system. It must be sufficient to appeal
to the tribunal of common-sense to affirm that there is
no reason why the law that defines our rights should be
either faulty or obscure ; and to insist that if it is simple
and convenient in one department, there is nothing to
prevent its being made so in another. Whatever, then,
lawyers may say to the contrary, the public may rest
assured that there is no ground whatever, save in the
undue reverence paid to certain refinements of antiquity
that have now neither meaning nor use, why the law
regulating estates in land should be more complex or
costly than that which regulates estates in ships, in
stocks, or in goods. Why it has not ere now been made
so will be indicated hereafter.

To take another instance of defect in a different
department, with which also the public has some general
acquaintance, attention may for a moment be profitably
directed to the more glaring faults in our system of
Criminal Law. Here the cardinal error undoubtedly lies
in the maintenance of the theory that crime is only a
hurt to an individual, rather than an injury and danger
to the State. In virtue of this theory, we throw all

the annoyance and trouble of prosecuting on the private person who has already suffered the wrong. Yet we are so sensible that this is unsound in social principle, that we do not leave it in his option to prosecute or not, but we compel him to prosecute, under the additional penalty of fine or imprisonment. And yet again, though we thus compel him to sacrifice himself to the public good, we take no means for ensuring that the resulting good shall be really obtained, for we leave the conduct of the prosecution almost entirely in his hands or in those of any attorney who may be disposed, for the scanty costs allowed, to undertake the vindication of public justice. The consequence is, that in cases of great importance we have to break through all these arrangements, and, in order to prevent crime going unpunished, the Home Office has to assume the position of prosecutor, for which it has no adequate machinery. So, again, in the detection of obscure crime, there is an equal failure of the system. Generally speaking, it is left to the not very acute intelligence of common policemen, guided by some inspector who has himself received no education save that of the ranks of "the force." In the case even of murder, our sole constitutional mode of inquiry, that of the coroner's inquest, can only act if the body is found, so that every case of disappearance goes necessarily uninvestigated; and where the case is mysterious and the inquest has returned its verdict, no further judicial inquiry can be made, unless (as in the case of the Road murder) the police bring a random charge against some specific individual, when of course they are confined to such evidence as actually bears upon the person selected for inculpation, and any means of extending it to facts that might bring guilt home to others is denied. For these scandalous defects in the administration of justice, the obvious remedy is the appointment of a public prosecutor, who should be charged with the investigation and punishment of crime, whether patent or obscure ; and should bring an educated intelligence to the direction of subordinate officers, exclude further annoyance of the innocent, and follow, by the highest professional skill, the clue of guilt till it finally results in conviction of the criminal by the constituted tribunals. In the want of such a functionary, England stands at almost solitary disadvantage with the rest of civilization ; and even so close at hand as in Scotland there exists a system which she might easily and profitably adapt to her own institutions.

The mention of Scotland may suggest to us another branch of the law in which the most unlearned may feel assurance that important amendment is possible. The distinctions between the law of different parts of the same kingdom is a serious inconvenience, and often an injury. It must not, indeed, be supposed that any legislation, however energetic, could sweep away all these discrepancies. As I have elsewhere shown,[1] there are distinctions in the legal system, springing from the opposite mental characteristics and habits of the people, which operate either through or in despite of law, even between different parts of England, and which we shall vainly, and hurtfully, attempt by legislation to

[1] "Principles of Reform—Political and Legal" (Smith and Elder, 1865). See the chapters on Assimilation of Law, and on the Marriage Laws of England and Scotland. I am most reluctantly obliged to refer to my own exposition of these topics, because I do not know that the questions they involve have been elsewhere examined.

remove. But, at least, infinite good might be done by removing superficial distinctions. We could not make the banking systems the same, but there is no reason why the practice of bankruptcy should not be identical. We could not assimilate wholly the laws of real property, for Scotland greatly values the permanent rights created by subinfeudation, for which England (except in Lancashire) has been content to substitute leases ; but we might make the forms of transfer of land the same in both countries. In other details, also, very much might be done. The establishment of a voluntary Register of Domicile would obviate many of the evils of the conflict of laws, and permit escape from some of the most intricate, costly, and painful of lawsuits. Even the assimilation of the mode of executing deeds would save many a lawyer's fee, and many a disappointment of intention. To those, indeed, who know the frequent inconvenience, and occasional impossibility that a man in one part of the island should comply with the technicalities of the law which affects his property in another, it would seem as if the differences in this respect (recently abolished in the case of execution of wills of personalty) were retained for no other purpose than to compel the employment of a double set of solicitors.

After these few illustrations of the defects of our legal system in point of positive law, let us proceed to glance at its administration in the Courts. Here we find confusion and uncertainty no less prevalent, and arising from similar causes. Because five hundred years ago the scholastic pedantry and contracted understandings of the judges converted law into a burden which no man could bear, an irregular means of redress

was provided by the Sovereign and the Church, in
the interposition of the Royal Chancellor, "to do
equity," or to compel conduct to be, not according to
the letter of the law, but "according to conscience."
This sort of interference was necessarily at first arbitrary ; but in time it grew systematic, and its exercise
was reduced to rules as strict as the procedure at law
which it modified. But when this practical end was
attained we did not abandon the machinery, though now
merely fictitious and superfluous, by which it had been
brought to pass. We still keep up the division between
the Courts of Common Law and Chancery, forcing a
suitor who seeks for one admittedly just remedy to resort
to the one set of tribunals, and, when he seeks for
another remedy, not less admittedly just, to resort to the
other, endowing him with rights sacred in one jurisdiction and unrecognised in the other ; maintaining theories
obviously contrary to the fact (as, for example, that a
mortgagee is in law the real owner of the estate, while
in common sense and in equity he is only the incum-
brancer), and this as if only for the mere purpose of per-
petuating conflict of systems ; and bringing us, at last,
to such a pass that our judges and barristers know only
one half of the law of England, and are confessedly as
ignorant of the other half as if they had received no
legal education at all. Yet the line of demarcation
which divides the two branches of legal science is so
artificial and unnatural that it is constantly found to
run through the middle of a subject, preventing any
one court or any one set of lawyers from dealing with
or even understanding the whole of the rights involved in the single subject with which they are

engaged. Thus, suppose the possession is sought of an estate, it must be at law, if the title accrues by descent, but in equity if by contract; if a will is impugned on the ground of the testator's weakness of mind, it will be investigated in the Probate Court, but the carrying it into effect is the sole prerogative of the Court of Chancery; if a merchant sues for a debt, he will have to seek justice at Westminster, but if he quarrels with his partner about their accounts, he must commonly come to Lincoln's Inn for redress. Illustrations like these might be endlessly multiplied.

Partly, too, from the different rules of different courts, the whole law, in so simple a subject as that of debt, has been placed on the most unjustifiable basis. The Common Law Courts preserve their traditional reverence for their own records, and for a seal attached to a paper instead of a signature. Hence, though both are now mere fictions, debts so constituted are allowed an unfair priority. A judgment debt is constituted by a mere warrant of attorney to confess judgment, and is the emptiest formality; a deed is constituted by the utterance of a few words and by a wafer stuck on the paper. Yet in the courts of law debts thus created must be paid, while the most solemn engagements in writing or otherwise are postponed. So, again, the law demands a consideration for a debt, only when it is not constituted by deed; but the condition is satisfied by a consideration of the most illusory character. Here a fictitious distinction is defeated by a fictitious evasion. But many of these fictions are not recognised in Chancery at all, nor in Bankruptcy, and therefore it may happen that a man gets paid what is owing him, or does not get paid, not by reason of the justice of his claim or the clearness of the evidence, but by reason of his getting it adjudicated in one court rather than in another. Yet, to every mind, however unlearned, it must be obvious that nothing could be more easy than to abolish all this network of tradition, fiction, and foolishness, and to establish in so simple and common a subject rules founded on the plain common sense of mankind.

It will probably, however, be answered that in all these departments we are already in process of improvement. The Real Property Acts, the Trustee Acts, the Court of Chancery, and the Common Law Procedure Acts, and the County Courts Acts, will be cited as evidence of the progress of legal reform. There is no need to deny that, before the Reform Act of 1832, the law was worse than it is now. That measure gave an impetus to progress which was felt even in the courts of justice, and in barristers' chambers. But thirty years have passed, and there is but little progress to show for a whole generation of work. A very few of the most flagrant inconveniences in the Law of Real Property have been swept away. The trading classes compelled the adoption of a simple and rational form of procedure for the recovery of small debts, and this so affected business in the superior courts, as to compel, fifteen years ago, the initiation of amendment in them. Justice is now not absolutely denied to the suitor by the impossibility of stating his whole case in the court in which he sues. But the illustrations of legal confusion and anomaly given above, are taken from our system as it still exists at the present day, after all the amendments that lawyers, during a whole generation of professed improvement, have introduced into it. And the mere statement of such absurdities still surviving, is proof that the work is being most imperfectly and tardily done.

What, then, is the cause of this scandalous position, and whence may we hope for remedy? The cause lies in the fact that no considerable part of the representatives of the nation have yet thought it worth remedy, and it has, therefore, been left very much in the hands of lawyers themselves. Now, there are inherent peculiarities in that profession which make it almost impossible that any rapid improvement in the law should come from within. Beyond all others, it worships success; and the barrister who gets business is influential, the barrister who has no business is powerless. But success does not always come from real ability and public spirit. Success is often due to the possession of qualities or connexions, that have no tendency to create or strengthen a desire to promote reform of the law. And in all cases when business does come, it is so engrossing as to leave scarcely the leisure to consider, far less to originate schemes of improvement. Moreover, the minds are very rare that see the need for improvement in arrangements under which they personally thrive. And rarest of all is the disposition to undergo a labour which seems invidious, and which, far from bringing gain to the reformer, will only impose upon him the difficult task of unlearning the lore of a lifetime, and beginning at the same point as the youthful student. Some few such minds there have been in the past, and some there are in the present generation, and to none can higher honour be due. But they are too scarce to make much advance against the dead inertia of disinclination, which the mass of the profession opposes to their efforts.

It is not from within, then, that, in the nature of things, we can expect effectual Law Reform to come. It must be forced forward by "pressure from without." But circumstances have hitherto made such pressure feeble. The classes that have till now been politically powerful in England are the landed class, the capitalist class, and the class of tradesmen. The intermediate class, comprising persons of modest independence, professional men, merchants and manufacturers in a moderate way of business, have not had much influence ; they have been in most constituencies overpowered by one or other of the extremes above or below them. But these extremes are precisely the classes that have least need to ask for any improvement in the law, and are most subject to the influence of those who are opposed to it. The landed class desires no change in anything. They are indeed happy husbandmen, for they do most fully appreciate the blessings of their position. To them a suit affecting the title of their estates is as a thunder-clap in a clear sky, a convulsion of nature to be neither foreseen nor provided against. In their dealings with their tenants, in their family settlements, in their mortgages, they resign themselves implicitly to fate and the family solicitor, and the idea of altering the law to make his proceedings simpler or his charges smaller never crosses their brain. The mercantile millionaire views the matter in the same light, though from a slightly different point of view. Time is to him the most valuable of all things,

and the costs of a lawsuit are far less than the cost of
the time necessary to reform the law. Both these classes,
again, are greatly under the influence, if not in private,
at least in electioneering matters, of the local solicitors
who are their election agents. A reform distasteful to
these gentlemen is pretty sure to meet with cold encouragement from the present class of members of Parliament. This power of the solicitors is openly avowed
and counted on by their own organs in the press whenever any measure that would affect their profits is in
agitation. And finally, the ten-pounder class is as much
below the sting of the law as these wealthy classes are
above it. Having compelled the establishment of the
County Courts, they have got all the law for which they
feel pressing need. The rest they do not understand,
and do not care for, because it seldom affects them.

From this apathy on the part of the great and powerful sections of the constituencies results the indifference
of Parliament, and from that indifference, added to the
reluctance of most of its own law officers, results the slug-
gishness of Government. The desire of all the parties is
to escape work, and to shirk responsibility. Notoriously,
the House of Commons, as at present constituted, cannot
be got to face the discussion of any measure involving
radical change, and it will not pass such a measure on the
recommendation of others. Thus among other pressing
subjects, Bankruptcy, which every one acknowledges to
be a matter in which the law is only an encouragement to
fraud and a cover to spoliation of creditors, is year after
year discussed ; a Bill is promised, perhaps introduced,
and then it is dropped because there would not be time to
discuss it before grouse-shooting begins. Thus, again, a

measure for the reform of titles to land, which can only
be effectual if made compulsory, is made voluntary, because the House knows it has not mastered the subject
sufficiently to be quite sure that its own measure will
not work harm. Thus, too, in the larger question of the
consolidation of the law, Commission after Commission
of lawyers has been appointed, has wrangled, and died,
with no fruit except a few criminal law statutes. Thus,
once more, when one of these Commissions had ventured
so far as to prepare something resembling a Criminal
Code, the result was referred to the Judges, of all men
notoriously the most prejudiced against change ; and,
without further investigation, Parliament at once proceeded to take their criticisms as conclusions, and to
abandon the measure without an effort to improve and
pass it. And thus, finally, we see that years after Lord
Westbury, as Chancellor, has made a speech in the
House of Lords recommending consolidation of the
statutes and decisions, a Royal Commission is appointed
to consider whether such a work is desirable, and how
it is to be done : though every one who has considered
the matter has long ago made up his mind that it is
desirable, and that the way to do it is to appoint
some one to do it, instead of appointing a new Commission to talk about it.

What is the remedy ? After having pointed out the
indifference to Law Reform of both the wealthiest and
the poorest classes of the present constituencies, it may
seem paradoxical to hope for advantage from the
admission of a class still poorer. And if that class
were to be influenced by nothing but its own selfish
and immediate interests, no doubt it would be vain to

q 2

expect from it much devotion to such matters. But
those are very much deceived who think that working
men desire admission to the franchise for nothing more
than to settle their own Trade Union rules, or to
discuss the question of fixing rates of wages by statute.
Whoever has any personal acquaintance with them
knows that, in a degree far beyond those above them,
they care for good government merely for its own sake.
Abuses in any department, however remote from their
own affairs, will find scant mercy at the hands of these
strong-minded non-electors. Of two candidates, one of
whom points out, and the other slurs over, absurdities,
in any part of our system, the reformer will always find
the majority on his side ; and if, after probation, he is
shown to have been negligent in the task he assumed, he
will know that his rejection next time is certain. The
mere fact that the law is obscure will, to those who judge
only by common sense, and without attempt to master
refinements, be its sufficient condemnation. Nor is it
true that occasions that will add the zest of personal interest will be absent. The working class, more than the
tradesman class, is affected by the real property laws,
for the latter seek generally to keep their accumulations
invested in trade ; the former have an inclination to invest
their savings in a cottage or a garden. There will not be
wanting men to show how much of these small savings
are absorbed in the costs of title ; and to stimulate an
agitation for a total reform of the system which, in such
a personal instance, is proved to be oppressive.

But it is to be remembered that this tendency will
be fostered and guided by a class which is fuller of
information, but at present practically powerless. It

has been pointed out that the class of moderate means
and yet of high intelligence, is practically, in most
constituencies, overpowered by those above or below
them. The people with incomes from £200 to £2,000,
are those whom either the ten-pounders or the men
of wealth swamp. But it is this class, including the
most active intellects of the nation, which feels most frequently the need of guidance or redress by the law,
while its means are not such as to make the costs other
than a heavy burden. Fully understanding the nature
of the grievance, these men will swell, with the force
of their intelligence, and practical or literary ability,
the demand for reform ; in which they will find new
and potent allies in the class that is below the influence
of attorneys, and above the influence of absorption in
their private trade or business.

But while all these elements will combine in operation, the great and vital influence will come from the
heightened earnestness, the stronger sense of responsibility for the State, which the enlargement of the Constitution will engender. When power is no longer the
hereditary appanage of a class, when the Government of
England is felt to be the administration of the affairs of
the community by themselves, there will spring up a state
of feeling which will be destructive of all manner of
traditional abuses. It is true that even then the help of
trained and skilful lawyers will be needed to construct
the improved legal system that the country will demand.
But legal ability will not be found wanting when it is
really called for. It dallies with the question now,
because there is no adequate impulse to compel earnestness. But when we have a nation in a position to insist

on earnestness, the earnestness will be given. Among
the higher minds the knowledge of what is wanting
exists already, and popular pressure will ripen it into
action.   Instead of speeches that show the evil, and
declare that a remedy ought to be elaborated by somebody else ; instead of Commissions to consider what every
one has decided upon ; instead of references to judges, who
are avowedly against any change whatsoever; we shall
see practical plans developed, work done, and obstacles,
that now are called insuperable, quietly set aside as
unworthy of real attention.   When the nation positively
insists on Reform of the Law, competent men will soon
show how thoroughly it may be effected.

VII.

THE ARMY.

BY GEORGE HOOPER.

THE management of military affairs by the House of
Commons is not a bad touchstone of its efficiency, as the
great business committee of the nation.

All imperfections in the Parliamentary representation
of the various interests involved in the administration of
each department of the State, must tend to produce corresponding defects in the practical conception of the
ends to be pursued, and as a consequence of this, in the
machinery by which they are to be achieved, and which
it is the duty of the House of Commons to maintain, to
repair, or to control. The action of the House will, in
the main, be dictated by what the classes represented
suppose to be their interests, modified by so much of a
large and enlightened public spirit as may habitually
animate its members.

Finance and commerce have been moderately well
dealt with, because finance and commerce have been
sufficiently represented to make themselves respected.
But in regard to the Army, and all that pertains thereto,

there are in the House of Commons few persons with
any knowledge of military matters, who do not belong
to the official and privileged classes; and, consequently,
army administration, in principle and detail, has been
subordinated to the interests and prejudices of a minority,
and to political considerations which assume the perfection of the present relations between classes in this
country. As an inevitable consequence, the House of
Commons in its treatment of the Army has been guided,
not by a single desire to create and maintain the most
efficient military machine, so framed as to draw to its
service all the available ability in the state, so organized
as to be adapted to the political necessities of our Empire,
so administered as to combine economy and efficiency;
but it has been guided by a paramount desire to make
the military machine only as effective as is consistent
with the maintenance of social distinctions, and the
permanence of a system of exclusion.

Mr. Disraeli once cleverly excused the action of certain
subordinate ministers upon a dockyard constituency with
the object of deciding an election, as an attempt to
bring the departments into harmony with the House of
Commons; and the same spirit, manifested in a different
way, has governed military policy and military legislation. Before Parliament was reformed in 1832, matters
were a great deal worse; but even a reformed Parliament,
which has swept away many abuses, has proved itself
to be, by its very constitution, incompetent to strike at
the root of the evil; and incompetent, because it represented and still represents the evil itself.

· It would, however, be unjust to say that the House of
Commons has done nothing towards the improvement of

our military institutions. It has sanctioned the establishment of a Ministry of War; it has insisted on the
education of officers up to a certain point; it has cheer-
fully empowered the government to improve the condition
of the private soldier, giving him more and better food,
better clothing, and, in many places, better lodging. It
has, through the War Minister, made some beneficial
changes in the organization of the Army. It has called
the Militia again into life, and dealt liberally with the
Volunteers. But it has done these things in an eleemo-
synary spirit as regards the men, and in other respects
as a concession to emergencies of the hour, or outcries
of the day; and in every direction it has limited its
reforms (as, indeed, from its faulty constitution it could
not help doing) by a rigid adherence to the principle of
preserving in the Army that spirit of monopoly and class
supremacy which has not yet been banished from
Parliament.

It is owing to the imperfect constitution of the legislative body, in relation to the country at large, and its
imperfect hold upon the Army and Army management,
that no large and masterly scheme of military policy
has governed the constitution and administration of the
Army, based on principles which are good, not for to-day
and to-morrow only, but for protracted periods of time.
Ever since the peace of 1815, we have lived from hand
to mouth. Nearly the whole work of Parliament and of
its ministers with respect to the administration of the
Army has consisted in cutting out abuses here and there,
as some disaster happened to make them notorious, and,
generally, under the influence of great external pressure;
but no minister has even so much as attempted radical

reforms like those effected in some other departments of the State. It is not the power of the House of Commons that is wanting in order to effect some of the most important of these reforms, it is the will. The governing classes consider their supremacy would be injured were the sale and purchase of commissions abolished; and still more, were a career in the Army thrown open to any one who should enter it as a private soldier. The theory —which seems to possess some minds—that labour exists in order that lucrative employment may be found for capital, has its counterpart in the practical arrangement according to which the promotion of the rank and file is limited, while more favoured classes monopolize the commissioned ranks. The House of Commons supports a system which cannot be justified on any reasonable principle, because it represents the commissioned ranks, and because the system of exclusion is in harmony with the disproportionate influence of particular classes in the State. No doubt the classes whose influence predominates in Parliament, believe this to be right; just as in 1815 a Parliament, still more exclusive, believed it right to pass a Corn Law for the purpose of keeping up rents ; just as the present Parliament believed it right to impose a rate to compensate cattle-owners for the loss of stock by the plague. The motives of the majority on such occasions as these may have been most pure ; but the character of their legislation is no less partial and selfish.

One consequence of the system of promotion based upon purchase, that exists in our Army is, that the officers receive no salary for their services, they are only paid interest on the capital they invest; and this again

gives them factitious rights of complaint and undue
influence at head-quarters. Some officers, of course, who
believe themselves aggrieved, never get redress; but
others, who are more powerful, do obtain what they
resolutely demand; while if they happen to be peers of
Parliament, they not only defend their own wrong-doing
in their places, they become accusers, and assail the
military authorities or the Minister of War. The indirect
effect of the purchase system, and the direct effect of the
exclusive system, have been to make the commissioned
ranks of the Army a sort of Club. The Commander-in-
chief himself is afraid to act upon the principle of selec-
tion, because he fears what he calls public opinion, but
what is really only the outcry of the Club. Seniority
and routine constitute the Magna Charta of mediocrity,
and, as the largest numbers come under that category,
they supply that opinion which prevails, and which the
Commander-in-chief fears. The bulk of the officers are
less adverse to favouritism than to such promotion as
recognises exceptional talents; for talent of the higher
kind is rare, while any one may become a favourite. It
may be asked, what has the House of Commons to do
with this? The answer is, Everything; since the House
of Commons alone maintains a system in which these
abuses are possible, nay, certain. The House of Commons
has not clothed its own minister with sufficient power to
cope with the influence behind the Commander-in-chief,
nor with the influence which the Commander-in-chief
himself may, and generally does, exercise.

There is at this moment a wail of alarm, because the
Army is not supplied with recruits; and there is an
outcry, more or less reasonable, for some comprehensive

plan of military organization. The House of Commons
will do something intended to quicken the supply of
recruits; but it will fail, because it will sanction only
paltry remedies, and will not go to the root of the matter
—the treatment of the private soldier. What happens
to the recruit? From the day he is attested he falls
under the influences of a method of treatment which an
enemy would say was intended to make the worst of
him. An ordinary man, who has grown up in ignorance
of the manners and customs of the British army in its
school and dwelling, could not enter a barrack-yard
without being both amazed and disgusted at the behaviour
of the teacher to his pupils. Nay, he need not enter
the yard. It is enough that he catch, in passing, the
tones, and hear the language of the drill-sergeants.
Brutality, contempt, insult, these are the principles of
training. Contrast the bearing and language of a sergeant
drilling volunteers with that of the same man drilling
regulars. Why is the difference so marked? Because
the volunteers would resent the manner thought good
enough for the rank and file of the Army. And how
short-sighted it is—for if the regulars do not suffer
more severely from this abominable system, what might
they not become were they treated like what they are—
men? Of course, there are rare exceptions, for it sometimes happens that a regiment has officers with a spirit
and enlightenment above the system they administer.
There are also fine natures which survive this systematic
degradation, but the bulk suffer from it far more than
they know or could express. And yet, with "nagging,"
bullying, worrying, drilling, as the rule of the service,
our military administrators are astonished at the short

supply of recruits, at the odious reputation of the Army among the people, and at the amplitude of the black list!

The relation between officers and men is the perfection of privilege. On one side is not merely a higher class— but one that is treated as radically different and permanently superior; and on the other side, not merely an inferior class, but one that is treated as radically different and permanently lower in the scale. So much is this theory acted on, that it governs the mode of training and discipline, and is held to justify the closing of the upper ranks to all, except a few favoured by accident or necessity. Officers are not treated as mere machines— men are; officers will not submit to insult—the private soldier often must. All officers are, in certain broad respects, considered equal; there would seem to be scarcely the equality of common citizenship between the officers and the men, except in the thick of the battle, or the hard labour of a siege. How then can recruits flow into the Army as they flow into all other callings, when there is neither pay, nor promotion, nor decent treatment, nor a fair share of honour to attract them? Here again, it be may said, that the House of Commons is not, and cannot be, responsible for this. Why not? We answer again, that the House deliberately upholds the system of which these are the fruits; that it maintains the lash, that it maintains the purchase system, that it keeps the private soldier always a private soldier, that it permits the qualified independence of the Horse Guards, that the Minister it appoints and pretends to hold responsible cannot, or will not, deal with the manifold evils of the system, and that the system does not open in the Army a career for all. Instead of making the most, our plan makes the least of the individual ability of each soldier. Repression, not development is the rule. Men are made machines to the prejudice of good soldiering. Bad characters, mainly the fruit of a bad system, were the curse of the famous Army which could go anywhere, and do anything. Abolish purchase, which the House will not do; abandon the lash, which the House will not do; educate and train, do not merely drill, drill, drill your soldier; give him a career, promote from the lowest rank up to the highest, treating the private soldier always as a man who may become an officer, and you will never lack recruits for the British Army.

As to constructing a comprehensive scheme of military organization, Parliament knows it dare not even attempt it; because, if that scheme went beyond certain limits,—if, for instance, it were based on a conscription even for home service—Parliament knows that its laws would not be obeyed. And why not? Because the House of Commons does not represent the bulk of the nation, upon whom it would impose this duty. *That* is an all-sufficient reason. There is no reciprocal confidence between the governing classes and the governed. In a moment of supreme danger Parliament might do what it pleased to save the State; but in quiet times, Parliament could not levy a corporal's guard by conscription. We cannot hope to obtain a wise, comprehensive, and acceptable military organization, from the House of Commons as at present constituted, and that is surely a capital defect.

The great break-down in 1854-5, may be directly

traced to the House of Commons, which, in its treatment of the Army, deliberately preferred the maintenance of privilege in the hands of a few, to an efficient system. The indignation of the House, the famous Committee of Inquiry, the obloquy heaped upon a few men, served admirably the purpose of a shield, to cover the real offender—the House of Commons itself. And so it will be again. If we enter on another war, similar deficiencies will appear, we shall meet with similar disasters; but should disasters unfortunately again happen, let us hope that censure will fall where it is deserved—not on a Lord Raglan, or a Duke of Newcastle, or a Commissary-General Filder, or a General Airey, but upon the system, and the Parliament which upholds that system.

Though the class which supplies, and is expected to supply, the rank and file of the Army, has few or no representatives in the House of Commons, the officer class is amply represented; and, indeed, a large number of officers appear in person in both Houses. And they make use of their position. Many officers of high rank have used their Parliamentary privileges for their own professional purposes; some to speak pamphlets on the part they had taken in disputed military incidents; others to contend for the privileges of their comrades in some special branch of the service. And the representation in Parliament of the military servants of the Crown, is so numerous, and their political connexion so potent, that attempts are often made in Parliament to control the judgment of the Minister even on minor points of military procedure, with which no legislative body should concern itself.

Although it is a matter of vital importance, very little

need be here said on the way in which the House of
Commons deals with the Army Estimates. Expenditure
no doubt depends on policy, but, when once the scale of
expenditure is fixed, frugality and economy depend on
administration. Practically, the House votes all, or
nearly all, the money when it votes the number of men.
In assenting to the demand of the Minister for men, it
surrenders its control, except over very small items. No
Member can place himself in the position of the Minister,
because no Member can take upon himself the responsibility of the Minister. It is all a question of confidence.
The Minister for the time being is supposed to have the
confidence of the House. If he abuse that confidence,
if he be lax and extravagant, he may be driven from
power. There is no other remedy. No representative
assembly can exercise a minute and effective control over
myriads of details. Those who are desirous of retrench-
ment are poorly informed, and those who are well
informed, in nine cases out of ten, have an interest in
expenditure. Hence each item of expenditure is well
fenced about, and fortified against attack. It must be
gross and flagrant to be cut off. The only really efficient
check upon extravagance lies in the appointment of
economical Ministers who feel their responsibility. At
present that responsibility is, not to the nation, fairly
represented, but to a Parliament, which does not represent
the nation, and which allows its dominion over military
affairs to be engrossed by a zealous and irresponsible
minority more or less interested in the maintenance of
a particular system. A good system might cost more,
but then it would be good, not a weapon which breaks,
when put to use, and wounds the hand which holds it,

instead of the enemy against whom it is directed, as our
system did in 1854.

Next to the constitution of the House of Commons,
which, if it were framed expressly to foster the grievances
heretofore specified, could not do its work better ; the
master evil afflicting the Army is the almost complete
independence of the Horse Guards. This is one of the
most startling of anomalies. Theoretically, the Secretary
of State is responsible for the entire management of the
Army and all that pertains thereto. Practically, he is
shorn of a large share of authority, and the chief officer of
the Horse Guards' staff is invested with powers that make
him practically independent of the Minister and of Parliament. The only department in which the Crown exerts
authority is the Army ; in some cases directly, in others
through the General Commanding-in-chief or the Commander-in-chief; and this in spite of the maxim that, as
the Crown can do no wrong, it must act through a responsible Minister. This is distinctly and directly unconstitutional. Parliament creates the Army, and pays the Army.
Parliament clothes, lodges, and feeds it. Without the
Mutiny Act, annually passed, there could be no Army ;
because there is no common or statute law applicable to
military offences. Without the consent of Parliament,
there could be no Army at all. Apart, then, from any
questions of efficiency or inefficiency, this abstraction
of the Army from the open and direct control of
Parliament, through the Minister responsible to Parliament, is a permitted violation of an essential constitutional principle—a standing infraction of the maxim that
the Crown cannot act except through a responsible
Minister.

The Sovereign should command and govern the
Army in the sense in which he declares war and makes
peace, appoints judges and governors of colonies and
dependencies, and commands and administers the
Navy. Lord Grenville declared it incompatible with the
principles of a limited monarchy to keep the military
distinct from the civil administration. But this violation
of constitutional usage, this direct and flagrant injury to
military efficiency, is what the House of Commons permits in defiance of the wise advice of some even of our
most aristocratic statesmen. It has refused to back its
own Minister, and, having done so, how can it give
reality to any indictment against him ? How can it
seriously arraign a servant for misfeasance, from whom
it has deliberately withheld powers essential to the
performance of his duties ? And, accordingly, the
thing is never done, unless it be at a crisis in the
struggle of parties, or in a time of panic like that
which raged during a part of the Russo-Turkish War.
And why does not Parliament, and primarily the
House of Commons, assert its authority and clothe its
Minister with full powers ? Because to do so would
interfere with the Club over which the Commander-
in-chief presides : and in quiet times, the Club is
all-powerful in the House of Commons. Officers and
statesmen, anxious alike for the efficiency of the military
training and for the administration of the Army, have
over and over again recommended the reform here indicated. But sound principle in this, as in so many
other respects, has been defeated by short-sighted and
interested mediocrity ; and the consequence is the halt-
ing, uncertain, unenlightened, and slovenly management

of a department which demands decision, vigour, open-
mindedness, accuracy, and quickness of insight. Can
we look for the great reform involved in the reduction
of the Horse Guards to its due subordination in a just
scheme for the administration of the Army, while the
House of Commons is constituted as at present? Privilege, monopoly, promotion by purchase, and too often
by favour, are the legitimate results in the Army of
a restricted representation of the people in Parliament.
Class views of management, and illegitimate action in
the name of the Crown, may be expected to prevail so
long as the House of Commons represents only certain
classes, and not the whole nation.

The shortcomings of the House of Commons in regard
to the Army are then but too manifest. Even the
warmest admirers of scant representation would not
crown Parliament with laurels for its achievements in
this branch of State business. It is beyond question
that the House of Commons hitherto has not been able,
because a most powerful section of its members has not
been willing, to insist on the supremacy of its own
Minister of War in all matters pertaining to his office;
that it permits an influence of an irresponsible character
to exist by the side of, and often to paralyse, a responsible
department; that it suffers an open system of buying
and selling places in the public service, and cannot
enforce its own regulations even in regard to the price
of those places; that it allows and even encourages
expensive habits, which make it practically impossible
for an officer to live on his pay; that in this way it
limits the area of supply, and in doing so, limits also the
available quantity of military talent; that it offers little

encouragement to such ability as by chance, and notwithstanding the system, finds its way into the Service; and that, to sum up the results of the system, the man who enters as an officer has almost no motive for exertion; and the man who enters as a private has no career—a state of things which effectually deprives our army of much valuable material for the making of soldiers. Drawing its officers from a very limited class, and conniving at the maintenance among them of idle and expensive habits, the House of Commons is compelled to leave the Army in the hands of a set of men, who from the influence of custom, tradition, and prejudice, are unable to devise and carry out any other system of training and discipline than one which treats soldiers as machines,—not as men, capable of intelligent co-operation. That section of the House of Commons which sees and deplores this state of things, is not strong enough to resist the powerful faction which is interested in maintaining it. But this is not all. Because the House of Commons does not represent the nation, it would not venture to enact, even if it had devised and desired, a comprehensive system of military organization, such as would effectually secure these islands from invasion, and enable the Government, should occasion arise, to vindicate the national honour and uphold imperial interests. These are among the shortcomings of the House of Commons, shortcomings which that House, as at present constituted, is powerless to overtake, and which materially strengthen the demand for an adequate amendment of the representation of the people.

VIII.

FOREIGN POLICY.

BY FREDERIC HARRISON.

"Afin d'éviter la Révolution démocratique par l'évolution sociocratique, le patriciat britannique doit autant régénérer sa politique en dehors qu'au dedans."—AUGUSTE COMTE.

WE can imagine with what shame an Englishman who remembered the reign of Elizabeth, the days of the great Defence and of the grand Design, must have watched the humiliations endured by her dastardly successor; how one who had heard the just voice of Cromwell ring across Europe, must have witnessed the vassalage of the later Stuarts; how the contemporaries of Marlborough must have groaned over the peace of Aix-la-Chapelle. All who can remember the Treaties of Vienna, and the place which our country held in Europe at the Peace, can understand the feelings of those men. But the process of humiliation, if less violent now than it was then, affords now less ground for hope. Our foreign policy has, in earlier times, been perverted by the folly of a king. It is now paralysed by the blindness of a class.

For a generation, our influence on the continent has
been steadily narrowing and sinking. Politicians of
every school are fain to accept it as a notorious fact.
No man can say what is the policy which this country
represents. It has sunk, through failure after failure,
into spiritless confusion. It fostered the malignant
jealousy against France, which had been its watchword
in the Coalition, until France broke loose in a convulsive
defiance. It passed from insolent oppression to petty
menaces, and ended in a feeble alternation of cordiality
and distrust. It encouraged the progress of Russia, so
as to place her for years in the centre of the councils
of Europe. This fatal blunder it next undertook to redress, in a war which began in imbecility, and ended in
waste. Year after year it bolstered up the fabric of
Austrian Empire, when that Empire was as obviously
destined to ruin as it flagrantly existed by oppression.
It was deaf to Italy and her claims, so long as it was
decent to be deaf; and then it contented itself with
patronage and words. The oppressions of Poland, the
plague-spot of Europe, it meddled with and talked
about, meeting ever unvaried discomfiture from the
oppressor, being faithless and pusillanimous in the eyes
of the victim. In Denmark it meddled and talked
again more eagerly and angrily than before, till it met
with a still more galling rebuff. Towards the people of
the United States it has acted with even a more fatal
spirit of perversity, and brought us far nearer to much
greater dangers. Towards uncivilized peoples, it is true,
our conduct has at least been consistent. It has been
consistently imperious. Towards the civilized, it is a
tale without coherence or result.

When Europe settled down at the Peace, this country
was by common consent the first in moral position, and
in material power. She had a definite policy to pursue,
and an organized government to wield it. Her word was
trusted, feared, and obeyed. In half a century she has
seen another, it may be others, pass steadily and surely
before her into that place of lead; and she is dependent
for a policy on the continent to chance or prejudice. Her
diplomatic influence, like her policy, has been stricken
with an inward paralysis. She promises and does not
perform, enjoins and is not obeyed, threatens and then
loses heart. She is without a purpose, without influence,.
and without allies. She stands irresolutely uneasy,
watching with half jealousy and half alarm her great
rival by position, and her great rival by race; not daring
openly to resist either, not sympathising heartily or combining with either. It is a policy which may be judicious,
but which certainly is not glorious, and not very safe.

There are persons to whom such language is incomprehensible; some who think that to doubt of one's
country's actions is a crime, some who are satisfied by
the show rather than the fact of a great position.
There is in our policy much that is well-meaning, a real
leaning towards freedom and progress, and many negative
virtues. But negative virtues are not enough for a great
nation, which has a part to fulfil in Europe. Fine words
in Parliament over the liberation of Italy or the wrongs
of Poland are a rather poor result for a nation's collective
action. To forswear, with high solemnities, the atrocious
doctrines of the Coalition and the Holy Alliance is
scarcely enough for the government of a people such as
this. In an age which is one long revolution, to abstain

only from reaction is to stand still; and to stand still is to obstruct. The nation which now professes that it has no policy but Non-intervention, professes that it has No Policy at all.

The pretentious Nihilism which marks our policy in Europe is indeed scarcely susceptible of any criticism but contempt. But there has been a critical question of recent times, capable of testing statesmanship, in which we may find matter for reflection. On the official bearing of this country towards the people of the United States, a thoughtful Englishman can hardly look backward without a shudder, nor can he look forward without dismay. The great struggle which has for ever decided the cause of slavery of man to man, is beyond all question the most critical which the world has seen since the great revolutionary outburst. If ever there was a question which was to test political capacity and honesty it was this. A true statesman, here if ever, was bound to forecast truly the issue, and to judge faithfully the cause at stake. We know now, it is beyond dispute, that the cause which won was certain to win in the end, that its reserve force was absolutely without limit, that its triumph was one of the turning-points in modern civilization. It was morally certain to succeed, and it did succeed with an overwhelming and mighty success. From first to last, both might and right went all one way. The people of England went wholly that way. The official classes went wholly some other way.

One of the great key-notes of England's future is simply this—what will be her relations with that great Republic? If the two branches of the Anglo-Saxon race are to form two phases of one political movement, their

welfare and that of the world will be signally promoted.
If their courses are marred by jealousies or contests, both
will be fatally retarded. Real confidence and sympathy
extended to that people in the hour of their trial would
have forged an eternal bond between us. To discredit
and distrust them, then, was to sow deep the seeds of
antipathy. Yet, although a union in feeling was of
importance so great, although so little would have
secured it, the governing classes of England wantonly
did all they could to foment a breach.

A great political judgment fell upon a race of men,
our own brothers; the inveterate social malady they
inherited came to a crisis. We watched it gather with
exultation and insult. There fell on them the most
terrible necessity which can befall men, the necessity of
sacrificing the flower of their citizens in civil war, of
tearing up their civil and social system by the roots, of
transforming the most peaceful type of society into the
most military. We magnified and shouted over every
disaster; we covered them with insult; we filled the
world with ominous forebodings and unjust accusations.
There came on them one awful hour when the powers of
evil seemed almost too strong; when any but a most
heroic race would have sunk under the blows of their
traitorous kindred. We chose that moment to give
actual succour to their enemy, and stabbed them in the
back with a wound which stung their pride even more
than it crippled their strength. They displayed the most
splendid examples of energy and fortitude which the
modern world has seen, with which the defence of Greece
against Asia, and of France against Europe, alone can be
compared in the whole annals of mankind. They deve-

loped almost ideal civic virtues and gifts; generosity,
faith, firmness; sympathy the most affecting, resources
the most exhaustless, ingenuity the most magical. They
brought forth the most beautiful and heroic character
who in recent times has ever led a nation, the only blame-
less type of the statesman since the days of Washington.
Under him they created the purest model of government which has yet been seen on the earth—a whole
nation throbbing into one great heart and brain, one
great heart and brain giving unity and life to a whole
nation. The hour of their success came; unchequered
in the completeness of its triumph, unsullied by any act
of vengeance, hallowed by a great martyrdom.

We stood by and saw all this, and vilified and falsified
it. Facts were distorted; characters were blackened;
random predictions of failure were showered forth. With
daily false witness and with daily curses the journals
of the rich perverted their cause, and covered their
chosen chief with gibes. Above all was heard one base
tongue, which fed the ill-will of a class. Those prophecies and forecasts stand now one and all refuted by
events; those calumnies live yet unrepaired; that evil
work is repented of, but cannot be undone. And all this
was for what? The governing classes neither dared nor
could follow up the bent of their wills. The nation
could gain nothing by this system of malevolent hostility,
by ill-will carried to the verge of war. With the
reckless journals that ministered to it, it was the echo
of the cynicism that reigned in drawing-rooms and
clubs. With the governing classes it was a wild impulse
to discredit the republican ideal, and to fan a reaction at
home. With the rich in general it was partly the aping

of fashion and partly the jealousy of their rivals in trade. One and all it has discredited. It has stamped them with political fatuity.

It was not merely that the governing classes lost character as statesmen by this conduct; they brought our country to the verge of great perils and have left her there still. One who knows what a war between the English and the American race arising out of such a cause would have proved in its reality, must shudder as he looks back on what we so narrowly escaped. A faction of political desperadoes were eager to drag us, the bulk of the wealthier classes were half-willing to drift, into this fratricidal war. It would have been one of the most obstinate and perhaps the most wanton in modern history. Once begun, its course could not have been foreseen, and no man can feel sure that, against those marvellous resources, even every advantage at the outset would have given us success in the end. It could have effected no useful and no conceivable result, but to gratify class prejudice, and adjourn the downfall of Privilege at home. It would have laid a lasting burden on our people, and inflicted on them terrible sufferings in a cause from which every sympathy and interest of theirs revolted. However much perplexity and pride would at first have dragged them into the struggle, in the end they would have taken things into their own hands by force, and purchased peace by civil convulsion at home. The oppressions and the sufferings laid on us by the Coalition war would have been renewed. Again they would have been met by the rebellion of every good instinct within us, a rebellion which this time would have succeeded at whatever risk and cost.

This great peril is not yet past. The anxiety, which diplomacy and journalism undisguisedly display to recall the tone of hostility they adopted, is proof that they see at last how serious a blunder they have made. Amongst the vices of the American people a morbid national vanity is not the least conspicuous, as both we and they have by this time good reason to know. Their political system has its own corruptions; their factions are neither inactive nor scrupulous. Now that the fine spirit to which in their trial they were strung has partially died out, it is not impossible that they may be goaded into an attempt to redress the injuries they believe themselves to have endured. Every traveller comes back from America with fresh stories of the depth and extent of irritation, and the ominous symptoms which exist that at any time it may burst into action.

It is beside the purpose to apportion whose would be the greater crime in a possible rupture with the United States. It is sufficient that we all know it to be a real danger. It is also beside the purpose to show that the first blow must come from them, or that when it comes we are well prepared to meet it. The true calamity is, that war between the American and the English race is far less unlikely than it used to be. We are not safe. As a nation which has a peaceful, but most arduous future to work out for ourselves, we are darkened by the shadow of this great possible calamity. The official bearing of this country is in the hands of the same men who but just now brought us so near to a war. It is animated by the same unfriendly spirit, tempered it is true by a tardy prudence. They have learnt and forgotten nothing by six memorable years. We are not safe in their hands.

Now on this great test question the people were and are as conspicuously right as the classes who wield the political power were and are conspicuously wrong. The superior information, the trained judgment, and the freedom from passion in the name of which the educated orders claim exclusive rule, did not hinder them from falling into one long tissue of misconception and blunder on the greatest question of our times. The ignorance, the impulsiveness, the want of critical power in the mass of the people, did not prevent them from seeing the truth and resolutely clinging to the right cause. These instincts and practical sense were found to be far truer political gifts than the literary advantages of their cultured neighbours. Like most political questions, it depended on right feeling and honest purposes, not on any mental qualification whatever. They never faltered throughout the struggle in their confidence in the national cause. They saw from the first how great Lincoln was, for he was of their own blood and bone. They spun no sophistry about tariffs, nor proved out of Jomini how Grant and Sherman were being drawn from their "base" to destruction. They did not think that the President was sometimes a "baboon," and sometimes an "ignoble tyrant." They never took Mr. Spence for a philosopher, and Mr. Fernando Wood for a statesman. Throughout the working classes all this while there was no doubt and no ill-will. It is the fashion to tell us that the risk of a rupture is owing to the dominance of Democracy there. Does any one suppose there would be that risk, or would have been

that risk, were aristocracy not dominant here? The
danger arises from the desperate antipathies of our own
ruling class. The masses of both nations are one in
heart. In a thousand meetings throughout England
there has been but one voice, friendship to the American
people and sympathy with their cause. From one meeting only ever came a voice of ill-will to them, crying
for succour to their enemies—and that meeting was the
English Parliament.

We are not safe whilst these men are the official
spokesmen of a nation which disowns them, whilst
they can drag it into a peril which of all others it
dreads. In some respects the risk and discredit to
our country are even augmented by their want of more
consolidated power. If they were a dominant oligarchy
of the old class their course would be clear, recognised,
and unfaltering. The world might think it arrogant
or unjust, but it would be known that it could not
be trifled with. But they are not a dominant oligarchy.
They are only the prescriptive officials of a Liberal
nation, with strong oligarchic prejudices. They are
dominant only in the smaller matters of administration,
and in obstruction generally. In the greater question
they are under a partial and indirect control. They
can drag us into the peril, but they are not strong
enough to drag us through it. They are ever drifting
into quarrels which their false position prevents them
from maintaining.

There is another branch of our policy in which this
cross purpose between the official and the national
current is conspicuous. Whilst in Europe our foreign
tendency is irresolutely liberal, and nervously peaceful,

in the East it is enterprising and high-handed. There is no question in which we have a definite national purpose but one, and that is, the forcing our commerce on the uncivilized world. The only foreign Minister who, for two generations, has left any mark on our policy, avowed it in justification of the aristocratic *régime*, that it opened ever new markets for our merchants, and fresh employment for our workmen. It gave the first wealth, and kept the second quiet. But this policy, though still in visible ascendant, has had its death-blow, and staggers at every step. It shocks the conscience and the good sense of all thoughtful men. It is counter to the instincts of the whole body of the people. Its hold grows weaker at each effort. The protests it calls forth grow louder. It is a thing of the past.

Turn to the history of our Eastern wars, during the last generation. The infamy of the opium war of 1837 has sunk very deep into the public mind. The second Chinese war, and the third, have left a memory which grows darker, and not brighter with time. The national vanity and the class cupidity they fomented have subsided; the denunciations they met from honourable men survive. The Japanese war, in turn, aroused still louder indignation, and the class who were indignant were far more powerful. There never was a more foolish laugh than that with which the official world defended the burning of Kagosima. The working classes are seriously ashamed and weary of these things. The men of thought who move them and whom they trust, are resolved that this wicked system shall end. Mr. Bright and Mr. Mill are their undoubted leaders. Where will the

system of mercantile buccaneering be when these men
are in power? Will they be found—*bellum cauponantes*
—traders in war? Are they the men "to make commerce
flourish along with, and by means of war?" This, too,
must change. The people have rejected the bait which
so largely corrupted the middle class.

The official diplomacy in civilized Europe is the old
system, out of all harmony with the new order of things,
which the Revolution called into being, and diametrically
opposed to the popular sympathies at home : it is, therefore, weak. The official diplomacy in the uncivilized
East is the old system also, vigorous and bold, but all
the more shocking to men of right feeling, and alien to
the popular instincts. This also is, therefore, weak ;
though it is usually imperious, and sometimes fierce.
Its habit of unchaining race hatred, however, will cost
it dear. It fights coloured men by means of the blood-
hound temper of white men's pride. The ruling classes,
perhaps, hardly know how the people's conscience revolts
at every appeal to this sinister auxiliary. There is not
one of these wars but degrades Government in their
eyes for its unscrupulous use of this spirit. New Zealand wars, Hottentot wars, Burmese wars, are stamped
with the old mercantile injustice, sometimes by the
old Colonist ferocity. The tone of the ruling classes
on the case of Jamaica, where both these were combined,
has given their authority a lasting moral blow. These
things do not pass away so easily, in spite of a confident
tone. Which will live longest and work most, the sneers
of the journals over the slaughter of Gordon, or the
protest of Mr. Mill and Mr. Bright? Society asks why
Government does no more to support its own officers

against clamour. Because it would cost Government too dear. These wars cost this nation some millions, but they cost more to the Constitution. Each outrage on our sense of justice strikes away a buttress from beneath the pedestal of the governing orders.

To sum up, there is something radically wrong in our foreign policy, quite apart from any particular case, or any personal mismanagement. Both the principal and the subordinate functions of that service are usually performed with conscientious ability; and this is eminently true at this moment. But why, with able Ministers, undeniably good intentions, and unflagging public supervision, backed by the boundless forces, both moral and material, which England can exert, is the foreign policy of England thus fitful and nugatory? That it is, on the whole, few will deny. The diplomacy of Prussia issues from a close bureau; that of the United States is popular both in origin and aim. Both are strong, the one in personal, the other in national unity of purpose. Our own system is neither the one nor the other, and loses the advantages of both. Its bureaucratic and its democratic side neutralize each other. When the hour of action comes, its knees are loosened by self-distrust. And the world now knows it.

This evil is twofold. In the first place, the system is out of all harmony with the real motive forces of Europe; secondly, it is out of all harmony with true popular sympathies at home. When it gets into the European movement it grows puzzled and irresolute, and can only cover its perplexity in a cloak of fine words. When it initiates a course for itself, it has the mortification to meet irritation and resistance within. This double source of weakness has reduced the influence of England, in spite of her moral and material power, in spite of the ability and industry of her statesmen, and in spite of Parliamentary control, to the second or even the third rank among the nations of the world. The hereditary directors of our policy are as a class more blind to the spirit of this age than any other ruling order in Europe, except the Austrian and the Spanish Courts.

It cannot be too often insisted that affairs on the continent have undergone an entire transformation since the French Revolution, that the key of the situation is the solution of the problems which that movement threw up. Those who fail to comprehend this necessity are the Rip Van Winkles of politics. They are talking of ideas which two generations have disposed of. The great influence which the Emperor Napoleon wields is due, quite apart from the position of France, to his thorough conception of this. He may mistake the current of things, and the relative strength of parties, but he never commits the grand blunder of dealing with Europe now, as if it was Europe of the past. He thoroughly conceives and feels the central Revolutionary ideas. Much that is good he attacks, and much that he strives for is evil; but in the general phases of the movement he is entirely at home. This gives him a strength to which he has no other title.

This is just the point at which our official action, with excellent intentions, love of justice, and honesty of aim totally breaks down. Our statesmen have, slowly, and much to their credit, shaken off the retrograde doctrines of the Coalition. It does them honour, though it hardly justifies the preposterous glory it receives. It is true

that since the days of Canning they have ceased to
lead the van in retarding the progress of mankind. But
having cast off one evil system, they are perfectly unable to adopt a better. They have no system. They
have settled in despair into that systematic negation,
known as the policy of Non-Intervention.   The real
current of the modern world is a thing which puzzles,
baffles, and alarms them.   They will not do battle
with it; but they dare not swim with it or guide it.
They have to deal with forces which they neither like
nor understand, all making towards an end which they
dread, but cannot foresee.   The result is inevitable—
indecision, expediency, and obstructiveness.   It is one
long *Non Possumus.* Till our statesmen can grasp the
true Revolutionary movement in Europe, their action
cannot step beyond the limits of a nervous and imbecile
Conservatism.

Then there is the second source of weakness—the
want of understanding with the people at home.   Up
to a certain point, the official authorities are supreme.
They can carry on wars in India without asking any
leave of the people.   They can begin wars in Japan,
though it remains to be seen if they can always finish
them, at their own discretion.   They can threaten a war
in Europe or in America, but it is very doubtful if
they could originate one.   Thus, whilst they have the
initiative everywhere, when the pinch comes in a great
question, they cannot get the support they require.   As
they began to feel this, our policy grew timid.   As other
nations began to feel it also, it grew contemptible.   The
foreigner now is really overrating this special source of
weakness, and presuming on it too far.   He may some

s 2

day be rudely undeceived. But it has been too often established not to be perfectly notorious. The affair of Cracow in 1846 first dispelled the impression of the power and determination of England to maintain the faith of treaties. The great convulsion of '48 came, and the policy of this country was seen to be balanced between aristocratic dismay and popular enthusiasm. The people yearned to support the heroic struggles of Italy, and the yet more desperate struggles of Hungary. Their heart thrilled and groaned whilst Kossuth, Mazzini, and Garibaldi sank. One hour of a great man, one sound from no uncertain trumpet, would have done it all. But the official classes, whilst wishing well for the cause of freedom, were scared by the vision of true Republicans. They could not believe in a cause which seemed to have neither Constitution nor double Chamber. So they confined themselves to protests and speeches, and, to the bitter indignation of their own people, continued to give to the worthy intentions of our policy an air of practical treachery. In fact, it was only imbecility.

Russia was the first to find out that England was a house divided against itself. She presumed on it too far, but the whole history of that pitiable time, when Ministers, as they artlessly said, "drifted into war," showed how far she was right. The people, however, took matters for once into their own hands ; and at length, maddened by the spiritless and old-world system in vogue, were all but taking matters into their own hands in a very rough and effective way. It would not be wise to tempt them so sorely again. The Italian campaign of '59 followed, and again the ruling orders were practically Austrian, and the mass of the people heartily Italian. A retrograde Ministry was thrown out by a happy accident, and thus we were preserved from taking the wrong side at the outset. It is far from impossible that, notwithstanding this change, we might have been found on the wrong side in the end. Happily, the war was abruptly closed by the caution and self-control of Napoleon ; and we were spared the probable consequences of the incorrigible belief of the official classes in the Balance of Power, and the Austrian Alliance. The Polish war came, and again a splendid opportunity occurred to place this country in its natural position as the colleague of France in guiding the progressive movement of Europe. Again, the English people throbbed to efface one of the deepest plague-spots in Europe. It was not a case simply of war, for all Europe was with us, or could have been roused. It was, again, a case for a great man, and a grand policy. It need not be said that our governing orders had neither to produce ; and would have kept both out of sight even if they had. Accordingly France was affronted, our people were disheartened, and our country was made a laughing-stock. Then followed the Danish war. Here diplomacy saw the danger, and earnestly laboured to meet it. But it worked by the old Cabinet and dynastic system of manœuvres. The people were puzzled and disgusted. And when the official orders appealed to them for support, it was doggedly refused. English diplomacy, in fact, again with the best intentions, pursued a course which looked very like, and was very like, practical treachery. And it endured the most conspicuous humiliation which it was possible, without a war, to inflict on a great power ; a humiliation which has left England with hardly a vestige of moral weight in the councils of Europe. The part taken by our politicians in the recent war in Germany, may be passed unnoticed. It was so small and was known to be so unimportant, that it was not taken into account by the powers of Europe. It need not be taken into account by us. The Danish humiliation was too recent for it to be otherwise. It was by this time well understood that Ministers might write despatches, but that neither the purse nor the arm of England was behind them ; that the policy of her Government was addressed, not to the foreign Cabinets, but to Parliamentary parties ; that menaces in their mouths were only the innocent, or rather the innocuous, artifices of debate.

These successive questions were united by a strict and natural bond. The events of '48 and '49 led on to the Crimean war ; that had its legitimate consequence in the Italian war of '59 ; the Italian war resulted in the Polish, as did the latter in the Danish campaign in Holstein. The three together had their inevitable issue in the wars of '66. We have thus, to the thoughtful politician, a very intelligible sequence of events, all phases of one comprehensive movement. Throughout, we see the great revolutionary problem of nationalities, the re-settlement of nations in harmony with their wants, feelings, and history ; the re-casting of the State-system into the new order of things in which dynasties, balance of power, and empires, shall be unknown. In all these movements, the governing classes and the people of England were divided, and in all, the first were wrong, and the last were right. In all, the official world took the wrong side, or were helplessly inert. Where they wanted to lead, the true power would not go ; and where it wanted to go, they would not lead. They are like the half-trusted agent of a firm, who can pledge its credit, but cannot effectively command its resources. They sit like some nervous horseman on an animal of too high courage for his skill. Both man and steed know it; he frets and chafes him with the curb; reins him in at the least show of life; and when he timidly gives him his head, the indignant animal jibs. But it is poor matter for a jest. For the end of this mutual distrust must certainly be some grand disaster.

Now, how is this to end? How is this distrust and antagonism to be cured? We cannot go back. It is obviously out of the question to expect that the people will ever surrender that share of power over foreign policy which they now have; or tamely entrust it without control to its present administrators. If they did, it would be even worse than the present condition of cross purpose and unstable equilibrium. There is nothing left except to go forward, to unite the nation again by giving a practical control in affairs to the popular element which is now the unrecognised, but ultimate arbiter. In other words, we need Reform. The present House of Commons acts as a sort of vast breakwater between public opinion and the Ministers. The full tide of the national will wastes itself in vain upon that stony obstruction. The House is much less popular and less responsive to public feeling than Ministries. It often gives them the means of resisting that popular element, whose wishes it is sent to express. And whilst the House is anti-national, so, too, our foreign policy will be.

This is essentially a Parliamentary question. It is

often said that whatever is done, is done by Ministries, that Parliament shows its liberal sympathies in eloquent debates; that after all the foreign policy reflects the tone of the governing classes and the preponderating influence of society. This is perfectly true, and Ministers are generally far more attentive to public opinion than Society or the House. But the truth is, that the whole political and social interest holds together as one system. Parliament, and the House of Commons in particular, is its official organ, and its responsible Head. Its nominal character as a representative chamber enables it to give an authority and justification to the acts of Ministers, which they never could obtain directly from public opinion. In foreign questions, the House is a venerable apparatus for enabling the territorial powers to manage things nearly as they will. So long as this solemn fiction retains its hold on men's minds, they will continue to do so. And the only way of effecting an immediate change in our foreign policy, is to effect a change in that House.

What should be the nature or the measure of this Parliamentary change, need not here be considered. The broad fact on which to stand is this, that to increase, or rather to create, the influence of the people within the House of Commons, would directly modify our foreign policy. It would bring it into harmony with the progressive movement of the world, and also with the real sympathies of the nation. It would give it strength, both within and without. Had the House of Commons contained but 100 men who shared the convictions of Mr. Mill and Mr. Bright, and real representatives of the workmen of the great towns would have been such men, our official policy in the American contest would have been utterly different. Here, as in the United States, a minority, conscious of a great cause, would have determined the action of all. No Reform Bill which has yet been discussed, perhaps no measure which could be devised, would do more for the present than plant in the House about a hundred men of this stamp.

Reactionists are fond of charging the enthusiasts of Reform with the chimerical promises which they hold out as the results of Parliamentary changes. There is much justice in the charge. But they usually commit precisely the same mistake in the chimerical forebodings in which they indulge. The terrors of Reform are just as shallow as the day-dreams of Reform, and for exactly the same reason. If the modification of the constituencies cannot possibly produce the millennium which the Radicals dream of, neither can it possibly bring about the deluge which Tories " abominate." The zealots on both sides are conjuring up ghosts of their own delusions. Of this extravagance, Mr. Leicester, the glass-blower, on the one side, and Mr. Lowe, on the other, are familiar types.

Those who actually administer the policy of this country, and certainly those who administer its foreign policy, will under any Reformed House of Commons be very much the same people as those who administer it now. The great difference will be that it will be administered in a very different spirit. The immense social power of the ruling class, their special habits and training, and their historical claims, will still make them the functionaries of the diplomacy of England. The entire absence of any such class, or any such class-power, the total contrast in the history of the two countries, make all comparison between the American system and our own essentially worthless. But even if Democratic licence such as that which undoubtedly disturbs and disfigures the foreign policy of the United States, were a possible result of Reform, it would still be an immense gain to be free from the contemptible and perilous condition to which our own is reduced. Many a professional diplomatist with small interest in home politics must sigh for the organic national vitality which the American statesmen can command in dealing with foreign nations. They can at least hold their own with the statesmen of kings and emperors, notwithstanding that they are directly in contact with their people. They can do this, only because they are so. But the true comparison is not between America whose social conditions are totally different, and England which has an historic class accustomed to rule, and, if they were in a less false position, not incapable of ruling. England can only be compared with England, and the true analogy is this. The change that we want to effect by bringing the foreign policy of this country again into harmony with the will of this people is the change which for a brief space came over the nation's bearing and fame when Chatham succeeded to Newcastle, when Canning succeeded to Castlereagh.

An objection is persistently made by the new "Constitutionalist" school which it is quite essential to face. As they seek to alarm the upper classes with the loss of privilege, the manufacturing classes with interference with Free Trade, the Economists with the prospect of over-legislation, so they would terrify the middle classes

altogether with prospects of war. The manœuvre is
skilful, and the argument not without force. The great
popularity of the existing political *régime* with the middle
class undoubtedly is this, that it guarantees systematic
no-government at home, and systematic non-intervention
abroad. Beyond question to give power to the people
would be the end of that Constitutional deadlock, that
absence of responsibility, that absolutism of private
interest, and that gospel of *Non Possumus* which now
satisfies the comfortable classes. It would be extravagant to assert that the political power of the people
would involve a system of war. But it is true that
a definite and determined policy might possibly in a
critical moment lead to a decisive and short struggle.
We are not in a millennium, and this terrible necessity
might again arise. But it may arise now. It does
perpetually arise now in Asia. The great thing to
provide for is that when such a crisis comes, the
course of England shall be worthy of this nation—on
the right side, not on the wrong. Rather a policy of
honour, and of duty with all its sacrifices, than a
huckstering timidity amidst the strong, and a huckstering rapacity amidst the weak.

The condition of Europe at this moment (April, 1867),
by common consent, is truly ominous. The dying throes
of Turkey and the ambition of Russia threaten commo-
tion in the East. Germany is forming herself into a
military empire : France is vieing with her in the rivalry
of arms. No man can say from whence the greater
danger to order arises. The situation on every side is
one of morbid action and reaction—a knot of vicious
circles. The confusion in the East is such as to force

the Western Powers to constant interference; but since they act without concert, and usually from self-interest, their interference does little but aggravate the confusion. The barbaric legions of Russia weigh like an incubus on the civilization of Germany, which, by causes both direct and indirect, is forced to a development in a military form. The attempt of Germany to effect a premature unity by violent measures arouses the pride, and even the fears, of France. The unwise though natural desire of France to hold her ground in the race of armaments reacts again on all her neighbours, and especially on the military and national jealousies of Germany. Who can say from what quarter aggression may first come?— whether from France, to maintain her ancient rank in Europe, or from Germany, to justify her new preten- sions to supremacy in arms?

For an imbroglio like this there is but one sound solution. It demands a genuine alliance of England with France; an alliance of which the avowed aim should be to promote, by peaceful and moral in- fluences, the progress of Europe towards complete re- settlement, to guarantee her against simple anarchy or aggression on the East, against violent and selfish dis- turbance of the existing order. The distinct purpose of such an alliance would be to throw the whole moral and material weight of England against the actual disturber of peace, whilst throwing it on to the side of orderly and permanent resettlement. Such an alliance must be offered first to France, because the sudden aggrandize- ment and immense power of Prussia have deeply alarmed the French people, and have given them, for a time, a sense of insecurity, which is intensified by the

novelty of the danger and their apparent isolation in
Europe. The French people doubtless overrate the
danger, which, however, is not wholly unreal; but the
only way to make them feel superior to it is to offer
them the friendship of England. On the other hand,
nothing short of such an offer can give us the title to
insist that, whilst guaranteeing our neighbours against
German aggression, we leave ourselves free to guarantee
both Germany and the smaller intervening States against
aggression from France.

The alliance of England is also due to France, because,
in spite of every objection which democratic rhetoric can
urge, the French people have a firmer hold upon, and
have done more than any other people of the continent
for the principles on which alone the political and social
reconstruction of Europe can be carried out. A willing-
ness on the part of the people of England to join with
France in this policy, whilst discountenancing, and, if
necessary, resisting, all military aggression (as being,
from whatever quarter it might come, the most flagrant
violation of the common policy), would at once supply
us with the conditions of harmony and repose in Europe.
This, and this alone, would satisfy the pride and allay
the fears of France, and withdraw her from miserable
schemes to promote her military prestige. With the
most liberal, and notoriously the greatest, of the other
European Powers on her side, it would be preposterous
for her to seek security in purchased fortresses, strength
in new conscriptions, or glory in annexed provinces.
Such a policy would be, for us, in the true sense of the
word, National in result, but peaceful in its machinery.
It would be a Policy Reconstructive and Non-military,

free at once from blind conservatism and from dynastic ambition. But such a policy is simply impossible without the accession to power in England of the popular element. The present system of government is incapable of it. For, if the military *régime* endangers Order, the oligarchic *régime* is incompatible with Progress.

Our foreign policy must either go backwards or go forwards, if England is to recover her place amongst nations. The clouding of her name is due neither to accidents or occasions, nor to the faults of parties or of men. There is something radically wrong within. An autocrat like the Emperor of Russia can conduct the policy of his country towards foreign nations with consistency and efficiency. So also can an organized bureaucracy like that of Prussia, or a traditional and oligarchic court like that of Austria. A real statesman who watches and rides upon the public opinion of the masses of his countrymen, and who understands his age, can do the same, whether with the machinery of Parliamentary majorities like Cavour, or without it like the Emperor Napoleon. Still more so can a free executive, like the President of the United States, who is the organ of a people at once united and energetic. Not so a Government which is none of these, which is neither a strong aristocracy nor a popular representation, which lives by the balance of factions, which rules by sufferance, which is alien to those for whom it professes to speak, and from whom alone it can derive either dignity or strength.

IX.

BRIBERY.

BY JAMES E. THOROLD ROGERS.

The worst blemish of our Parliamentary system, we are often told, is bribery. But the tolerance or connivance which the crime of giving or offering bribes meets in the House of Commons is far worse than the corruption of electors. Men notoriously guilty of the offence, suffer no discredit if they escape conviction, and are held to be blunderers only if they are detected; for the knowledge that a man has obtained his seat by bribery carries with it no social reproach.

The gift and the receipt of a bribe are not the only hindrances which intrigue puts in the way of a free Parliament, a true reflex of public opinion. The end of representation is equally frustrated by coercion, by the machinery of a precarious but beneficial occupation of agricultural land, by the easy servility of traders or shop-keepers, by the cabals of Parliamentary agents, and by the trick of casting election expenses on the candidates. When the House of Commons discusses bribery, and cognate malpractices, it does not visit the offence, except capriciously, on the real culprit, the man who offers the bribe, but contents itself with declaiming on the immorality and corruption of constituencies.

But it is impossible to believe that the House is in earnest, when it professes horror at the practices which in one shape or other have seated more than half its members. It has never cared for the disinfectants by which a purer atmosphere might be created ; it has itself increased corruption by the Conveyance of Voters Act. Any expedient which enlarges the cost of elections, and supplies the elector with the means of recording his suffrage at the charges of the candidate, is a form of bribery. Such too is the character of all arrangements, which give the rich man an advantage in elections over the man of moderate means ; for, so far, they make wealth and not ability the test of fitness for legislative functions.

The majority of the House of Commons is seated either by bribery, or by profuse expenditure. The revelations at Yarmouth, Lancaster, Reigate and Totnes, are only a small part of that which is known familiarly among agents. In many small boroughs it is not the practice to petition even against notorious bribery, because it is known that exposure would lead to disfranchisement. But much of that horror which is expressed or implied in Parliament at the corruption of the towns whose delinquencies have been described in detail, is mere affectation. Men buy a seat as effectually, though not quite as openly, as they do an estate or a sum in Consols. Some people whose candour is excessive, boldly defend the practice. The advocates of nomination boroughs can hardly condemn it, for it is the strongest outwork of the existing oligarchy. They treat it as one of the safeguards to what the Queen's Speech calls, confidently enough, the balance of political power; though how a monopoly can be "a balance," it is difficult to explain.

Again, even though there be no evidence of direct bribery, the charges of elections, especially in counties, are enormous. The average cost in each of the twenty-six contested county elections to the present Parliament was nearly 12,000l., a charge which completely excludes any but the very wealthy from competition, and indisposes even the most wealthy from contemplating a dissolution with any other feeling than disgust. As a consequence, the tranquillity of many counties is rarely disturbed by a political conflict, and in most cases an arrangement is entered into between the landowners, for the purpose of preventing a dispute which might impair the fortunes or endanger the return of sitting members.

The influence of the great landowners is generally secured by precarious but beneficial tenancies. A leaseholder can scarcely be dependent on his landlord. It is difficult, however, for a tenant from year to year to be independent, since he can hardly migrate from his farm without a loss. And if a tenant at will who rents land at its full value finds himself unable to exercise his own discretion at an election, how much more passive must they be, who barter their vote for a beneficial holding? It is notorious that political influence is maintained in many counties by that form of bribery which makes it a tenant's interest to please his landlord, a tenant's loss to thwart him.

The payment of the expenses of elections by candidates

t

is as unconstitutional as the expenses are excessive. In early times elections were undoubtedly conducted at the charge of the constituencies, who also paid wages to their representatives. Public opinion has extinguished the practice of paying salaries to Members of Parliament, chiefly, it may be presumed, because there is an impression that a trustee should not be hired, even when the duty is unwillingly undertaken. It would be thought, for example, indecent, if the office of a juryman were paid handsomely. Such a service is part of the claim which society may justly make on the time and capacity of its members. But no man is constrained to be a Member of Parliament; and it is contrary to the public interest that any man should make Parliamentary life his profession, or the source of his maintenance. Yet, though one may call on the man who offers to serve the public as a legislator to do so gratuitously, it cannot be expected that he will assume the office at great charge to himself, and then fail to reimburse himself for his outlay, either in improving his own fortunes, or in promoting the interests of his own order.

But the Legislature has not only sanctioned the practice of putting on the candidate the charge of elections, and, in cases of notorious bribery, those of a Commission of Inquiry on the nation; it has also increased those charges by direct enactments. Nothing can justify, on public grounds at least, the Conveyance of Voters Act. If it be admitted that infirm or indolent voters should be carried to the poll (and there are far cheaper ways by which their suffrage might be recorded), nothing can be alleged in favour of transferring the charge of this service from the constituency in whose interest they are supposed to vote, to the candidate, who should have at heart not his own interest, but the general good of his constituents and the community. The result, if not the purpose of the Act, has been to cripple the choice of constituencies, by narrowing the field of candidates. All the laws and customs which permit elections to be matters of expense to candidates, are direct encouragements of bribery. They familiarize the minds of candidates, agents, electors, and the public at large, with profuse and reckless expenditure. People have come to look upon a Member of Parliament as necessarily a rich man, and a rich man who has undertaken to spend his money freely. Illegitimate follows "legitimate" expenditure. When elections are accompanied by vast expenditure on the part of the candidates, the more ignorant or less scrupulous electors naturally think that a part of what is spent ought to enrich themselves. Even contributions to local charities have become a form of bribery. If it is desired to destroy this deeply-rooted cancer of our politics, even these should cease—at least for a time. Is there any reason why high-minded men of large means should not agree to deny themselves the satisfaction of contributing to the charities of the place they represent, so long as their benevolence serves to justify a great evil?

The personal canvas of electors almost necessitates bribery. There is no reason why electors should have any other intercourse with candidates, than such as is afforded by the speeches and the interrogatories of a public meeting. Electors who need to be personally argued into voting for Mr. A. or Mr. B. had better not vote at all. When Parliament is really resolved to put down bribery, it will forbid the employment of agents altogether.[1]

Far wiser than the Conveyance of Voters Act would have been an enactment that no contract entered into for the payment of election expenses should be pleaded or maintained in a court of law. To compare what should be with what is :—Lord Ranelagh was lately cast in a suit for the expenses of the inchoate contest of Middlesex. It seems that he never was actually a candidate. It is averred that he sacrificed a seat elsewhere, in obedience to the suggestions of his party. The Court lamented his case, suggested that his club had been shabby, and gave a verdict against him. In other words, they recognised an association compared with which no trade union could be equitably condemned. The common law, we are told, is hostile to maintenance and champerty; but a club may maintain a political suit in defiance of the public interests, and the *campi partitio* is in this case a conspiracy against a free Parliament, and an intrigue for the redistribution of offices.

The House has shown in other ways its reluctance to detect and punish bribery. The decisions of its Committees in contested elections are capricious, partial, and attended with enormous expenses. Among the oaths and declarations which it exacts from its Members, it has never inserted one which would be worth all the rest,—that by which the Member should declare that he has not been seated by money payments, by promises,

---

[1] It is worth while to state, that in the election of burgesses for the Universities, the candidates never address the constituency, much less canvass their supporters.

or by indirect influences. An oath is probably not a very powerful sanction ; but if a competent tribunal for the trial of elections were appointed, an anticipation of the infamy of perjury, and the penalties which would be levied on convicted candidates, might make men afraid to bribe. But it is idle to expect a just scrutiny of elections from Committees of the House of Commons itself.

A long time has passed away since the interests of freedom required that the House should insist on taking cognizance of disputed returns. The judicial functions of Parliament had their meaning and their justification, while the contest lay between the Crown and the representatives of the people. It is now a century and a half since the Crown has interposed its veto,—nearly a century since it has intrigued in elections. Tradition has confined the monarch to social functions, and debarred him from immediate political action. There is no longer any reason why the nation, which is most interested in the choice of representatives, should not sit by deputy on the qualifications of those who have been elected.

Temporary judges of elections could be found among that class of lawyers which supplies revising barristers. There is, indeed, no absolute necessity that they should be lawyers at all, though it would be far more convenient that they should be. Perhaps, however, the dignity of the House of Commons would require that such investigations should be conducted by judges of the superior courts. Those against whom bribery has been proved, should be treated as misdemeanants ; and, if they have taken the oath denying bribery, should be made liable to the penalties of perjury, and, in all cases, to some of the consequences of legal infamy. In the course of time, and in the event of other remedial measures being adopted, these judges would be rarely invited to fulfil their functions. Were vigorous means taken to repress bribery, the practice would soon be eradicated.

But there are two other remedies which should be adopted, fully and immediately. Without them, no guarantee can be given for the purity of elections, for the legitimate development of a representative system. With them, the necessity for a widely extended suffrage is less urgent, though the grant of it would be almost immediate. These are, the transfer of all electoral expenses from the candidate to the constituency, and the adoption of the ballot in the act of voting.

As is the case with nearly every Reform in our representative system which is now demanded, an enactment that the charges of elections should be borne by the constituencies, would be merely the restoration of one among the many landmarks of the English constitution, which have, at some time or other, been removed. The travelling expenses, and the wages of knights and burgesses, were legally demandable for centuries after the Parliaments of Edward I. It is absurd to suppose that these personages were mulcted with any charges at their election.

But in urging the propriety of this Reform, there is no need to appeal to antiquarian researches, or to the history of mediæval Parliaments. The intrinsic advantages of the change are sufficiently manifest. The line which separates the legal charges now levied on the candidate, from the illegal payment of money or money's worth for votes, is seen to be almost imperceptible, whenever an attempt is made to state the principle on which the distinction rests. The law which mulcts the candidate in the payment of travelling expenses, operates as a barrier against the admission of men whose capacity for the public service may be large, but whose means are too small for the required outlay. In the public interest the continuance of such a charge is indefensible. Equally indefensible is the law which divides among the rival candidates the cost of hustings and polling clerks, and the other machinery of elections. The purpose of an election is, not to give social rank and political power to an individual, but to obtain the honest and diligent performance of an office of great trust. It is impossible to believe that when the cost of selecting a public servant is paid by the person selected, his service will satisfy the trust reposed in him.

But the existing practice makes bribery familiar, venial, shameless. Political morality needs far stricter sanctions than even private duty, because its obligations are weakened by distribution, and only occasionally brought into notice. Our electoral system, instead of awakening the public conscience, encourages a casuistry which is no better than a trap. Why, indeed, if some part of the charge of being returned, not a little of which is voluntarily incurred, can be legally demanded from the candidate, should not other kinds of voluntary expenditure be tolerated ? In the days when this country attempted to defeat the protective tariffs of other countries by encouraging smuggling, it was adopting a policy which stimulated the practice of smuggling into the United Kingdom. An expedient which was held to be almost

patriotic when used against the revenue of other governments, was with difficulty conceived to be immoral, when
the operation was extended to the revenue of our own
Government. And similarly it needs a nice sense of
comparison, to detect a difference between laying a
mulct on the candidate, applauding subscriptions to local
charities, permitting an agent's house to be a relieving
office for needy or importunate electors, allowing a
sportula after the election is over; and downright
bribery. If, however, the payment of any sum, however
small, towards the expenses of an election were made
illegal, it would be easy to define the practice which the
House of Commons denounces in words, and virtually
sustains.

The vast cost of an election explains the continuance
of the Septennial Act. Many political thinkers have held
that this Act gives too long a duration to the representative's office. It is true that, on an average, Parliaments do not last much longer than the three years'
term which was once their legal tenure. This indirect
limitation has been rendered necessary, because, in the
ordinary course of things, a Parliament which has been
sitting some years becomes unmanageable or negligent.
But the cost of elections enables the Minister to use the
power of dissolution in controlling the votes of Members
who cannot afford to be independent, because they shrink
from the expenses of a fresh election. A dissolution
should take place, or not take place, as the interest of
the country demands ; and the interest of representatives
should neither hasten nor retard it. Many of those who
voted against Reform in the last session, are supposed to
have been influenced by the dread of a fresh election.

Indeed, Members were found candid enough to acknowledge this motive in their vacation speeches.

A dissolution of Parliament does not imply, under
our existing arrangements, any general appeal to the
country. In the case of the nomination boroughs, the
dissolution is a farce. The charges of a contested election
in boroughs are large, but not necessarily oppressive. In
the counties a contest is enormously costly. It has been
observed, that in the twenty-six counties, or divisions of
counties, in which a contest did occur at the last general election, the average admitted charge was nearly
12,000l.[1] With such a prospect, there is a dearth of
candidates ; there are conventions between the leading
families ; and an attempt to disturb the sitting Members
which no one would deny to be a public right, is in
practice considered to be a private wrong. Hence,
political feeling is almost extinct in the counties ; and
since the expense of the conflict equals a small fortune,
the great landowners control the counties completely,
partly by coercion, not a little by the barrier which the
cost of a contest opposes to a free Parliament. It is
probable, that this narrowing of the field of competition
is just as effectual a protection to the political power of
the great landowners, as their direct influence over the
tenant farmers. Were the Chandos clause repealed,

---

[1] There were 56 county-seats contested at the general election of 1865.
I have seen the returns of the election expenses of only 50 of these. They
amount to 291,836l. ; the average charge for each seat being 5,836l. Allowing this amount for the six seats the returns for which I have not seen, the
total amount of the election expenses incurred in respect of the 56 county-
seats contested at the last general election, is 326,852l. The rateable value of
the contested counties is 22,274,293l., that of the uncontested counties is
37,421,208l. The total rateable value of all the counties (contested and uncontested) is 59,695,501l.

but the charges of a contest still laid upon the candidates, it is not probable that any great change would ensue.

The only objection which could be alleged against laying the cost of an election on the constituency, is that it would encourage contests, and stimulate the ambition of a far larger number of candidates.   In itself, a contest is no evil.   But small as would be the burden of an election, when distributed among the ratepayers, it would still be felt ; and, while sitting Members who have given satisfaction would be safe, the constituency would discourage needless conflicts.   Besides, means could easily be devised for checking an unwarranted candidature, even if public opinion in the several constituencies were not sufficiently energetic for the purpose.   Honest men do not make up their minds as to the rival merits of candidates on the day of election, still less when the conclusion of the polling is at hand ; and it is not difficult, if an election be pure, to anticipate the difference between reasonable chances of success and a hopeless attempt.

But the advantages—those, namely, of a larger supply of qualified candidates, and the discouragement of corruption—are great and manifest.   The man who buys his seat does something more than debauch certain venal electors.   The constituency for which he sits is not represented ; the votes of some other constituency really represented, are neutralized.   Besides, a man who sits by corruption, is likely to use his vote for private ends.   The like objections apply, though with less force, to those who sit by large though legal outlay. Put the expenses on the constituency, and the choice is sure to be free.   When compared with a chargeable

election, a free seat is vastly more likely to be occupied
in the public interest.

If all the charges incurred by the candidates for the
counties, during the last general election, were not only
legitimate, but incapable of reduction ;—if we cannot, for
example, look for the repeal of the Conveyance of Voters
Act, or the reduction of the charge of agencies ; if it
could be shown that every penny spent in these county
elections was not only legal, but necessary ;—the cost
when distributed over the rateable property of the contested counties, would have been comparatively slight.
It amounts to about $3\frac{1}{2}d.$ in the pound. Now, the
levy of such a rate once in four or five years is no great
sacrifice for the advantages of a free Parliament, for the
liberation of the counties from the control of noblemen
and squires. It would be money well laid out if it
awakened the landed interest (by which I mean not
the landowners only, but the various classes who are
engaged in agricultural operations) to a regard for their
own interests ; now indirectly represented at best, and
often neglected or compromised for the sake of a small
section of the community. If the whole charges of the
county elections of 1865 were collected by a rate from
all the counties contested and uncontested, they would
amount to about three-halfpence in the pound.

It is not enough that the charge of a contested election
should be borne by the constituencies : in order to secure
a free election, it is necessary that they should bear the
cost of disputing a return, when there is *primâ facie*
evidence of corruption or violence. Corruption and violence are crimes, because they interfere with the lawful
exercise of admitted rights; and therefore, in accord-

ance with the general rules of municipal law, the criminal should, if possible, pay the charges of prosecution if his guilt is established. Once make it the interest of constituencies to put down bribery, and with the aid of the law they will do it. With the fear of a rate before them, they would be vigilant enough. Men who smile at bribery now, would be urgent to annihilate it, if it bore unpleasant consequences on detection.

The second remedy is the Ballot. The objections to this method of recording the franchise are either trivial or ill-founded. It is said that secret voting is not an English practice. On the contrary, the practice is all but universal, open voting being adopted in Parliamentary elections only. It is said that it leads to a reticence on political questions; whereas, on the contrary, men are much more likely to discuss and decide on public questions openly, when there is no fear that the vote they may give at the poll will be watched. It is said that it would be an advantage to dishonest electors only, who would promise one candidate and vote for another. What of this? The promise would be made, under such circumstances, to such candidates only as are suspected of a wish to force or corrupt the elector. It is doubtful whether men would waste time, even in small constituencies, in canvassing such doubtful electors; and even if they did, it does not seem that it is an unpardonable sin to elude an impertinent or malicious querist. At all events, the impossibility of ascertaining whether a promise had been kept would discourage canvassing; and canvassing is one of the greatest evils of our electoral practice.

But of all the arguments alleged against the use of the

Ballot, *i. e.* the rule that the act of voting shall be secret, the most completely unsound is that which avers the franchise to be a trust, and adds, that a trust should be exercised with all conceivable publicity. In the language of logicians, both major and minor premisses are false. The franchise is not a trust, and it does not follow that if it were, it should be exercised openly.

To constitute a trust, it is necessary that the trustee should act always and entirely for the benefit of another. His trust is vitiated, if he has any personal interest in that for which he has been constituted a trustee. There is no better example of a trust than the office of a juryman. If it can be shown that he has an interest in the acquittal or condemnation of the person put into his charge, he is peremptorily and at once disqualified for the office. If it could be proved after conviction and sentence, that a juryman had interested motives, it would be sufficient cause for setting aside the verdict, and annulling the process. The duty of such a trustee, as of every trustee, is to exercise a discretion uninfluenced by prejudice or interest. His office is absolutely incompatible with passion, fear, self-interest, sympathy, —the host of feelings which are stirred up when political debate occupies men's attention.

The franchise is not a trust, but a property, which forms part of full citizenship. It is a means for bringing the opinion of the elector to bear indirectly upon public policy, since the vastness of modern societies makes it impossible that he should exercise a direct suffrage. But it would be extravagant to assert that the opinion an elector may form of what is good for the State is not, or that it ought not to be, largely coloured by his opinion of what is good for himself, or for those in whose welfare he is more immediately interested. Where his own interest and that of the State appear not to coincide, a sense of duty will sometimes lead the voter to prefer the public interest; but the selfish vote of a minority is more commonly corrected by the no less selfish vote of a majority. However this may be, the "public opinion" to which the practice of open voting makes the voter responsible, is, if not the opinion of a landlord or of a master, the opinion of a crowd as selfish as himself, and more tyrannical. Free discussion is the surest source of honest voting. And free discussion is rather helped than hindered by the ballot.

Even, however, if the trust were ever so sacred and disinterested, it does not follow that it should be exercised publicly. I have already alluded to the function of a juryman. The suffrages of a jury are gathered secretly, and any gossip about the views taken by individual jurymen would, if traceable to the person who circulated it, be held to be a breach of decorum, if nothing worse. It is doubtful, indeed, whether juries could be induced to act, unless their voting were allowed to be secret. It is plain, too, that the rule—peculiar, I believe, to English criminal law—that a jury must be unanimous, is an incidental, and not an essential condition of the method in which they deliver their suffrages.

So with examiners. The office of an examiner in the Universities is a trust of a very serious kind. But, in one at least of the Universities, examiners vote secretly in the distribution of honours, and, as far as the outer world is concerned, in elections to scholarships and fellowships. It has never been said, although much has been charged against the method of election in these cases, that the secrecy which attends it is an evil. Above all, secret voting, apart from the check that it puts on illicit practices, has the inestimable advantage of securing on a most solemn occasion decency and quiet. Excited as public opinion often is in the United States, the polling-booth is undisturbed by violence and law-lessness. The Ballot reduces the power of dominant parties, and gives depressed interests the chance of a hearing. No community which once adopts the Ballot abandons it. In English elections a clamorous, and often lawless crowd surrounds the polling-place, and intimidates every voter on the unpopular side. Where the voting is secret, such a crowd will not be collected, because it can learn nothing from the silent process by which the vote is recorded. The debate which leads to a political conviction may be, indeed always will be, open ; the record of that conviction may be, and should be, silent. The objection, that voting should be open, because the elector exercises his privilege on the part of the unenfranchised, may be a good argument for extending the franchise. But the riot and intimidation which attend ordinary elections are conclusive reasons for adopting an expedient which checks the violence of mobs, because it offers no object for attack.

So grave are the evils which attend not only corruption and intimidation, but the very show of political partisanship at the hustings, so imperceptible is the line which separates legal from illegal expenditure, that the best fruits of Parliamentary Reform will be lost, unless the change be rapidly followed by an Act which puts all expenses on the rates, and protects not the voter only, but the suffrage by the ballot. With these remedies, the privilege of the franchise may be safely conceded; without them, the refusal of the franchise is only more dangerous than its concession. If the Conservative party, which supported Sir Rainald Knightley's resolution, and the Liberal party, which has always affected the strongest sympathies with electoral purity, are honest in their professions, the change will be made; and a true reform in the representation effected. Without them, there is risk that the widest suffrage may only mean a fresh barrier to capacity and intelligence, a new buttress to bare wealth; and the distribution of seats, a mere shuffle of the cards.

X.

THE PROGRESS OF THE WORKING CLASSES.

BY J. M. LUDLOW AND LLOYD JONES.

[The following pages form part of an Essay written, at the request of the Editors, for the present collection. The writers found it impossible to do justice to the importance and the extent of their subject in the space that had been reserved for them : and their work has accordingly assumed proportions better suited for independent publication.[1] Under these circumstances they have liberally given permission to the Editors to make such extracts as appeared most necessary for the purpose of this volume.

One of the writers of the Essay was, in the year 1832, a working man in Manchester, having already wrought at his trade (then a highly paid one) in the south of Ireland and in Dublin. In the course of the following years, he had occasion to travel through the whole of Lancashire and the surrounding counties, and subsequently to visit almost every large town in England and Scotland, residing for some time in Leeds and Glasgow, as well as in London, and mixing everywhere with the most energetic and active-minded members of the working class.]

INFLUENCE OF THE WORKING CLASSES ON LEGISLATION AND POLICY, 1832—1867.

THE questions which test most closely the intelligent forethought of the working people of Great Britain, and prove most clearly the value to the country of their power

[1] The whole essay will shortly be published by Messrs. Strahan.

u

in influencing the course of legislation, are those which
have originated amongst themselves, and which have been
carried to a practical solution chiefly by their exertions.
The question of Factory Labour is a strong case in point.
Under the old system, children and women were worked
in the factories sometimes twelve, sometimes fourteen,
and sometimes even more than sixteen hours a day ; and
notwithstanding the dreadful effects of this continued
drudgery visible in many ways, the employers as a
class believed that any interference, come from whom
it might, to check or modify such a practice, would inevitably end in the destruction of the cotton trade.
Those who remember the short-time agitation, and who
were so far mixed up with it as to understand the
spirit in which it was carried on, cannot have forgotten
the determined hostility of the factory owners to that
measure.[1]   The few men from outside the working class
who engaged on the side of the latter in this struggle,
were regarded by the employers with a most intense
dislike.   The present Earl of Shaftesbury—then Lord
Ashley,—John Fielden, Michael Thomas Sadler, Richard
Oastler, and some others fought nobly in this cause, and,
for their disinterested and unflagging labours, deserve
to be gratefully remembered.   But as Inkerman has been
called " the soldiers' battle," so the credit of this arduous
conflict, ending as it did, triumphantly, belongs in the

---

[1] It is impossible at the present day to read without a smile, in the Parliamentary Debates of 1832-3, the speeches of the opponents of factory
legislation—including some whose names we will not be cruel enough to quote
—so lugubrious are the prophecies they contain of certain ruin to the country
if measures should be passed, which have since been followed by a tide of
unparalleled prosperity.   In short, were it not for differences of name, one
would fancy it was Messrs. Creed and Williams descanting on the proximate
ruin of the iron trade in 1866-7.

sacrifices it called for, as well as in the blessings it has brought to the community, to the working men of England.

The question was taken up warmly by men engaged in every kind of labour. The factory operatives themselves were, indeed, for a long time far more apathetic— nor can this be wondered at when the facts of their degraded condition are remembered—than those belonging to other branches of industry, who were drawn into the agitation more by their sympathies than by their interests. These men gave their money, their time, and their energies, to the forwarding of this question, not because they themselves suffered directly from the evils of factory work, but because they saw around them the dreadful havoc it was making. But as the agitation went on, it gradually took in large numbers of the factory people.

As early as February 1, 1832, Mr. Sadler presented a petition from 10,000 operatives of Leeds, chiefly employed in the factories, praying the House of Commons to adopt some means for limiting the duration of the labour of children so employed, and numerously-signed petitions were in the course of the same session presented from almost all the chief factory centres,—from Bradford, a petition with 9,000 or 10,000 ; from Huddersfield, one with 10,000 ; from the workers in the power-loom factories in Glasgow, one signed by between 6,000 and 7,000 in two days ; besides the monster petitions of 130,000 and 138,000, presented by Mr. Sadler and Lord Morpeth ; the latter, however, in particular, signed to a great extent by persons belonging to the agricultural population of Yorkshire.   In the next session these numbers increased.

Bradford sent 12,000 signatures in place of 9,000 or 10,000 ; Leeds, 16,000 instead of 10,000. After Lord Ashley had taken charge of the question, he declared (June 3, 1833) that "he had just as much right to say that he was empowered to speak the sense of the operatives, as any honourable members had a right to say that they were empowered to speak by their constituents. Delegates had been sent to him from the manufacturing districts on the subject, and they had been as fairly elected as any member had been by any constituency. . . . Four delegates were in London who had been elected (the vote having been taken by universal suffrage) by the operatives of the West Riding of Yorkshire and Lancashire." In vain were the workers assured by those who opposed them that short hours would bring short wages, that their children would be compelled to run in idleness about the streets, and that women who then earned good wages would find themselves without the means of decent and comfortable sustenance ; and, above all, that foreign competition would, to a certainty, drive the cotton trade of the country into the hands of continental rivals, whose operations were not interfered with by the unreasonable outcries of misled mobs.

To these assertions the working men paid little regard. If need were, they declared that they would take the smaller wages ; but they were determined, whatever became of the cotton trade, to rescue their wives and children from the excessive toil that was killing them.[1] Upon one occasion, they exhibited the factory children

---

[1] See, for instance, Mr. Sadler's speech of February 10, 1832, in which he said "he had been before numerous meetings, some of them attended by 20,000 individuals, when the question had been broadly put to them ; namely, will you consent to a diminution of wages ?"

in a great street procession just as they left their work,—
stunted, distorted, and pale as spectres ; a sight amongst
the saddest ever seen on this earth since labour became
a duty of life.

This procession of factory children took place one
Saturday afternoon, on the occasion of a visit from
Oastler and Sadler to Manchester. As it passed along,
the people who lined the sides of the streets seemed awe-
struck ; and when at Peterloo, where they were to be
addressed by the two gentlemen named, they struck up
a hymn, asking God to bless those who were labouring
on their behalf, their plaintive voice sounded like an
appeal to the Great Father to deliver them from the
crushing oppression under which they suffered. On
hearing this, men and women burst into tears, and, though
delayed for years, from that hour the short-time Bill was
safe.

   *   *   *   *   *

The protective legislation as to mines and collieries
has followed pretty much the same course as that relating
to factories. It cannot be said that it originated in the
efforts of the miners themselves as a class ; otherwise the
shocking state of things which was disclosed by Lord
Ashley in 1842, could never have subsisted unheeded.
But from the moment that a way of improvement was
opened by the first Mines' Inspection Act, the men made
the question their own, so that great as has been the
influence exerted by the working class on factory legislation, it has from that time been perhaps even greater
upon mining legislation ; whilst, owing to the wide
divergence of habits which generally separates the under-
ground from the surface worker, that influence has had to

be almost exclusively exercised by the class affected alone. The Mines' Inspection Act of 1860, for instance, may be considered to have been the work of the miners themselves. We have before us the "Report of the Delegates of the Amalgamated Association of Miners of Lancashire, Cheshire and Yorkshire, upon the means of obtaining the Improved Mines' Inspection Bill, 1860 ; " which shows that, the former Act expiring in 1860, the men took time by the forelock, met in conference at Leeds, 9th to 12th November, 1858, at Ashton-under-Lyne, 2nd to 7th May, 1859, drew up a form of petition for an improved Act, appointed a council to obtain signatures and conduct the general business, fixed upon a treasurer, and arranged for an amalgamated fund to meet expenses ; that addresses were issued, information obtained and circulated, meetings held, delegates sent to London in July 1859, and again on the 19th February, 1860, who first obtained from the Home Office the bringing forward of a new Bill, then watched that Bill through its whole progress, through both Houses, until it finally obtained the Royal Assent, August 28th, when they left London. " In the afternoon and evening," they say, "often into morning, the delegates were in the House of Commons, explaining their case and reasoning with the opposition, *so that in hot weather and bad atmosphere, after miles of walking and hours of standing, they were so weary as to long for the pit, the pick, and home again."* And although they could not get all they asked, yet they obtained an Act which, say they, " is a decided advance upon the old one, and, if fairly worked, will prove of incalculable physical and social advantage to the operative miners in future "—the cost of the Act to the operatives, the delegates tell us, amounting to nearly 900*l.*

The Bakehouses Act is also the result of many years' agitation of the subject by the class affected.

*   *   *   *   *

A whole group of enabling Acts expressly state that they are passed only to regulate or encourage existing forms of activity. Clearly the legislation embodied in these Acts has been anticipated by the spontaneous efforts of the working class. The Building Society, the Co-operative Society, the Friendly Society, are not the creations of Parliament, but the working man's own creations. Each has had—as the Trade Society, the Arbitration Council, is having now—a pre-parliamentary history, culminating or to culminate in some blue-book or blue-books of a Select Committee, which ends by recognising the fact that the institution exists, and has succeeded in maintaining itself outside of the law, and deserves or requires to be brought within it. And in every instance, we believe, in which these Acts have been amended, delegates have been empowered or sent up by the group of bodies affected by such amendment, who have conferred with the Government or with private members on the subject, and, when belonging to the working class, as they generally have done, have never failed to impress those with whom they came in contact with a high sense of their shrewdness and business capacity.

*   *   *   *   *

It is more difficult to measure the influence which the working classes have exercised over legislation of a more general character, or over general policy. That influence has often been exerted in ways of which few are cognizant.

Take the following fact, which has never been mentioned in print, and is probably known to very few but those who, like the writer, were actors in it :—When the first grant of 30,000*l.* was proposed by the Government for educational purposes, it was regarded as the narrow end of a very dangerous wedge by many ; especially by those who dreaded the strengthening of any influence not exercised by themselves. A certain section of the Church party in Manchester called a meeting in the Corn Exchange, to oppose the Government proposal.. Canon Wray presided, and the Rev. Hugh Stowell was one of the leading speakers. A body of working men, favourable to national education, having taken the matter into consideration, decided that their views should be represented. To this end each of them agreed to go to one of the shops where the tickets for the meeting were to be had, and get as many as they could. In this way they secured considerably above one-half the tickets, and quietly distributed them amongst safe men in certain large workshops, with instructions to attend in their " go-to-meeting" clothes. They did so ; and to the astonishment of the chairman and the speakers, decorously and quietly, without speech-making or amendment-moving, negatived all the resolutions except the vote of thanks to the chairman, and then dispersed and went to their homes as quietly as if nothing particular had happened. So far as the writer is aware, the conveners of the meeting never knew how their intended "pronouncement" against State-aid to education was defeated. But it was owing to the good sense of a number of working men that Manchester was saved the obloquy of declaring against a measure, of which all its then clerical opponents lived to avail themselves, and which they also, we would fain trust, lived to feel heartily ashamed of having opposed.

The war against the compulsory newspaper stamp, again, was one which, though it might be led by the publishers, could never have been carried to its eventual triumph without the rank and file of working men, always ready to support the unstamped newspapers. Much interesting matter might be supplied as to the heartiness with which many working men threw themselves into this crusade, hawking about the cheap papers at the peril of imprisonment, which was often no idle one.

To pass on to other questions, it is certain that, at a time when the working men of England had, God knows, grievances enough of their own to complain of, they never turned a deaf ear to pleadings for the rights of the African slave ; that anti-slavery meetings were always largely attended by the working class. In 1839-40, when an attempt was made by the British India Society to popularize the subject of Indian reform, a lively and intelligent interest in the subject was manifested by the working men in all large towns in which it was ventilated, and that interest has never wholly passed away.[1] In the agitation for the repeal of the Corn-laws again, notwithstanding the opposition of the Chartist body, and of some of their most trusted leaders (such as Richard Oastler), who were sincerely wedded to Protection, the working classes took a large part. Besides their " Working Men's Anti-Corn-Law Societies," numbers of them were

---

[1] At a sea-side town last autumn one of the writers of this paper found the secretary and shopman of a Co-operative store more alive to the horrors of the Orissa famine than nineteen-twentieths of the persons he is in the habit of meeting.

enrolled members of the League, and filled its meetings in hall and theatre, whilst the pen of their own Ebenezer Elliott gave the stamp of poetry to the cause.

But there is one crowning instance, fresh still in all our memories, in which the working classes may be said to have decided the policy of the country, when the voice of the people proved truly to be the voice of God.

At the time when every evil influence under heaven seemed combined to force England into abetting the slaveholders' secession, when famine and blockade-runners' profits, the French despot and the *Times*, the country party and the ship-owners, Mr. Carlyle and half the piety of England, were urging us on a course which all now feel would have been one of headlong and ruinous folly, the working men of Lancashire stood firm and fast to the holy principle of human freedom. Sublimely patient, far-seeing beyond speculators and statesmen, they could meet in the midst of their own deep distress, caused by the continuance of the war, to congratulate Abraham Lincoln on his proclamation of emancipation; and, when any expression of sympathy with the cause of the Union was sure to meet with fierce scorn or self-complacent derision in the House of Commons, as well as on every " 'Change" throughout the country, they never wavered in their firm faith of its ultimate triumph.

USE MADE BY THE WORKING CLASSES OF IMPROVED LEGISLATION.

We have now to prove by facts that the improved legislation of the last thirty-four years has not been a dead letter,—that the working classes have known how to avail themselves of it, for their own benefit and for that of all classes of the community. To any thinking mind, the growth of general prosperity is sufficient to prove the fact.

But let us examine the question more in detail. Take first the Factories Acts, and their results.

The common prediction of the opponents of those Acts was that they would reduce wages, that they would diminish production, and that the workers would throw away the leisure afforded to them. The exact contrary has happened; wages and production have increased, and a very large number of the workers at least have known how to make excellent use of their leisure.

The wages of factory hands, in fact, rose in the years between 1844 and 1860 from ten to twenty per cent. The number of spindles at work in the fifteen years, between 1850 and 1865, increased from 17,099,231 in the former period, to 30,387,267 in the latter. The number of yards of cotton cloth produced in 1830, when factory owners worked all the hours they thought proper without remonstrance or restriction, was 914,773,563; whilst in 1860, thirteen years after the ignorant operatives and "sentimentalists" had tied their hands, they produced 4,431,281,728, an increase of 384 per cent.

In the case of the Factories Acts, a measure recommended by every consideration of humanity and justice was successfully carried into practical operation by the efforts of the working men in the manufacturing districts, assisted by a few benevolent and enlightened Parliamentary leaders, in opposition to all that power, wealth, and position could bring to bear against it; and this measure, instead of bringing injury to any class, has been a blessing and a profit to all concerned.

We do not for a moment wish to give the Factories Acts credit for the whole value of these results, which are undoubtedly due in a great measure to other reforms of the period above enumerated, and in particular to the Repeal of the Corn-laws, and the general improvement of our fiscal system. But it is undeniable that the rise in wages, the increase in production, and the development of protective legislation have proceeded simultaneously; that the one has not hindered the other.

A result, however, which is more directly traceable to protective legislation, has been the improvement in the health of the workers. The most cheering evidence to this effect is contained in a paper by Mr. Robert Baker, one of Her Majesty's Inspectors of Factories, " On the Physical Effects of diminished Labour." [1]

" There is," he says, " a gross increase of workers of 92 per cent. ; the increase of females being 131 per cent., and nearly as many children as there were formerly ; *and yet all the diseases which were specific to factory labour in* 1832 *have as nearly as possible disappeared.* We seldom or never now see a case of in-knee or of flat-foot ; occasionally one of slight curvature of the spine, arising more from labour with poor food than from labour specifically. The 'factory leg' is no more among us, except as an old man or woman limps by, to remind one of the fearful past. . . . The faces of the people are ruddy, their forms are rounded, their very appearance is a joyous one." We omit other evidence to the same effect.

---

[1] Read before the Bradford meeting of the Social Science Association, in 1859.

Let us now turn to the effects of the educational machinery of the Factory Acts. And here let us at once dispose of an objection which has been made to that machinery, viz. that it has driven children into those employments which are not subject to inspection. That this has been the case to some extent may be inferred from the fact that the number of children employed in factories has diminished instead of increasing. In 1835, there were 56,455 children at work in factories ; in 1838, only 29,283 ; in 1858, 46,071, population meanwhile having largely increased. It is moreover remarkable, that of the figure last mentioned no less than 44,769 were employed in England, 1,188 in Scotland, and 114 in Ireland. The contrast between these numbers will serve to explain the different views which have been taken of the results of the Act north and south of the Tweed. Thus Mr. J. D. Campbell, Sub-inspector of Factories, in a discussion on " Educational Tests for em- ployment,"[1] " gave it as the result of his observation, that the educational clauses of the Factory Act had almost totally failed in the Glasgow district; and he believed he might state that this was the experience of the other inspectors also. Parents preferred sending their children to those trades where they would get full wages. Even when children were sent to factories under the half-time system, they went, as soon as they got the opportunity, to other places where they got full wages ; and the con- sequence was that owners of factories would have nothing to do with half-time youths."

This testimony is irrefragable as far as it goes, though little creditable to either Scotch employers or operatives.

[1] Social Science Transactions, 1860, p. 419.

But from England the testimony is far other.   Mr. Redgrave, in a paper read before the " Congrès International
de Bienfaisance " in 1862, says :—" Before the Factory
Act passed the Legislature, but few of the children had
any opportunity of attending school. . . . For the last
thirty years every child under thirteen works in a factory
for only half the day, and attends school for three hours
on the same day.   At this time upwards of 54,000
children are so attending school, making good progress
and attending to the earnings of the family."

So Mr. E. D. J. Wilks, Secretary to the British and
Foreign School Society, in a paper read before the Social
Science Association, at Bradford, in 1859,[1] says of the
Educational Clauses of the Factory Acts : "I have no
hesitation in avowing my conviction, based . . . upon
actual, long-continued, and widely-extended observation,
that, generally speaking, their operation has been most
healthful, not only in an educational, but also in a social
point of view . . . The results have proved the principle
sound in theory, wise in legislation, and practical in
working.   Evils that were dreaded have not been realized,
and advantages of a kind that could hardly be anticipated have accrued."   Among the last may be reckoned
the fact, more pregnant in social consequence, perhaps,
than any other ascertained in this age, of the superiority
of the half-time over the whole-time system, as a means
of education, or, in other words, of learning *plus* work
over learning alone.   Wherever good factory schools
have been provided, it has been proved, to use the
words of Mr. E. Chadwick, at Glasgow, so far back as
1860, "that in three hours the half-timers eventually

[1] Transactions, p. 363.

obtained as much book instruction as the children de-
tained in the same schools for five or six hours daily ;
the fairly taught half-timers were . . . intellectually more
apt than the long-time scholars, taught by the same
teachers, and under the same system." [1]

Mr. Akroyd, at the Congress of the Social Science
Association in 1864, said that " he and his father had
been opposed" to the half-time system, but he now
"advocated the extension of the principle embodied in
the Act to all classes of workers, and argued from experience that the measure which had been so beneficial
to the children in the factory towns, would be equally
advantageous for those in the agricultural districts." [2]

Experience has thus shown that the educational results
of factory legislation, wherever its provisions have been
efficiently carried into effect, have been as cheering at
least as the physical ones ; and if it has failed on this
head in some districts, it is simply because the principle
remains too restricted in its application.

And now let us look at the more general results. " The
Factory Acts," says Mr. Edmund Potter, " were resisted
by many of us as economically unsound, and as an unjust
interference with the rights of labour and capital. *They
have been socially beneficial. . . .* The cotton district
population has rapidly and soundly improved during
the last thirty years. . . . No working population has

---

[1] With education, morality has greatly improved among the factory hands,
the females especially. In one Bradford mill, "where 500 girls were employed,
the average yearly number of illegitimate children did not amount to more
than three, and those were mostly to suitors, who afterwards married the
mothers," says Mr. J. James, in his before-quoted paper, read before the
Social Science Association, in 1859.

[2] Social Science Transactions, 1864, p. 479.

existed in the kingdom of so high and healthy a moral and physical standard."

In 1832, sinking as they were daily under the burthen of over-toil, both premature and excessive, the factory population was below, not above the general level of the working class. This condition of things is now, by competent observers, alleged to be reversed.

At the height of the Cotton Famine, the Rev. J. P. Norris, in a paper "On the Half-time System,"[1] said : " It was only last week that one of the largest employers of labour in Manchester, speaking of the patience and fortitude with which a population of many thousands of operatives are now enduring an unprecedented amount of privation, said to me, 'I know nothing in the range of my experience more remarkable than the development of the Lancashire character in the last fifteen years ;' and he ascribed it chiefly to the beneficent operation of the Factory Laws, adopted as they have been by the master manufacturers as their truest interest."

" The masses," says again Mr. Redgrave, in his paper on " Factory Inspection in Great Britain," read before the " Congrès International de Bienfaisance," in 1862, " have proved themselves worthy of the boon conferred upon them ; they have not abused the gift ; their intelligence has increased ; their habits have improved ; their social happiness has advanced ; they have gained all, and more than, they expected from Factory legislation ; and they have not been intoxicated with success. Much might be said of what the operatives have done with their leisure hours ; how evening schools have been frequented ; various mutual improvement societies have been appreciated ;

[1] Social Science Transactions, 1862, p. 278.

how the Easter and Whitsuntide holidays have been spent in more rational enjoyments than formerly; how the intelligence, subordination to authority, and the general tone and bearing of the operative have kept pace with the advancement of the age."[1]

But perhaps the most remarkable result of the Factory Acts has been their effect upon the employers. As some of our quotations have already shown, from being the virulent opponents of legislative interference the manu- facturers now, for the most part, cordially accept it, and as Mr. Redgrave truly says, " are now generally the fore- most advocates of improvement,—promoting the erection of factories and schools, the establishment of educational institutions, donors of parks, baths, washhouses, for the express use of the factory operatives." Hence those magnificent establishments, such as Saltaire and Akroydon, which have come to rank among our national glories ; hence the princely public benefactions of the Crossleys, and of so many others. It would scarcely be too much to say, that the humble factory worker, through his perseverance in enforcing righteous legislation, has been the great civilizer and moralizer of his employer.

We may seem to have been devoting too much time to the subject of factory legislation, especially in the cotton districts. But this is, in fact, a typical instance in many ways. In the first place, it must be recollected that our cotton exports alone amounted, in 1860, to 52,000,000*l.* out of 135,000,000*l.*, or nearly five-thirteenths of the whole. Again, it is in the cotton districts that the system of protective legislation to the worker has had its longest trial (extending now over a generation), and

[1] Page 52.

has had its results, through the exceptional calamity of the cotton famine, most severely tested. A system which has stood the double ordeal of time and of an unprecedented temporary strain, cannot be a bad one.

We have, therefore, every ground for concluding from the thorough success of protective legislation in the cotton districts, that slowly but surely, in proportion to the time during which, and the extent to which it has been applied, it is working similar effects in all other employments to which it has as yet been extended. Even as respects those which have been only brought into the system by the Factory Acts' Extension Act in 1864,[1] there is evidence that beneficial results are being obtained, whilst the employers, taught by the experience of their fellows, readily co-operate in carrying out the Act. "There can be no longer any doubt," says Mr. Baker, June 5, 1865, "that the wisdom of Parliament in assimilating the hours of employment one to another in various trades will be productive of the happiest results."

*   *   *   *   *

Consider now how far the working classes have availed themselves of the several enabling Acts in their favour which have been passed since 1832.

Space will not admit of detailed reference to the proceedings of the many thousands of Benefit Societies existing in England. Mr. Charles Hardwick, in a paper read at the " Congrès International de Bienfaisance," was perhaps under rather than over the mark, when he said that the entire Friendly Societies of Great Britain possessed reserved capital amounting to twenty millions

---

[1] Under this Act about 50,000 workers were added to the 775,534, who, in 1862, were employed in the various trades comprised in the system.

sterling.[1] Nor must it indeed be supposed that the exercise of the working man's forethought in the way of insurance is confined within the Friendly Society, or only tends to the use of the later facilities for Government Insurance. Several of the ordinary insurance offices are largely used by the working class. We are here quite out of the range of statistics, but we may quote as an instance, the " British Prudential Insurance Society," which, we are informed by a correspondent, has issued in Durham and Northumberland 32,500 policies, most of them to working men.

But,—to proceed to a form of providence more distinctive of the working class,—Building Societies, again, are now firmly established in all great centres of industry, —Liverpool, Manchester, Leeds, Birmingham, London, &c.; and in these places the men may be counted by tens of thousands who, in addition to having a sick and burial fund to rely on, have also homes provided in which they are their own landlords, or in a fair way of becoming so. Messrs. Chambers, in their tract on " Building Societies," describe with considerable fulness the gratifying results attending their operations in Birmingham. The statute, within the provisions of which they act, was passed in 1836, but their existence dates only from 1847, when the Freehold Land Societies started with the intention of manufacturing forty-shilling freeholders, by purchasing estates in bulk, and subdividing them amongst their shareholders. That object is now quite a matter of secondary consideration. The shareholders may not care less for the freehold, or the political power it confers;

---

[1] Some further details may be found in Mr. T. Y. Strachan's paper on Provident Institutions ; Social Science Transactions, 1863, p. 663.

but their leading desire is to add a house to the land, and thus secure free homes. At the time when the writer visited Birmingham, from 8,000 to 9,000 of these working men's homes were erected. The aggregate number of enrolled members was 10,000, the annual receipts 150,000*l.*, and fully 90 per cent. of the persons enrolled were working men whose wages varied from 12*s.* to 40*s.* per week. One group of these societies, doing business in the same office, during sixteen years have received 520,000*l.* in millions of small sums, and not a penny had been lost by error or default. It may be added that upon the committees, managing this group of societies, "there are not more than two or three middle-class men, and not one of the upper classes;" and "the same proportion is said to exist in all the other Birmingham Societies." [1]

Mr. Hole, in his admirable work on "The Homes of the Working Classes" (London, 1866), gives later details. About 9,000 working men in and around Birmingham have supplied themselves with superior dwellings of their own. . . . "In six societies, comprising 14,973 members, the amount of money actually received up to June 1, 1865, was 865,000*l.*, and the amount advanced on mortgage was 561,000*l.* ; of which the sum of 302,500*l.* has been absolutely redeemed, leaving 259,000*l.* now due on mortgage. These societies are only those connected with the Freehold Land Society ; but there are several other

---

[1] The moral effect of these societies was testified to by Mr. J. A. Stephens, before a committee of the House of Commons. "Freehold Land Societies encourage provident habits, diminish drunkenness, induce the working classes to invest their earnings and behave better ; so much so, that twelve years ago, when the population was 50,000 less than now, 420 police were necessary, but with this increase of population there has been a decrease of police, and 327 are now sufficient to preserve the peace."

societies in Birmingham whose operations may be safely estimated at about half as much more." The progress of these societies in the West Riding of Yorkshire is still more remarkable. Mr. Dibb, the Deputy Registrar of Deeds for the Riding, stated in 1858 that the number of deeds annually registered on behalf of such societies had risen from 31 in 1843, to 637 in 1857, the numbers in quinquennial periods having been,

From 1843 to 1847	192
„ 1848 „ 1852	1372
„ 1853 „ 1857	3044
Total	4608

Mr. J. Arthur Binns wrote in 1859 of the then four principal Societies of the West Riding, that they had received during the previous year, 222,522*l*., and had advanced on mortgage 632,457*l*. The "Leeds Permanent [1] Building Society" alone had, between 1848 and 1858, received in subscriptions, 519,568*l*.; in loans, 103,226*l*.; and had advanced on mortgage, 340,692*l*.; the cost of management being 8,102*l*., or 1*l*. 5*s*. 6*d*. per cent. on receipts—a higher figure than in two of the others. By 1864, the receipts in subscriptions had risen to a total of 1,200,598*l*. 6*s*.; in loans, to 251,461*l*. 4*s*. 6*d*.; the advances, to 749,864*l*. 6*s*. 11*d*.; the subscriptions received in 1864 alone amounting to 150,567*l*. 3*s*. 7*d*.

In Sunderland the progress of these Societies has been no less signal. From a letter by Mr. John Robinson,

---

[1] Building Societies are either "terminating," *i. e.* established for a certain period, or "permanent." They are, again, either "mutual," where every member looks to becoming a house-owner, or "investing," where members are admitted who merely seek a profit for their money. Minor distinctions, as of " Starr-Bowkett Societies," &c. we need not enter into.

dated July 11, 1866, and published in the *Sunderland Times*, it appears that the number of Societies in operation in the borough in 1859 was 40, in 1866, 60, being an increase of 50 per cent. in seven years ; the members numbering 13,401 against 3,823 in 1859 ; the capital, 1,768,025*l*. 10*s*. against 582,001*l*.

It would be difficult to procure an accurate return of the number of Building Societies in England, and the number of persons in the aggregate belonging to them ; but as there are few forms of association so general, and as nearly all the great popular societies of the kingdom have Building Societies attached to them, they must be very numerous. Mr. Baines, in 1861, estimated the number of members at 100,000, their annual subscriptions at 1,750,000*l*., the amount advanced by them to their members at 6,000,000*l*. Latterly, says Mr. Chambers, these institutions have been introduced into Wales, between which and the borders of Scotland there are now few towns without them. Throughout England and Wales there are said to be 2,000 Land and Building Societies, comprehending more than 20,0000 members. The money paid into these societies now amounts to eleven millions, of which upwards of eight millions have been invested in property." Not the least interesting feature of the Benefit Building Society consists in the facilities which it affords to benevolent employers and others for providing houses for the working classes.

No form of association, however, proves so much in favour of the moral and intellectual progress of the working people as Co-operation. No other system is so intricate in its organization, so complicated in its workings, so exacting in the demands it makes on the forethought and reasonableness of those who enter into it, and at the same time so completely the result of the working man's own thoughtfulness. Working men matured the plans, experimented on them, and carried them out to a successful issue, without advice or aid from any one outside themselves. The Co-operative store system is an arrangement to promote economy of expenditure amongst its members. It has to provide for buying all sorts of merchandise of the best quality, at the lowest price; for selling at a sufficient profit; for recording sales, so that the profits realized may be distributed again amongst the purchasers, in proportion to the extent of their purchases; with much more that can only be carried out successfully by a wise supervision, a steady application to business, and an exercise of intelligence and honesty of a very high order. Curiously enough, the first attempt at Co-operation was made somewhere about the time when the various other forms of Association which have been noticed were either coming into existence, or striking those roots which have since nourished their vigorous growth. Co-operative Stores were meant chiefly as a defence against the inroads of the distributing classes on the working man's pocket; and also as a means of promoting ready-money dealings, and the prudence in expenditure which usually accompanies such dealings. It would be difficult now to conceive the state of things that then existed. The back streets of the manufacturing towns swarmed with small shops, in which the worst of everything was sold, with unchecked measures, and unproved weights. The customers at these shops were the persons who drank and danced as long as they had money, and who, when they had none, had no other resource than the "stuff shop." The business to the shopkeeper was profitable, when he got regularly paid on the Saturday night; but regularity in payment was not the rule, and great losses were sometimes suffered. The business upon the whole was a bad one. Hence, when Co-operative Stores first began their much needed operations, the general indebtedness amongst the working people made success almost impossible. At this early period nothing was known of the admirable plan on which they are now worked. At that time a certain number of persons supplied the capital in small shares, and divided, in proportion to the capital invested, whatever profit was made. Such concerns had no special attraction for artisans, or for the public, nor could they furnish any guarantee against fraudulent dealing.

The first true beginning of the Co-operative Store movement, was the Rochdale Equitable Pioneers' Store, and the chief ground of its success was the admirable plan upon which it started, a plan which cannot be too often stated or too closely studied. The great difficulty with the first stores was to bring custom, and, failing in this, they broke down. In Rochdale, however, they said to the public, "Invest in the trading capital here, and you shall have five per cent. on your money, inasmuch as we bind ourselves not to put it to risk by speculative trading, no credit being given. In the next place, whatever remains as profit after paying interest on capital will be divided as bonus on the amount of money spent in the store by each member." The advantages of this proposal soon began to make themselves apparent.

Presuming a hundred men invested twenty shillings each, one shilling each would be due to them at the expiration of the year, as five per cent. interest on their separate investments. They had each done precisely the same as investors, and each was justly entitled to the same reward. But custom is as necessary as capital for the production of profit, and in contributing this all-important element they almost necessarily differed from each other. The family income made a difference, the number in the family made an important difference. In fact, a poor workman with a large family was a far more profitable customer than a well-paid artisan with a small one. These poorer men, therefore—the most difficult to move, because usually the most incumbered by debt—were the most directly appealed to by the new plan. There was no interest in buying inferior articles and selling them at high prices, no temptation to adulterate anything sold, no inducement to give short weight or measure, inasmuch as anything taken from the consumer by fraud, would go back to him again as increased bonus. And as everything purchased had to be paid for in ready money, the whole frightful system of indebtedness, which up to that time crushed the people, must disappear. Their growth has of a natural consequence been very rapid. Rochdale made 32*l.* 17*s.* 6*d.* profit in 1845, its first year, 80*l.* the second year, and 117*l.* 2*s.* 10*d.* the third year. Whilst in the June quarter of 1866, the most recent document at hand, the business done is stated in the Committee's report as follows:— "The total cash received for goods sold this quarter is 60,904*l.* 9*s.* 6½*d.*, being an increase of 3,587*l.* 0*s.* 2½*d.* compared with last quarter. The profit this quarter is 6,917*l.* 0*s.* 2½*d.*, which after allowing 275*l.* 18*s.* 6*d.* for depreciation of fixed stock, and 137*l.* 7*s.* 4*d.* for the educational fund, will allow a dividend of two shillings in the pound to members." [1] These figures show a business of nearly a quarter of a million a year, done at a profit of 24,968*l.*, of which sum 23,315*l.* goes back again to the members as bonus on purchases, the economy of management being so great, that including interest on capital, the working expenses amount only to 2 per cent. on the returns. But this is not all. There is also in Rochdale a Corn-mill Society, doing business with the stores of the neighbourhood, which during the same quarter did a business of 50,212*l.* 18*s.* 0*d.*, or at the rate of 200,000*l.* per annum. There is a large Cotton-mill as well, but we have no returns by us of its business. Now if it be considered that Rochdale is returned in the last census as having a population of 38,000 inhabitants, and 7,700 inhabited houses, it may be seen at a glance what proportion of its people are engaged in this co-operative business, especially if it be borne in mind that the members of these stores are nearly all heads of families, and in this store alone there are somewhere about 6,000 members. In Halifax, the co-operative store, in the number of its members, is on a par with Rochdale ; at the end of 1865, according to the Registrar of Friendly Societies' returns there were 5,775 persons belonging to it. The cash received for goods, however, only amounted to 147,963*l.*, and the profits to 12,541*l.* There is also here a large

---

[1] This paragraph is added. " The Committee regret that the dividend this quarter is the smallest we have had for the last five years. And one of the principal reasons is on account of the Butchering department yielding so small a gain, which is caused by the great restrictions arising from the Cattle Plague."

Flour-mill, and as the inhabitants and the number of inhabited houses are much the same as in Rochdale, the proportion of persons engaged in co-operation compared with the number of inhabitants may be taken as about the same in both towns.

Mr. Tidd Pratt's return for 1865 shows that the number of Societies certified to December, 1864, was 651, of which, however, only 417 had sent returns, whilst 52 had been dissolved. The 417 returning Societies held together 761,313*l.* of share capital, owed 112,733*l.* on loan ; they had done business for the year to the amount of 3,063,088*l.* for goods purchased, 3,373,837*l.* for goods sold ; had a balance of 136,923*l.*, possessed assets to the amount of 1,105,685*l.*, and were accountable for 273,480*l.* of trade liabilities. Thus their balance in hand exceeded their loan capital, and their trade liabilities were less than a quarter of their assets. Sounder conditions of trade can hardly be imagined. The 148,586 members who composed them were scattered nearly all over the country, but far more thickly through the manufacturing districts.

The total number of co-operators is not very easy to estimate. On the one hand, whenever different co-operative bodies exist for separate purposes in one town, the same men are generally members of both. But on the other hand, if we take into account the fact that 182 societies had sent in no returns ; that 216 certified since December 1864, were not included in the return, which is made up to 31st December, 1865 ; that another twelvemonth has elapsed since then ; and that a vast number of societies never register at all, we shall see that the figure of 148,586 members must be below the reality, rather than above it. Let us take it

at 200,000, and let us suppose that three-fourths of these
are engaged in retail shop-keeping, the last third in
wholesale trade or in some process of manufacture,
whether that of flour, as in the corn-mills, so flourishing
especially in Yorkshire, or of some other.   What does
this show?   That nearly 150,000 of the working class
have raised themselves collectively if not individually by
this means alone, into the position hitherto occupied by
the shop-keeping class, forming the vast bulk of the 10*l.*
occupiers in boroughs; whilst about 50,000 — whose
business requires premises, if not of freehold tenure, at
least held for some fixed interest or term of years,—
have raised themselves collectively in like manner to a
position equivalent to that of the independent classes of
county voters, freeholders, copyholders, or leaseholders.
And yet, according to our present electoral system, it
would only be a mere handful out of the number who
could be entitled to vote.   Let it be observed, moreover,
that this co-operative movement has lately successfully
traversed the critical experiment of a cotton famine; that
it is growing officially, as Mr. Tidd Pratt's return shows
us, at the rate of over 200 Societies a year; representing,
say at 150 members each, 30,000 men, to whom must be
added over 8,000 a year for the increase of numbers in
existing bodies; in all nearly 40,000, of whom at least
three-fourths must be taken to belong to the working
class, commonly so called.

But the co-operative movement cannot be sufficiently
appreciated unless it be followed into its higher branches,
—wholesale trade, or production.   What an instance of
developed capacity in the working class is shown by that
" North of England Wholesale Co-operation Society,

Limited," of Manchester, which, as its advertisements in the *Co-operator* tell us, after two years of life, is now doing business at the rate of a quarter of a million sterling per annum ! Many other instances are omitted.

For productive purposes, however, co-operation is now passing over into the form of the Limited Company under the Joint Stock Acts, in which we fail to trace it, except in individual cases. Several co-operative mills and other establishments are thus registered as joint-stock companies. The rapid spread, under this form, of the "Industrial Partnership," or "Partnership of Industry" system, is especially to be noticed. It would have been impossible, if the worker were not by this time admitted by his employer to be capable of being, as a shareholder, associated more or less closely in the management of large concerns ; or as a mere bonus-receiver, of being stimulated to greater exertions by the hope of a distant addition to the amount of his wages. This system is now, under various modifications, being applied by Messrs. Briggs and Co., and the South Buckley Company to mining ; by Messrs. Crossley to the carpet manufacture ; by Messrs. Fox, Head and Co. to iron works ; by Messrs. Greenings to another branch of iron manufacture ; by the Cobden Memorial Mills to the cotton manufacture ; by Messrs. Wardle, and by Messrs. Lloyd and Summerfield, to the earthenware and glass manufacture ; by Mr. Goodall of Leeds to printing, &c. &c. The principle is being adopted by the working class in their own undertakings, as by the "London Co-operative Cabinet Manufacturing Society, Limited," or by the "Framemakers and Gilders' Association, Limited," —the latter a most noteworthy instance of success in co-operative production. Thousands of working men are in these various establishments learning to enter into the position, to share the interests of the employer class.

Not the least remarkable feature of the co-operative movement, as well as of that of the partnerships of industry which has grown out of it, is its connexion with education. The example set by the Rochdale Equitable Pioneers, of its reading-room and educational fund, has been followed by many co-operative bodies, in Lancashire especially.[1] Thousands of pounds have thus been raised by the working men, as a voluntary rate on their co-operative success, for purposes of self-improvement. And it is from the example thus set them by the working classes that the founders of the new "Partnerships of Industry" have borrowed the provision embodied in the articles of association of several of them, which authorises their directors, before recommending a dividend, to set apart a reserve fund, for the purpose, amongst others, of "creating and maintaining a fund for establishing and supporting a library, news-room, workmen's club or other educational benefits for the servants of the Company."

The co-operative movement is, however, no doubt still in the main confined to our manufacturing, mining, and coast districts, though gradually creeping into the small towns of the agricultural districts; as in Essex, in the shape of co-operative stores; or even laying hold on

---

[1] Four societies figure in the returns of 1866 as contributing over 100*l.* a year, to an educational fund, viz., Rochdale, 537*l.*; Bury, 261*l.*; Oldham (King Street), 150*l.*; and Bacup, 144*l.* It must be observed, moreover, that the educational fund being often, according to the Rochdale pattern, a rate of two and a half per cent. on profits, it goes on always increasing with the success of the society.

agriculture, in the co-operative farms of Suffolk.[1] The spread of general education is, we believe, slowly paving a way for it on all sides.

*   *   *   *   *

But we must meet now another question, that of intemperance. Allowing to the fullest extent the frightful reality of the evil—the vastness of the sums squandered away by the working classes on this form of self-indulgence—one striking contrast offers itself to those who can look back to the days before 1832, between that time and this. Drunkenness was not then felt as an evil thing by the working class; the active war upon it, which is now being carried on everywhere within the bosom of that class, was not thought of; moderate men there might be, but the energetic, aggressive abstainer was not to be found. The temperance movement is now powerful enough to have split into two, each section energetically carrying on its own work. And although it may be difficult to estimate the total number of abstainers,[2]— which number itself would, thank God! give no idea of the habitually sober,—certain it is that thousands of enthusiastic men have been labouring for years in this cause, chiefly among the working classes; and though not satisfied with the result of their labours, they know they have not been labouring in vain.

---

[1] See an interesting paper by Mr. John Gurdon, in the Transactions of the Social Science Association for 1864, p. 693.

[2] Mr. Baines, in his speech of 1861, reckons the number of Temperance Societies at 4,000, that of Teetotallers at "not less than" 3,000,000, of whom however, perhaps more than half were under fifteen. There were thirteen large associations, employing forty paid lecturers, with an annual income of 22,000*l.*, three weekly newspapers, circulating 25,000 copies weekly, six monthly magazines, circulating 20,000, &c.

Nor must it be considered indeed that the various temperance bodies are the only organizations directly warring against drunkenness among the working classes. Whatever may be thought of its policy, it is unquestionable that the "Sunday League" is largely supported by working men, and that the main ground of their support is this, that the opening of public museums, gardens, and places of entertainment will be a powerful check to drunkenness. The same consideration operates to enlist their support in favour of working men's clubs and institutes, and of other places or forms of popular entertainment.

The free opening of parks, libraries, galleries, whilst operating as a check upon drunkenness, affords also a powerful argument in proof of its decrease. The Crystal Palace, again, to whatever extent it may be frequented by all other classes, could never have maintained itself without the working class, which in turn, thirty years ago, would have been incapable of enjoying it. They now resort to it, in their days of leisure, by the thousand; they crowd thither in tens of thousands on the occasion of a Foresters' Fête, or other like holiday of their own. Mr. F. Fuller, in a letter addressed to the *Times* on December 31, 1866, and since largely circulated, declares that " ever since it has been opened, about a million and a half of persons have profited by it in each year; and in the present year no less than 2,067,598 persons have visited the building, . . . and out of the 18 or 19 millions of people scarcely 18 cases of drunkenness and disorder have appeared in the police reports." In presence of this single fact, is it possible to believe in a general increase of drunkenness?

The circumstances indeed of different localities, not necessarily far apart from each other, vary widely in this respect. The more common experience is, we believe, that of the Rev. Alexander Macleod, in a paper read before the Social Science Association in 1861, where he says that the "real problem" lies in the lowest classes ; that whilst in others there may be individuals, "even families and little coteries entangled in the evil, the only *class* in society where the evil does not seem to be yielding to the influences which have been brought to bear against it, are the very poor. I do not mean," he emphatically adds, "the industrial poor. I do not mean the class which would be admitted to the suffrage if the 5*l.* rental were made the condition of the vote. I mean the classes which underlie these."

On the other hand, it is undoubtedly the fact that in many instances it is not the worst paid trades that are most given to drink. The Sheffield trades, almost generally, are a case in point. The Spitalfields weavers, glad to earn 8*s.* a week, are habitually temperate ; the coalminers, earning nearly or quite four times that amount, the puddlers, who, in turn, easily double the miner's figure of wages, are too often drunkards. There are, it must be admitted, "conditions,"—to use Mr. E. Chadwick's words[1]—" in which high wages mean only excess in drink." And he quotes the instance of a retailer of coals near Manchester, "who refused to give credit to any man who earned more than 24*s.* per week, because he found from experience that if he did so, he never got paid." So far from being universally true is the theory

---

[1] See Social Science Transactions, p. 89.

y

that the lower you get in the social scale, the more you will find drunkenness and improvidence to prevail.

It must, too, never be forgotten how largely drunkenness is, in a real sense, involuntary—the result of ill-ventilated workshops, unhealthy employment, inadequate lodging-room, and similar causes. In many cases, it is even compulsory.

However this may be, let it be remembered that numbers of the working class rank as advocates of general measures against drunkenness; and either (as the supporters of the Permissive Bill) would place the local suppression of public-houses in the hands of a body —the ratepayers—partially, and in some cases only to a very trifling extent, composed of their own class; or (as the "Alliance") would suppress the trade authoritatively everywhere; and we shall perhaps see grounds for viewing in a different light whatever amount of drunkenness does still exist among the working class, and for considering that the political enfranchisement of that class would afford one of the most effective means towards checking that vice, so far as it can be influenced by legislative enactments. Indeed, the United Kingdom Alliance, in their Report for 1865-6, declare that "a Reform Bill, from whatever Government it may be ultimately accepted, must strike at the root of publican domination, and must therefore be an important Alliance gain."

WHAT THE WORKING MEN HAVE DONE FOR THEMSELVES WITHOUT HELP FROM THE LAW.

We have seen a little of what the working men have done since 1832, the Law favouring them. Something must now be shown of what they have been able to do, the Law not favouring them, or at least affording them but the most niggardly measure of protection in their undertakings.

Prominent among such are, of course, the Trade Societies. Without entering into any discussion as to the origin of these bodies, we may say that in 1832 their only objects generally were to keep up wages and limit the influx of apprentices. Now, however, they frequently support their members in sickness, pay burial fees in case of death, assist those who are out of work, and, in some cases, give considerable sums to such of their members as are incapacitated by accident, as well as annual payments to such as are unfitted for labour by age. In Great Britain, at present, the number of persons who belong to these bodies may be stated at 400,000, the largest individual body being that of the "Amalgamated Society of Engineers," founded in 1851. This Society, the year before the great lock-out, which occurred in 1852, had 11,829 members, and a balance in cash of 21,705*l.* 4*s.* 11½*d.* That fierce fight with the employers brought the number of members down to 9,737, and the reserve fund to 17,812*l.* in 1853. At that time it was thought that trade unionism had received its deathblow. This calculation was premature. Last year this giant Society numbered 30,984 members, with an income of 75,672*l.* 6*s.* 2*d.*, and a clear balance in hand of 115,357*l.* 13*s.* 10½*d.* It had 229 branches in England and Wales, 32 in Scotland, 11 in Ireland, 6 in Australia, 2 in New Zealand, 5 in Canada, 1 in Malta, 8 in the United States, 1 in France. The total amount expended by it had been, during 15 years—

	£
For "donation," *i. e.* assistance to those out of work, including strikes	279,840
For sick benefit	115,127
Superannuation	26,935
Accidents, &c.	12,400
Funeral benefits	34,600
During 13 years for assistance to other trades	9,415
Benevolent grants (12 years)	6,400
	£484,717

The Amalgamated Society of Carpenters and Joiners, affords another instance of these vast trade organizations. Much younger than that of the Engineers, having been established in 1860, by December 1865 it numbered 134 branches, 5,670 members, and a fund of 8,320*l.*; having paid away 6,733*l.* 11*s.* 5½*d.* in the year in benefits. By February, 1867, it had 190 branches· and 8,191 members.

Another large and interesting body is the "National Association of Coal Mine and Ironstone Miners of Great Britain," the "Transactions" of whose "General Conference" at Leeds in November 1863, form a volume of 174 pages, published in London (Longmans) and Leeds. No more valuable document can be consulted as to the spirit of self-help which is stirring amongst our working classes.

Later data as to the strength of these societies generally are contained in the "Report of the Conference of Trades' Delegates of the United Kingdom held in the Temperance Hall, Sheffield, on July 17, 1866, and four following days." At this Conference accredited delegates attended for societies comprising from 180,000 to 200,000 men. At a subsequent Conference held at Manchester, January 1–4, 1867, delegates representing and paying for 59,750 members were present. A similar Conference has since sat in London. Yet some of the largest Societies were unrepresented at all three; and the number of society men represented even at the first cannot be reckoned at half the total number.

Even the large amalgamated Societies themselves do not give a measure of the power of organization, the capacity for social action, manifested by the working man in this his own peculiar province. Many towns have local associations, formed of distinct Societies. Such are the London Trades' Council, representing 60,000 men; the Sheffield " Association of Organized Trades," comprising 5,000 men, and 33 trades; the " Amalgamated Trades of Preston," &c. &c. The Conferences—whether of single trades as a whole, or of many trades together—which are held, sometimes at stated intervals, sometimes only on specific occasions, are no less interesting than their standing organizations. Nor can we overlook a still further development of the Trade Society's work. At the Sheffield Conference, above mentioned, the " International Association of Working Men," comprising 12,000 members, was represented by two delegates; and a " Workmen's Congress," was held in Geneva (November, 1866), at which the English delegates took a decided lead, gave form to the proceedings, and carried most of the resolutions proposed by them, showing themselves the most practical and business-like group in the strange assembly.

It is true that all this power of organization, instead of being accepted as an evidence of social development, is treated only as a cause of alarm to other classes. " I shall not refer to the subject of strikes," said Mr. Lowe, in his speech of May 3, 1865, on Mr. Baines's motion for

Reform, " but it is, I conteud, impossible to believe that the same machinery which is at present brought into play in connexion with strikes, would not be applied by the working classes to political purposes. Once give the men votes, and the machinery is ready to launch those votes in one compact mass *upon the institutions and property of the country.*" As if the Amalgamated Society of Engineers, with its 30,000 members, which, in 1865, spent 14,070*l.* 4*s.* 9*d.* in "donations, sending members to situations, and beds for non-free members;" 13,785*l.* 14*s.* 9*d.* for "sick benefit, stewards, and medical certificates;" 5,184*l.* 17*s.* 4*d.* for "superannuation benefit;" 4,887*l.* 6*s.* for "funeral;" 1,860*l.* for "accidents," &c. were not an " institution !" As if the working man's labour were not as truly "property" as that capital which it enables to accumulate ! As if it were likely that the great trade societies should have accumulated their capitals of thousands of pounds, tens of thousands, nay, in the case of the Engineers over 100,000*l.*—invested them, as many of them have, in Post-office Savings Banks at 2½ per cent. ; rendered tens of thousands of widows, and of sick men, of the aged, disabled, dependent upon those funds,[1] in order to " launch " votes in a compact mass at institutions or at property ! The calumny is one so preposterous that it surely needed an unreformed House of Commons to listen to it, and it goes far to justify the Trade Societies in claiming such a measure of political reform as will render the like impossible henceforth to be uttered, with-

---

[1] "The unions do more than merely raise the wages. They are a great benefit in this respect, that they are the means, I believe, by their sick funds, by their accident funds, by their death funds, by their funds for supporting men when out of employment . . . of keeping men off the poor rates."—Lord Elcho's speech at Dalkeith, *Times,* January 23, 1867.

out calling forth a prompt and indignant reply from the representatives of the people.

No greater mistake can be made than, as journalists and politicians are apt to do, to treat the mass of members of Trade Societies as dupes, idlers, drunkards, or incapables, their leaders as knaves, strikes for higher wages as their common object. The more these Societies are examined, the more apparent it will be that they represent almost invariably the bulk of the able, industrious, and provident workmen in each trade ;[1] that they are habitually well governed by men fairly elected by the members as the most trustworthy, respectable, and intelligent amongst them ; that they prevent far more strikes than they encourage.

No Trade Society could maintain itself, of which the members were not habitually at work, and sufficiently thrifty to put by something for their contributions ; of which the leaders were not careful to keep their men at work as far as possible, honest enough and judicious enough to reckon on their punctual payment of the moneys required to carry on the operations of the society.

---

[1] Where the men in a trade generally are given to drink, or any malpractice, of course the Society men will not be free from such tendencies. Yet a friend, a member of the bar, at one time secretary to the committee of a conservative candidate for the city of London, who has been much connected with the working class, writes thus on the subject of Trade Societies :— "Though a Tory in politics, I am a strong supporter of Trade Unions, and think that every member of a union ought to have a vote as such, precisely the same as the members of the trade-guilds had in former years, and the members of the city companies (which originally were nothing but Trade Unions) have now. . . . I believe the respectable working man would like it better than any other enfranchisement, and we should obtain the cream of the working classes. According to the rules of Trade Unions a man is liable to fine and even expulsion if not steady, sober, honest, &c., so that it would be impossible that any man of disreputable character could have a vote as a Trade Unionist. A franchise of this kind would be far better than a brick and mortar one."

Employers often complain of the difficulty of dealing with working men, whilst nevertheless they have in their hands the terrible argument of dismissal, and their dealings are confined to a few dozens, hundreds, very rarely thousands of workmen. How much more difficult must it be for the officers of Trade Societies to deal with those same working men, when numbering as many thousands often as a large establishment might employ hundreds, where they can use no other arguments than those of their own honesty, ability, good sense, and good temper? Sometimes the temporary leaders of a trade society may be hot-headed and unwise; but the permanent officers will almost invariably be found picked men of their kind. An examination of the accounts of the leading societies will show that their business is managed with great economy. If any charge can be brought against their management, it is that they cost too little, not too much; and if those who take money for public services are to be denounced as "vampires," it may be said that the Trade Society vampire is the most ill-used creature of that species in existence.[1]

A strike is as much a calamity to a trade society as it is to any one else. It is in time of peace, when work is plentiful and wages high that the society flourishes; the immediate effect of a strike is necessarily to deplete its coffers and circumscribe its resources. The provisions as to strikes which occur in trade society rules, show clearly that they are viewed only as necessary evils. To take one instance out of many. The Coachmakers say:—" No shop or town shall be allowed to turn out on their

---

[1] Mr. Odger, well known as secretary of the London Trades' Council, receives for his services to that body 2s. 6d. per week.

own responsibility; but, in the event of any oppression or dispute, the secretary of such town, in conjunction with the members, shall furnish the Executive Committee with all the particulars of such grievance, who shall determine whether it be expedient to summon delegates, and if found necessary to do so, the Executive Committee shall send one delegate, and the town secretary, where the grievance takes place, shall summon one delegate from each of the two nearest relieving towns; should the delegates fail to settle the matter amicably, they shall represent the case to the Executive Committee, who shall determine whether it be necessary to call the men out or not." Surely it is impossible to surround a declaration of war with more precautions and formalities. Would to God it were as difficult for an English Ministry to involve the Empire in hostilities as it is for a Trade Society to enter upon a strike! Let it be observed, moreover, that strikes are expressly discountenanced by many Trade Societies in their rules; that one of them (the Smiths) boasts of being "the Original Anti-Strike Society;" and literally every Society, which can do so, boasts of the length of time during which it has carried on its operations without striking.

But the most remarkable evidence on this subject is afforded by the proceedings of the Sheffield Conference. A resolution having been proposed by Mr. Odger, to the effect that the various Trade Societies of the United Kingdom should be invited to join the proposed amalgamated society of all the trades, "for the purpose of resisting lock-outs in any trade so connected, and in rendering pecuniary and moral support to such branches as are necessitated to seek the same," several amendments were proposed, in effect for the purpose of empowering the association to aid strikes, but were withdrawn, or rejected by large majorities, the vice-chairman saying: "You will observe that we came here not to form a trades' combination for the advancement of wages either one way or the other, but to resist those great evils of lock-outs and to discourage strikes."—"If they led trades to believe," said another speaker, "that they would get the support of the trades of the country on all occasions of strike, strikes would be precipitated by the action of this organization, and it would be a complete failure in a short time."

Are these merely idle words? Surely there is evidence of their reality in the remarkable and growing feeling of the working classes in favour of legalized arbitration as a substitute for strikes. In how many instances has arbitration been offered by the men, and rejected by the masters—by the engineers in 1851-2, by the Preston weavers repeatedly in 1853, the West Yorkshire miners in 1858, &c. &c.! In how few—the Staffordshire ironfounders' case seems the only prominent one in point —has it been offered by the masters, and rejected by the men! In many instances arbitration is required to be resorted to by the rules of societies. Sometimes they have even succeeded in obtaining legal means of settling disputes by arbitration. Thus, in the London printing trade, a scale of prices was agreed to at a general conference of master-printers and compositors in 1847, which was embodied in a deed, and has formed the subject of legal decisions; disputes may be settled by an arbitration committee, consisting of three masters, nominated by the master in whose office the dispute has arisen, and three journeymen, not employed in such office, nominated by the journeymen, with a barrister for chairman ; in practice, however, disputes in this trade are settled without difficulty. In the Potteries, the agreement contains a clause that " if any dispute arise between the parties as to the prices or wages to be paid by virtue of such agreement, the dispute shall be referred to an arbitration board of six persons, to consist of three manufacturers chosen by the masters, and three working potters elected by the working men"—a system, we are told, which " has been much tried, and worked most successfully in ninety out of a hundred cases."[1] At Macclesfield, a court of conciliation was formed, in 1848, between the silk-weavers and their employers ; and during the four years of its existence no strikes took place, until it was broken up by an employer refusing to abide by the award ; and " no sooner was the board broken up than strikes commenced."[2] At Sheffield, amongst the carpenters and joiners, a code of working rules was drawn up between masters and men, in May last ; and on the employers' own proposal, a committee, composed of an equal number of employers and workmen, meets monthly, to discuss and decide by a majority all differences that may arise on one side or the other ; and many cases on both sides have been satisfactorily decided by it. " I may add," writes the intelligent secretary to the Amalgamated Society of Carpenters and Joiners, from whom we learn the above fact, " that in at least twenty towns our members have succeeded in getting codes of working rules

---

[1] Report of Trade Societies' Committee of Social Science Association, p. 282 ; see also Report of Select Committee of the House of Commons on Masters and Operatives, 1860, Mr. G. Humphries' evidence.

[2] Ibid.

mutually agreed to by the employers and themselves, each binding themselves to give two, three, four, or six months' notice of any alteration either may require, and if they are unable to agree, to settle all their differences by arbitration. For all practical purposes, strikes are impossible in such places."

Again, the Board of Arbitration of the Nottingham hosiery trade state,[1] that " having now had six years' experience of the practical working of the system of arbitration, as opposed to strikes and lock-outs, it is thoroughly convinced that, in a free country, where workmen and capitalists have a perfect right to enter into combinations, the simplest, most humane, and rational method of settling all disputes between employer and employed is arbitration and conciliation. The Board is strengthened in this conviction by the fact, that during the past two years the demand for hosiery has been, in several branches of trade, of an exceptional character, and labour, in some departments, unusually scarce ; and notwithstanding the workmen have preserved their trade unions, by having a central authority to appeal to, composed equally of employers and employed, all questions calculated to produce irritation and lead to disputes have been promptly settled, all inequalities in the rates of wages have been adjusted, the manufacturer has been enabled to accept his contracts without apprehension and execute them without delay, and the rights of workmen have been zealously looked after and strictly preserved."

Again, the Bill, originally brought in by Mr. Mackinnon, late taken charge of by Lord St. Leonards, and now passing through Parliament, for establishing Courts of

---

[1] See *Times*, of January 29, 1867.

Conciliation, has been, as is well known, warmly supported by the Trade Societies. Not long ago, a letter was published from Lord St. Leonards, stating that delegates, representing upwards of 100,000 working men, had expressed themselves in favour of his Bill. This is itself only half the truth ; for at the Sheffield Conference, at which, as before stated, from 180,000 to 200,000 workmen were represented, a resolution was unanimously passed "highly approving" of the establishment of such Courts, "exceedingly regretting" the withdrawal of the Bill, and "pledging" the delegates present to "use every exertion to obtain the establishment of such Courts."

But let us see what the working men claim to have achieved by means of their Trade Societies. "It is said," we read in a speech by Lord Elcho, at Dalkeith,[1] "that the unions led to the abolition of serfdom in 1799, when in Scotland men were transferred like chattels with the pit. Through the action of these unions, it is said, that women work no longer in pits, while children's labour has been limited ; that education below twelve years is prescribed for every boy before he is admitted into the pit ; that the truck-system has been abolished, that inspection has been obtained, and that the payment of wages at public-houses has been stopped. Further, I am assured that it is through the action of the unions that there is less violence attaching to strikes ; and that, among other things, workmen do not have their ears cut off, as they used to have them last century, by their fellow-workmen ; *and I believe it is so.*"

We are far from being mere partisans of Trades Unions. They are at best one-sided and one-eyed.

[1] See *Times*, January 29, 1867.

Existing simply to protect or further a single class interest, they appear to us far inferior to Co-operation, which seeks to harmonize warring interests ; aiming only at improving the condition of the wages-receiver, they are lower in conception than whatever tends to abolish the thraldom of wages-receiving itself. And yet we believe, not only that they constitute the most powerful of all the self-evolved agencies operating upon—energizing, if we may use the term—the working class ; but that their improvement and development afford the most convincing proof of the progress of the artisans of England.

We have endeavoured to show, by means of the Trade Society, and subsidiarily, of the Board of Arbitration, what the working class has done outside of the law in the way of organized effort.   But besides any actual organizations, there are certain facts of a more general character lying within this sphere, which we must briefly characterise.

Foremost among these has been the gradual approximation of the working man towards other classes.   Less than twenty years ago, there lay between him and the men of any other class—except in a few special instances —a sort of fog of distrust, which almost prevented either from discerning the true lineaments of the other.   That fog has now in great measure rolled away.   In almost all large trades and towns, the man of another class who wishes and deserves to have working men for his friends, need not search very long for those who are in turn worthy of his friendship, and will bestow theirs upon him.   Benefit Societies, Building Societies, Industrial and Provident Societies, Working Men's Colleges, Working Men's Clubs and Institutes, &c. form an ever-increasing number of meeting-points, material as well as moral, between class and class, which are gradually binding each with each by closer links of fellowship. Into the ranks of authorship working men are passing—not always rising—continually. They have taken part repeatedly in the proceedings of the Social Science Association, either by contributing papers to its transactions, or by joining in its discussions.[1] The Secretary of one of the great Amalgamated Societies has made his appearance in the rooms of the Statistical Society, and perhaps the day is not far distant when even the Political Economy Club may deign to invite some working man to tell his views and experience on some of those economic questions which so deeply affect him.

The growth of loyal national feeling among the working class is another remarkable fact of the period. The

---

[1] We cannot resist the pleasure of referring to the candid and pathetic paper, on "The Chain and Trace-makers of Hadley Heath and its vicinity, and their Employers; or, Union and Disunion, and their Consequences, by Noah Forrest, a chainmaker," in the "Transactions" of the Social Science Association, for 1859, p. 654.

On the other hand, it has been made a matter of complaint by the Sheffield "Association of Organized Trades," that Mr. Dronfield's paper, entitled "A Working Man's View of Trades Societies," read at the Sheffield Congress, October 5, 1865, was not only not printed in the Transactions for the year, but not even mentioned in the Summary of proceedings; that the discussions which had special reference to the questions more immediately affecting the working men's interest are omitted in the Report, except as respects Courts of Arbitration, and that no mention is made of what was said by the trades' delegates on the occasion. Mr. Dronfield's position in Sheffield, and among the working class at large, should alone have secured to him more courteous treatment, nor can the writer of these lines forbear to express his opinion (as a member of the Social Science Association, and formerly on its Council), that Mr. Dronfield's paper would have been a valuable addition to the slender volume of the year's Transactions.—[J. M. L.]

positive disloyalty which was so prevalent in 1832, in
1839, in 1848, which even fifteen years ago was wide-
spread, has almost universally disappeared.   The Queen's
reception at Wolverhampton last year—Mr. Bright's
rebuke to the able but unlucky member for the Tower
Hamlets a few months ago—are events which would
have been impossible in the last generation.   Among the
most striking evidences of this altered change of feeling
has been the participation of the working classes in the
Volunteer movement.   Though their hearty co-operation
has too often been damped by official red-tapery, or the
snobbishness of Lords Lieutenant and Commanding-
officers on the one hand, and on the other by the ill-
judged opposition of one of the chief organs of working
class opinion ; it is nevertheless certain that, whenever
they have been encouraged to do so, working men have
largely entered into the Volunteer corps, and are con-
tinuing still so to do, and that working men officers
have shown themselves capable and efficient.[1]

No less remarkable, however, has been the growth
amongst the working class of what, if the term were not
becoming a cant one, we might term international sympathies.   During the great continental war, a foreigner
could hardly go abroad in our streets without being

[1] The decay of religious feeling among the better educated working men is
on the other hand proclaimed by the ministers of religion, and was made the
subject of a remarkable " Conference" with the working classes, at the
London Coffee House, on Monday, the 21st January last.   Very hard things
were certainly said of churches and ministers by working men on that occasion.   And yet those who, like one of the writers who was present at the
afternoon sitting, could look back some nineteen years nearly in their intercourse with working men, could not but feel what a change has been wrought
in the interval, even to make the bringing together possible for such an object
of so large a body of working men—many of them at the cost to them of a
half-day's wages.

mobbed, simply because he was a foreigner. One signal instance of such mobbing occurs in the period which occupies us ; but, however unjustifiable legally, what a progress in the moral sense of the worker does it exhibit, when English draymen could deem themselves called upon to avenge on an Austrian general the floggings of Hungarian women ! ' But there are facts of a far less questionable nature, which will occur to the mind of every reader. The sympathy shown for Kossuth, and in a still larger degree for Garibaldi, show the growth amongst our working class of an interest in the politics of the world which is limited by no considerations of birth or language. That, after the vast emigration to America, Lancashire operatives should have learnt to sympathise with a kindred nation, and through newspapers, written in their own language, to understand its politics, is not surprising. But what ties with them had this Hungarian, this Italian, that they should surround either with such enthusiastic popularity ? Surely a class which can appreciate the simple manhood of a Garibaldi has risen to manhood itself. Surely the men who can take so lively an interest in the destinies of foreign nations are fit to share in ruling their own.[1]

We here conclude this sketch. Lengthy as it may seem, we are ourselves chiefly conscious of the gaps which are left in it, of its shortcomings and deficiencies. Such as it is, however, we venture to think it abundantly proves what we sought to show, viz.—That with the exception of certain quarters of the metropolis, and of our larger

---

[1] Even the class-sympathies of the English working man are expanding beyond the limits of his country or his language : witness the London "International Association of Working Men," with its 12,000 members, and the Geneva Conference above referred to.

towns, where, through the gradual withdrawal of the
wealthy, then of the comfortable classes, either to other
quarters, or to country residences, the poor have been
left alone to become poorer, more ignorant, and more
degraded ;—of certain other towns and quarters of towns,
where, through some sudden influx of prosperity, or
again, through the demolitions caused by railways or
other public works, the population has become accumulated under bad sanitary conditions, often in dwellings
hastily run up by speculators, and has so fallen a prey to
similar evils ;—or, lastly, of particular trades which have
either remained exceptionally depressed through peculiar
circumstances, or in which, conversely, through exceptional
prosperity, the rise in the price of labour has outstripped
the development of the legitimate wants of the worker—
the progress of the working class, since 1832, has been
general and continuous.[1]   We are far from saying that it
has been as rapid—that it has been carried as far—as it
might have been ; that the working man has made the
fullest use of the opportunities which have been offered

---

[1] Even the agricultural class, we believe, has participated in that progress—
partly through the spread of education, partly through economic causes—such
as the general development of wealth, the depletion of the agricultural labour-
market by means of public works, emigration, the growth of manufactures.
Among the most cheering signs of such progress, to our minds, are the movements which have taken place within the last year or two among the farm-
servants of Kent, and the Scotch ploughmen, for raising their wages, and
bettering their condition.   But, in the Southern counties perhaps especially,
there is very much yet to do.   Dr. Drew, in a paper on " The Moral Effects
of the Poor Laws," read before the Social Science Association, in 1865 (Transactions, p. 556), tells of a Sussex labourer's wife, who said that her husband
had joined a sick-club, but she " persuaded him to leave it.   Why should a
poor man pay 1s. 6d. a week just to screen the parish ?... We know very
well why the gentry and farmers try to get up such clubs ; but poor people
here know better than to spend their money just to save the rates."   So alien
is still all idea of association or forethought to these Sussex hinds.

to him. But we believe, nevertheless, that the history of no people under the sun will show a period of the same duration in which, without any great political or social revolution, so great a progress has been achieved by the working class, and that chiefly through influences which God has been pleased to evolve from the bosom of the class itself.

Without, therefore, in anywise subordinating political reform—the means—to social reform—the end,—we wish to express our conviction that the time has come for the working classes of England to exercise, as of right, a far larger share of political power than is at present doled out to them. They are not perfect ; but their faults and their vices, if not always the same as those of the classes already in possession of political power, have at least their equivalents among those classes. They are not perfect, but the vice with which they are most taunted is, by the most ardent opponents of that very vice, made a ground, not for withholding the suffrage from them, but for extending the suffrage to them. The most advanced section of the Temperance party declares that they are the victims of the publican, not his friends, and that "any Reform Bill" is "an Alliance gain."

The account here given of the influence on legislation of the working classes while still unenfranchised, and of their progress by efforts of their own outside the sphere of legislation, affords good ground for hope as to the results of their enfranchisement. The legislators returned by their votes will give Parliament a more prompt and accurate knowledge of their circumstances and wishes ;

the measures necessary to assist their progress will be carried with fewer drawbacks and less delay : while, as time passes on, the working classes themselves will learn from political responsibility and intercourse with statesmen, to take a larger view of the interests of their own class, as inseparable from the interests of the nation.

THE END.

R. CLAY, SON, AND TAYLOR, PRINTERS, LONDON.

www.ingramcontent.com/pod-product-compliance
Lightning Source LLC
Chambersburg PA
CBHW021121270326
41929CB00009B/991